CRITICAL RACE SPATIAL ANALYSIS

CRITICAL RACE SPATIAL ANALYSIS

Mapping to Understand and Address Educational Inequity

EDITED BY

Deb Morrison, Subini Ancy Annamma, and
Darrell D. Jackson

STERLING, VIRGINIA

Published by Stylus Publishing, LLC.
22883 Quicksilver Drive
Sterling, Virginia 20166-2102

Library of Congress Cataloging-in-Publication Data

Names: Morrison, Deb, 1970- editor. |
Annamma, Subini A., editor. |
Jackson, Darrell D., 1975- editor.
Title: Critical race spatial analysis: mapping to understand and
address educational inequity/edited by Deb Morrison,
Subini Ancy Annamma, and Darrell D. Jackson.
Description: Sterling, Virginia : Stylus Publishing, 2017. |
Includes bibliographical references and index.
Identifiers: LCCN 2016052907 (print) |
LCCN 2017017377 (ebook) |
  ISBN 9781620364253 (Library networkable e-edition) |
  ISBN 9781620364260 (Consumer e-edition) |
  ISBN 9781620364239 (cloth : alk. paper) |
  ISBN 9781620364246 (pbk. : alk. paper)
Subjects: LCSH: Educational equalization--United States--
Statistical methods. |
Educational evaluation--United States--Statistical methods |
Discrimination in education--United States. |
Minorities--Education--Social aspects--United States.
Classification: LCC LC213.2 (ebook) |
LCC LC213.2 .C754 2017 (print) |
DDC 379.2/6--dc23
LC record available at https://lccn.loc.gov/2016052907

13-digit ISBN: 978-1-62036-423-9 (cloth)
13-digit ISBN: 978-1-62036-424-6 (paperback)
13-digit ISBN: 978-1-62036-425-3 (library networkable e-edition)
13-digit ISBN: 978-1-62036-426-0 (consumer e-edition)

Printed in the United States of America

All first editions printed on acid-free paper
that meets the American National Standards Institute
Z39-48 Standard.

Bulk Purchases

Quantity discounts are available for use in workshops and for
staff development.
Call 1-800-232-0223

First Edition, 2017

We situate ourselves in a lineage of scholarship and activism committed to resistance against white supremacy, anti-Blackness, and interlocking systems of oppression. We thank the scholars who came before us who have forged this path, those who do the work with us currently, and those who follow to push this work forward. We hope this body of work improves the lives of historically marginalized students, families, and their communities.

CONTENTS

PART ONE

INTRODUCTION

SEARCHING FOR EDUCATIONAL EQUITY THROUGH CRITICAL SPATIAL ANALYSIS

Subini Ancy Annamma, Deb Morrison, and Darrell D. Jackson

The black students, every one of them, had vanished on the way to school. Children who had left home on foot never appeared. Buses that had pulled away from their last stop loaded with black children had arrived at schools empty, as had the cars driven by parents or car pools. Even parents taking young children by the hand for their first day in kindergarten, or in pre-school, had looked down and found their hands empty, the children suddenly gone.

—Derrick Bell (1989, pp. 102–103)

I n Bell's (1989) work on desegregation he had the character Geneva Gay from the story, "The Chronicle of the Sacrificed Black School Children" imagine a scenario where Black[1] children are removed from the public spaces of schools through an unknown phenomenon. Though many may cringe at the idea of little Black bodies disappearing from the world without a trace, Bell's larger point was to reveal the ways that Black people had experienced this same kind of fate through the racialization of educational inequities. Or, as Du Bois (1935) wrote in the article "Does the Negro Need Separate Schools?" from which Bell drew his title for the story opening this chapter, "There are many public school systems in the North where Negroes are admitted and tolerated, but they are not educated; they are crucified" (1989, p. 329).

It is in the racialized spaces of schools where this book is situated. Temporally and socially, racialized educational inequities have been well documented. Our goal was to integrate a critical spatial dimension, not to replace either the historical or the social, but to enhance. Historically and socially, it has been well known that as schools were integrated, Black teachers and principals were removed from schools, so in fact the integration was only within the student body. Moreover, a race-neutral policy, one that sought to treat all kids the same, meant treating the Black and Brown children "just like" the white ones—that is, requiring Children of Color to meet the same academic and behavioral standards as white children without the assumption of competence or caring. This neoliberal focus on equality versus equity negated the complex and deep history of racial oppression in the educational and social spaces of America in favor of the reproduction of the status quo (DeCuir & Dixson, 2004).

A critical spatial analysis of any educational inequity requires the researcher to interrogate this paradox from a holistic framing, asking multiple, interconnected questions: (a) Why was the education philosophy to treat these Children of Color integrating white spaces, whose historical, social, and spatial experiences varied so much from white children, similar to their white peers? (b) How is power inscribed and reinforced in the bodies of the white children and removed from the bodies of Children of Color by using the treatment of white children as standard? and (c) How did Children of Color resist then, and continue to resist now, the mechanisms schools used to reproduce social inequities in their physical and internal spaces? Since integration, including Students of Color in physical spaces did not mean their internal spaces were ever considered. Said differently, as Black and Brown bodies of adults were erased from the spaces of public schools, simultaneously the internal spaces of the Children of Color were disregarded and punished. These unjust geographies of public schools continue to result in racialized educational inequities into the present day (Soja, 2010). In a speech given in France, "The City and Spatial Justice," Soja (2008) discussed the term *spatial justice*, explicitly addressing spatiality and justice from a theoretical perspective. He built on the foundations of Michael Foucault and Edward Said to understand the intersections of space, power, and knowledge in order to expose geographies that perpetuate or disrupt inequities in both processes and outcomes. Soja recognized the possibility to (re)examine space in education as more than a simple background where education happens; instead he built theory that allowed researchers to search for ways the space of schools (at all scales) both contribute to and resist inequities. Almost every author in the present volume references Soja's (2010) work as he provided many of us the opportunities to reconsider our work through a lens of critical spatial theory and methodology.

The purpose of this book, however, is not to provide a microanalysis of Soja's entire body of work; it is also not an introduction to critical race theory. Soja's work is a starting point for a wider analysis, and critical race theory is used as just one way to engage racialized inequities in education. Instead, the purpose of this book is to examine racial inequities in education through a critical spatial lens, situating the spatial temporally and socially. Therefore we did not dictate the theories or methodologies that authors should use. Instead, we encouraged authors to draw on their own contexts to use and develop theories and methodologies that work in their own spatial contexts by asking authors to examine how spatial analysis can be used to highlight educational inequities and search for solutions. This book is unique in that it adds a spatial analysis lens to the historical and social lenses, more commonly utilized in education research, to examine racial inequities in education.

This book, then, is organized to resist the racialized dimensions of these unjust geographies and to consider their intersections with other marginalized identities. To that end, the book is arranged both thematically and multiscalarly. Thematically, the book is set up similar to an empirical study wherein it moves from the purpose to an example of the theories in which we situate our spatial search for justice (Part One: Introduction), followed by potential methodologies with which to do the research (Part Two: Case Methodologies and Tools), to empirical findings of studies from across the United States (Part Three: Case Examples). *Multiscalar* refers to the idea that there are *macro-geographical* (global), *meso-geographical* (regional), and *micro-geographical* (local) scales which are not "discrete layers detached from one another. . . . They are interconnected and, like spatiality itself, are . . . socially produced" (Soja, 2010, p. 213). This book is structured multiscalarly, in that it moves between the local, regional, and global scales of analysis.

In Part One, the idea of critical spatial analysis and more specifically critical race spatial analysis are introduced. In this chapter, the authors connect the expanded work of this book to the historical roots of Edward Soja.

In Chapter 2, Véronica N. Vélez and Daniel G. Solórzano extend Soja's call for a critical spatial analysis by rooting it deeply in critical race theory, thereby developing critical race spatial analysis. This macro-theoretical chapter lays the foundation for the book, rooting spatial analyses in critical commitments to studying injustice.

In Part Two, authors provide examples of innovative ways to critically engage with spatial research. In Chapter 3, Subini Ancy Annamma shares how education journey mapping was created and utilized to explore the education trajectories of historically oppressed students, including the physical spaces of schools they encountered, the ways internal spaces of students were impacted by structural violence, and the spaces between the physical and internal.

In Chapter 4, Deb Morrison and Graham S. Garlick do not develop new methodologies; instead, the authors reclaim the tools of geospatial analysis, which have often been used in positivist and problematic ways, and reappropriate them within an explicitly critical framework.

Leigh Anna Hidalgo explores the augmented fotonovela in Chapter 5. Hidalgo researched the phenomenon of payday lending as a predatory act and used the augmented fotonovela in order "to force audiences to see and hear my community and fully recognize Latina/o immigrants in Arizona as the dignified and resilient people they are" (this volume, p. 70) All of these methodologies were built within a critical commitment to understanding racialized outcomes *and* resistance from a spatial perspective, highlighting the voices of People of Color in data collection and analysis. In addition, each of these methodologies and tools has the potential to link the scales together, situating the micro within the meso and macro scales.

Part Three contains case studies that vary in scalar focus. The authors of Chapter 6 zoom out to the city level of Los Angeles using historical documents. Exploring the spatial and temporal, Daniel G. Solórzano and Verónica N. Vélez dig through meso-scale archives and expose how sections of the city were formed through a critical lens. They found that white spaces contained racial covenants in order to keep People of Color out and that spaces occupied by People of Color were underresourced through redlining.

In Chapter 7, Benjamin Blaisdell explores how the concept of redlining can be applied to classroom interactions wherein teachers segregate supposedly integrated classrooms. In this micro-scaled example, the author also illustrates how redlining can be used as an analytic tool for teachers to change their practice.

Chapter 8 takes a broader perspective as Mark C. Hogrebe and William F. Tate IV explore regional scales of educational opportunity and access as a "visual political literacy project" (this volume, p. 128). The chapter examines the extent to which districts across Missouri offer access to advanced coursework in mathematics at the high school level.

In Chapter 9, Federico R. Waitoller and Joshua Radinsky explore the meso-scale of Chicago in the era of school reform. Exploring data representations and the narratives they tell from a critical perspective, the authors argue that these representations must take into account intersections of race and ability, or Children of Color in special education will be ignored within education reform. The authors find that this invisibility of the most marginalized allows educational injustice to flourish and only a critical examination of these trends will disrupt these inequities. In each of these chapters, the authors situate their own scaled research within a larger meso-scaled discussion of racialized inequities. This is purposeful as the editors believe that no individual can be understood as acting alone without context; instead, we all function within a structure of white supremacy and racism.

In Chapter 10, the concluding chapter, Deb Morrison, Subini Ancy Annamma, and Darrell D. Jackson draw connections across sections, and elucidate tensions and possibilities for future research. We recognize that spatial analysis is not a solution that will heal entrenched educational inequity on its own. Instead, we hope to address the limitations of a singular dimension analysis (e.g., only social *or* spatial *or* historical) and highlight the potential when using the spatial in conjunction with historical and social-critical analysis. This focus on spatial analysis allowed authors and editors to reimagine a right to the city (Soja, 2010), and specifically a right to education for People of Color. If we demand this right, then the first step is recognizing how this right is denied through systemic racial inequities.

We believe the thematic organization of this book reflects a symmetry of building empirical research with theory situated in literature, methods, and then cases. Moreover, the commitment to multiscalar work is essential. It reflects the commitments of this book's editors and contributors, as well as the intellectual forerunners who laid the path long ago. Du Bois (1935) recognized the need for a critical spatial, social, and temporal analysis when it came to educational inequities. He wrote,

> We shall get a finer, better balance of spirit; an infinitely more capable and rounded personality by putting children in schools where they are wanted, and where they are happy and inspired, than in thrusting them into hells where they are ridiculed and hated. (p. 331)

Du Bois's words guide us as we think about how educational inequities are reproduced in the temporal, physical, and social spaces of schools and how those inequities are resisted by Children of Color and the communities from which they originate.

Note

1. Similar to Neil Gotanda, we purposefully choose to capitalize Black while leaving white not capitalized. We encourage readers to read Gotanda's (1991) piece (p. 4n12) to understand why he makes these stylistic commitments, which we adhere to for analogous reasons.

References

Annamma, S. A., Connor, D., & Ferri, B. (2013). Dis/ability critical race studies (DisCrit): Theorizing at the intersections of race and dis/ability. *Race, Ethnicity and Education, 16*, 1–31. doi:10.1080/13613324.2012.730511

Bell, D. (1989). Neither separate schools or mixed schools: The chronicle of the sacrificed black school children. In *And we are not saved: The elusive quest for racial justice* (pp. 102–122). New York, NY: Basic Books.

DeCuir, J. T., & Dixson, A. D. (2004). "So when it comes out, they aren't that surprised that it is there": Using critical race theory as a tool of analysis of race and racism in education. *Educational Researcher, 33*(5), 26–31.

Du Bois, W. B. (1935). Does the Negro need separate schools? *Journal of Negro Education, 4*(Summer), 328–335.

Gotanda, N. (1991). A critique of "our constitution is color-blind." *Stanford Law Review, 44*(1), 1–68.

Soja, E. W. (2008). *The city and spatial justice*. Paper prepared for presentation at the conference Spatial Justice, Nanterre, Paris. Retrieved from: https://www.jssj.org/wp-content/uploads/2012/12/JSSJ1-1en4.pdf

Soja, E. W. (2010). *Seeking spatial justice*. Minneapolis, MN: University of Minnesota Press.

2

CRITICAL RACE SPATIAL ANALYSIS

Conceptualizing GIS as a Tool for Critical Race Research in Education

Verónica N. Vélez and Daniel G. Solórzano

Lorena has lived in Barrio Rosas[1] her entire life. Today, like most days, her father picks her up from school in his blue truck full of gardening tools and heads toward the Westside. He will work on two more homes before they return to the Barrio for dinner. As the blue truck merges into the noisy city traffic, Lorena gazes out the mud-splattered window and smiles. From the freeway she can see the colorful houses of her neighborhood and hear echoes of her brother playing soccer in the streets. Closing her eyes, she can almost smell the cinnamon cookies from Doña Luca's Repostería [bake shop]. If they work quickly enough, her father will buy her one on their way home—their special secret. As the truck makes its way north, her smile fades into a frown. In those still, green hills was a different world she entered only to work. It was a mostly residential area comprising expansive homes and lush gardens. Despite her frequent visits, it never ceases to feel foreign to her. It felt colder there, and no children played in the streets. In front of the huge lawns she feels small, insignificant, as if the wide streets could swallow her up so quickly and quietly that no one would even notice. As her father exits the freeway and the noise of the traffic fades away, Lorena's hands clench into clammy fists. She feels as if the wide windows glared at her, reminding her that she just didn't belong. Although most days she remained silent, she had moments when her discomfort was overwhelming and she would ask her father for the hundredth time why he didn't find more work on the south side, closer to their Barrio. Lorena's father, an immigrant from Guatemala, would smile and remind her in a proud voice that in America, the streets belonged to everyone. And besides, the money was better on the north side. Out of respect Lorena would agree. Yet deep down she wondered if, as her abuelita often said, her body was "telling" her something important. She understood, through her tension and anxiety, that streets were not just streets. In college she would gain evidence to support this feeling; people in the north didn't just enjoy greener grass. They also had fewer health problems, well-resourced schools, and enough political power to determine where freeways were even built. She learned that her instinct was right. Certain parts of the city were designed to keep out people like her. Even if there was no physical fence separating the north from the south, the barriers were just as real and even more vicious in the ways they shaped people's experiences and life opportunities.

Lorena's story reflects the tensions common to working-class People of Color[2] who learn to navigate between the wealthy neighborhoods where they work and the communities dealing with poverty in which they live. Separated by more than just a variance in income, communities are often bounded by streets and freeways that define differences in power and opportunity. While these physical markers appear meaningless—they are simply slabs of asphalt—we argue that they signify deeper socially constructed borders that reflect institutional practices of racial exclusion. What Lorena *feels*[3] is symbolic of the ways People of Color are systematically denied access to positions of power and how the construction of social spaces reflects this dynamic. We ground our work in an acknowledgment of the enduring nature of institutional racism and focus this chapter on the possibility of "the map" to provide an innovative, critical perspective on the intersection of race and space as one manifestation of larger structures of dominance.

The opening vignette is based on a real Lorena,[4] who was one of our undergraduate students and described to us her experiences working with her father in response to several maps constructed with digital mapping technologies known as geographic information systems (GISs). We originally designed these maps to help us understand and define the geohistorical and geopolitical markers of race and racism in South Los Angeles, specifically along the Alameda Corridor,[5] and their impact on the educational experiences of Students of Color. Unknown to us at the time, Lorena's home community was the focal point of the maps shared in class. Her response, referenced in the opening vignette, has since given these maps a more nuanced meaning, one infused with her lived experience, her memories, and her stories (see Cherrie Moraga's "Theory in the Flesh" in Moraga & Anzaldua, 1983, p. 23). The maps, in essence, became part of an embedded countercartographic narrative (Knigge & Cope, 2006) that poignantly illuminates Lorena's understanding of the relationship between the social and the spatial and how power can intervene at this intersection to mediate her lived experience. Lorena's response, along with those of the many other students, parents, community organizers, and researchers with whom we have shared these maps, became a driving force for this project: to critically theorize the relationship between space and race, particularly the role of "the map" in this process, and to develop a methodological approach to the study of space and mapmaking that could rightfully be called an antiracist practice.

With that in mind, we began to develop questions to guide our process. We looked for models in the field of education that employed GIS mapmaking, a device most often used by geographers and urban planners, as a methodological and conceptual tool to reveal how these sociospatial relationships impact students and their families. A few examples emerged that introduced GIS as a visual display of spatially related demographic and statistical data concerning schools (Tate, 2008; Hogrebe

& Tate, 2012; Riles, 1966; Caughey, 1967; Horng, Renee, Silver, & Goode, 2004). But few sought to provide a critical approach for using GIS in educational research or find ways to display qualitative educational data through GIS technologies, and, even less so, to use GIS to tell a *counternarrative* as an intentional strategy to challenge racism and other forms of subordination within the field of education. We began to ask ourselves: What types of education-related questions could GIS help us answer? What would it take to reenvision GIS as both a conceptual and methodological tool for critical educational research and practice? How could GIS be utilized to challenge racism and other forms of subordination?

Although the use of GIS within educational research and practice is only beginning, it offers a whole range of exciting possibilities to help answer these questions that build from transdisciplinary work in geography and other social sciences that have long been attentive to concerns about spatial processes and locational attributes (Lefebvre, 1991; Harvey, 1990; Soja, 1989, 1996, 2010, 2014). Employing numerous forms of spatial data, empirical studies on "space" have included everything from geopolitical inquiries about spatial models of international cooperation and conflict (O'Loughlin & Anselin, 1992), to urban and regional studies that explore the spatial "mappings" of an array of socioeconomic variables (Bronars & Jansen, 1987; Dubin, 1992), to feminist geographic research that explores the construction of gendered identities across space (Jones, Nast, & Roberts, 1997; McDowell & Sharp, 1997). While most of these studies reference larger geographic frameworks on spatial theory, by utilizing a transdisciplinary approach to address a range of questions and implications related to space they help us imagine new avenues and possibilities for examining educational interests about the important social, cultural, political, and historic role of space and place[6] as they relate to schools.

Educational inquiries that explore the spatial dynamics of schools and their communities, however, are not unique. Wild (2002), for example, explores how racially integrated schooling environments foster larger, more inclusive, multiethnic communities within the working-class districts of Los Angeles. Taking a more historical approach to the development of space, Monroy (1999) explores the complexity of the cultural formations of space for the identity development of Mexican youth in Los Angeles during the 1920s. Haymes (2003) utilizes a social geographical approach of urban space and critical pedagogy to suggest a *pedagogy of place* for Black urban struggle. Tate (2008) deepened our understanding of geographies of opportunity (Brown & Lauder, 2006; Pattillo, 2007; Wilson, 1996) by using GIS and spatial data to question whether the advancement of science in certain regions positively impacts educational outcomes. These examples highlight just a few instances of a growing body of critical scholarship interested in the role and construction of space within educational research. Yet we find that one of the most important methods for the study of space—the map—has been underutilized. And those methods that begin to explore the possibilities of mapmaking in educational research, as noted previously, fail to see their "maps" beyond visual representations of quantitative data, a shortcoming that many critical geographers warn could lead to reinstating the dominant power hierarchies that critical research on space hopes to dismantle. We argue that the employment of maps in critical educational scholarship must treat the technique of mapmaking as both an epistemological and methodological approach that requires attention to issues of positionality, power, the varied construction of knowledge, multiple subjectivities, and the politicized nature of representation. Only by doing so can critical education scholars, particularly those interested in investigating the role of race and racism in the construction, maintenance, and transformation of space, expect to use maps as a discursive technique and tool to imagine and redefine spaces connected to schools as ones where racism and other forms of subordination no longer exist.

This conceptual chapter, then, hopes to serve as a starting point for not only conceptualizing the purpose and uses of GIS maps in educational research today but also proposing an approach for the construction of maps as a critical tool that aligns with the goals of and critiques put forth by critical race theorists in education. The goal throughout is to make evident to readers our thought process and theorizing steps toward the development of this approach. To do this, we begin our first step by situating our work within critical race theory (CRT) and its applications within the field of education. CRT provides the overarching theoretical framework from which we draw our understandings of space, derive our guiding questions, and frame our proposed mapmaking practice as antiracist. We particularly highlight the work of W. E. B. Du Bois in helping us articulate the relationship among space, race, and power from a CRT standpoint. Using CRT as our guide, we are then better equipped to navigate and incorporate the transdisciplinary connections of research on space and place within critical race work in education. In this second step, we journey into geographical developments on race and space and draw from visual sociology on the use and practice of visual representations of space, such as the map. Although much of these conversations and advancements on the study of space are occurring outside the field of education, we argue that schools and their varied spaces are intimately connected, so much so that a critical investigation of schooling and student experience, especially the role of race and racism, necessitates a sensibility to issues of spatial location and processes. As a way of accomplishing this, our third step introduces and defines GIS mapmaking as an important methodological and conceptual tool for exploring, analyzing, and visualizing the relationships between schools and spaces, particularly their connection to the dynamics of race and racism. By addressing the epistemological premises, critiques, and applications of GIS through the lens of CRT, we offer an approach that utilizes maps in powerful ways to spatially analyze the role of race and racism in the historical and contemporary context of schools. We define this approach as *critical race spatial analysis* (CRSA). Finally, in our last step, we conclude by addressing the importance of GIS to critical race scholars and activists in education, particularly as an antiracist practice that seeks to transform racism and other forms of subordination.

Critical Race Theory

CRT originated in the late 1970s from the work of lawyers, activists, and legal scholars as a new strategy for dealing with the emergence of a post–civil rights racial structure in the United States. This structure, they argued, was maintained by a color-evasive[7] ideology that hides and protects white privilege while masking racism in rhetoric of "meritocracy" and "fairness" (Bonilla-Silva, 2001; Delgado & Stefancic, 2001; Ladson-Billings & Tate, 1995; Solórzano, 1997; Solórzano, 1998; Solórzano & Yosso, 2002a; Solórzano & Yosso, 2002b). Premised on the belief that the civil rights struggle and numerous legal decisions, such as *Brown v. Board of Education of Topeka, Kansas* (1954),[8] granted equal opportunities to all citizens, color-evasive ideology argues that race is no longer a decisive factor in the distribution of resources. The danger of color-evasive "racism," though, is that it disregards the "enormous and multifarious implications of the massive existing racial inequality" (Bonilla-Silva, 2001, p. 80). It denies that institutions continue to perpetuate racism, and its "reasonable" and politically correct style has made it both a popular and "moral" position, creating an "almost impenetrable defense of postmodern white supremacy"[9] (Bonilla-Silva, 2001, p. 162). CRT powerfully emerged within this context as a framework aimed at undermining color-evasive ideology through a deconstruction of its racist premise.

CRT draws from several disciplines, including civil rights, ethnic studies, gender studies, and critical legal studies, to examine and transform the relationship among race, racism, and power (Delgado & Stefancic, 2001; Solórzano, 2013). Mari Matsuda (1991) defines *CRT* as

> the work of progressive legal scholars of color who are attempting to develop a jurisprudence that accounts for the role of racism in American law and that works toward the elimination of racism as part of a larger goal of eliminating all forms of subordination. (p. 1331)

Thus, CRT is motivated by social justice and characterized by a passionate activism to eliminate racism as part of a broader effort to end subordination on gender, class, sexual orientation, language, and national origin lines (Solórzano, 1998). Some of the basic tenets or themes of CRT include the reexamination of history through the eyes and voices of People of Color and interest convergence, the belief that racial reform only served to promote whites' self-interest (Bell, 2004; Delgado & Stefancic, 2001; Solórzano, 1997, 1998).

CRT today is characterized by various new subdisciplines that "challenge civil rights activists to rethink the ways they conceptualize race and civil rights" (Delgado & Stefancic, 2001, p. 101). For example, Latina/o critical theory (LatCrit), as a branch of CRT, emerged to explore and deconstruct race-neutral or color-evasive ideologies within historical and cultural contexts in an effort to challenge racial or ethnic subordination as it particularly affects Latinas/os. LatCrit has now become an important theoretical lens to more fully examine how multiple forms of oppression based on immigration status, language, culture, ethnicity, and phenotype intersect to shape the experiences of Latinas/os (Solórzano & Delgado Bernal, 2001). Although originating in the field of law, CRT has crossed disciplinary borders. Within the field of education, for example, CRT is providing educational researchers with a lens to explore the role of race and racism in the educational experiences of Students of Color and their communities.

A CRT approach in education seeks to expose and challenge the ways race and racism mediate to produce educational inequality both in and out of the classroom (Solórzano, 1997, 1998; Solórzano & Delgado Bernal, 2001; Solórzano & Yosso, 2001a, 2001b, 2002a). It employs the following five elements that frame its methodological use within research (Solórzano, 1998; Solórzano & Delgado Bernal, 2001):

1. the intercentricity of race and racism with other forms of subordination,
2. the challenge to dominant ideology,
3. the commitment to social justice,
4. the centrality of experiential knowledge, and
5. the transdisciplinary perspective.

Through these elements, CRT allows educational researchers to "see," deconstruct, and transform the oppressive educational realities that affect Students of Color and their communities. In this way, it has aided us in helping define and examine the relationship of space and place to these realities and the way that GIS can function as a critical race tool in our research and practice toward a transformative end. Using CRT as our frame, we developed the following questions to guide our work and theoretical explorations in this area:

- How do race and racism shape the spaces within and connected to schools, give them meaning, and condition the experiences of students and their families?
- How can GIS, specifically, be used as a methodological and conceptual tool for spatially analyzing the role of race and racism in the historical and contemporary context of schools?
- What pedagogical possibilities does GIS hold for teaching and learning about the relationship between race and space?

Understanding Space Within a Critical Race Framework

In order to address these questions, we first needed a definition of *space*. Rather than turning to other disciplinary fields for answers, we decided to begin our search within our own traditions as critical race scholars. W. E. B. Du Bois immediately came to mind. In his foundational work, *The Souls of Black Folk*, Du Bois (1903/1999) poignantly defined and articulated the intersection between space and race as the *color-line*:

Since then a new adjustment of relations in economic and political affairs has grown up . . . which leaves still that frightful chasm as the color-line across which men pass at their peril. Thus, then and now, there stand in the South two separate worlds; and separate not simply in the higher realms of social intercourse, but also in church and school, on railway and street-car, in hotels and theatres, in streets and city sections, in books and newspapers, in asylums and jails, in hospitals and graveyards. (p. 66)

Although Du Bois first articulated his notion of the color-line more than 100 years ago, his words bear contemporary significance.[10] His words highlight the way *space* comes to be defined and experienced as the conceived and constructed reality of a racist society. In his writing, Du Bois explored both the breadth and depth of racism's influence in determining who will occupy certain spaces along the color-line and the opportunities that are then afforded to individuals based on which side they have been assigned. In describing southern communities in the United States during the period he was writing, for example, he described the intricacy of form and shape the color-line assumes while noting that its function still serves the same purpose; namely, that of separating, dividing, and shaping the experiences of individuals based on their social "location" to "the line." He wrote,

I know some towns where a straight line drawn through the middle of the main street separates nine-tenths of the whites from nine-tenths of the blacks. In other towns the older settlement of whites has been encircled by a broad band of blacks; in still other cases little settlements or nuclei of blacks have sprung up amid surrounding whites. (Du Bois, 1903/1999, pp. 106–107)

It isn't difficult to imagine how the notion of the color-line could be applied today. Continued segregation in schools and neighborhoods, educational tracking, and gentrification are just a few examples of where the color-line could be appropriately applied as a concept to examine and understand our social world at present.

Drawing from Du Bois's work, the color-line is key in framing a CRT understanding of space. It exposes the central role of race and racism in the purposeful construction of the physical, perceived, and conceptualized notions of the spaces that make up our social world. The lens of CRT makes visible the fingerprints of white supremacy in shaping every urban and rural neighborhood, city center and suburb, school and prison, and their social construction as "safe" or "ghetto," "rich" or "poor." The color-line powerfully defines privilege and opportunity, as well as subordination and marginality, as the spatial markers and consequences of an inherently racist U.S. landscape. Yet the color-line cannot just be seen as an oppressive delineation within a CRT framework. It must also be viewed as a space of antiracist transformation and possibility (see hooks, 1990).

Lorena's story that opened this chapter also reminds us that the physical constructions of nearly every city, such as freeways, separate along racial lines. These boundaries are both physically seen and experienced in feelings of inclusion and exclusion, and the realities of opportunity and oppression. Regions of the city are constructed both through policy and daily cultural practices. Predominantly Latina/o neighborhoods such as Lorena's are products of structural issues such as immigration waves, economic shifts, and exclusionary housing practices that historically limited the areas where non-whites could purchase homes. In conjunction with these larger social forces are the ways people create cultural communities characterized by everything from particular markets, spaces for work and play, and even language practices. One aspect of these communities is how people in their daily lives make sense of structural issues. As seen in Lorena's story, not all interpretations of regional divisions are the same. While Lorena's father holds onto an all-inclusive conception of freedom and access to all neighborhoods, Lorena intimately acknowledges that this access is limited for her and her family to acts of work and service. This limited access for Lorena signifies the reality that her community also doesn't have equal access to a range of social, economic, and political rights and resources. Yet Lorena's father reminds us that there isn't one way to make sense of how power plays out in space. Lorena's and her father's presence in wealthy, white neighborhoods also reminds us of the porous nature of borders and regional divisions and how each area enables the other to exist. For example, that there are non-white areas fundamentally depends on the existence of white ones. Lorena's family, and many more like them, navigate between the areas of the city, push on their boundaries, and construct multiple meanings for each space.

Exploring Transdisciplinary Connections in the Study of Space, Race, and Schools

According to Delaney (2002), interest in race, racism, and racialization has grown substantially in the field of geography over the past 10 years. Today, a growing body of work exists that can be referenced about geographical inquiry on the topic (Bonnet, 1997, 2000; Delaney, 2002; Dwyer & Jones, 2000; Jackson, 1998; Kobayashi & Peake, 2000; Neely & Samura, 2011; Pulido, 2000; Price, 2010, in press; Rose, 1970; Silvern, 1995; Zavella, 2000). Much of this work has emerged from a critical line of transdisciplinary work on spatial theory that includes the well-known and well-referenced work of Lefebvre (1975), Harvey (1990), and Soja (1989, 1996, 2000, 2010). A few broad categories of research in this field include examining spatial distribution and interaction of the processes of race-based segregation, economic issues such as labor market participation among People of Color, and political geographical inquiry that examines the spatial effects of the civil rights movement and affirmative action, for example (Peake & Schein, 2000). The impetus for this effort rests in the belief that "no geography is complete, no understanding of place or landscape comprehensive, without recognizing that American geography . . . as the spatial expression of American life, is racialized" (Kobayashi & Peake, 2000, p. 392).

For geographers exploring this area, the process of racialization becomes a way to differentiate racialized groups, assign them stereotypical characteristics, and establish sociospatial segregated conditions as way of maintaining and reinforcing racist

ideologies. Kobayashi and Peak (2000) argue that this is one of the most enduring and fundamental means of organizing society. Many geographers interested in
how ideologies of race, racism, and racial consciousness, or racial formation (Omi
& Winant, 1994), constitute space, and vice versa, argue that space can be viewed
as a form of *enabling technology* (Delaney, 2002), through which race is produced.
This suggests that "race . . . is what it is and does what it does precisely because of
how it is given spatial expression" (Delaney, 2002, p. 7). This perspective aligns with
a fundamental premise of geographical theories that stress how the social and spatial
mutually constitute each other, in that social dynamics, such as race, don't simply
exist in space but are reinforced and constituted by it (Delaney, 2002).

Theorizing about the importance of race and racism in geographical inquiry
has furthered research into the complexities of how spaces become racially constituted. Some are examining how racial formations are a product of historically specific
geographies (Kobayashi & Peake, 2000). These geohistorical accounts incorporate
historiography to illuminate how historical processes of colonialism and labor markets, for example, interact with race-based ideologies and other ideologies of power
to produce the highly textured, power-laden aspects of space. In line with a critical
race theoretical approach, geographers in this camp are exploring how "whiteness,"
in particular, is crucial to the study of race and space because to understand "the nor-
mativity accorded to 'white' landscapes . . . [requires] . . . a reopening a view of past
landscapes where the terms of today's normalization were laid down" (Kobayashi &
Peake, 2000, p. 400). Accounting for "whiteness" aligns with critical race theoretical
frameworks in that it acknowledges "white" spaces as racialized spaces, unmasking
the normative and manipulative power whiteness has "to mark 'white' as a location
of social privileges" (Kobayashi & Peake, 2000, p. 393). Thus, the "inner city," the
"border," and "the prison," for example, aren't the only places we investigate in our
quest to understand the relationship between race and space, but also the "gated community," the "safe streets," and the "good schools." Beyond historical approaches,
the study of the racialized elements of a range of spaces across different scales has led
many critical geographers into the field of anthropology, gender studies, legal studies,
sociology, labor history, and postcolonial studies, to name a few (Peake & Schein,
2000). The transdisciplinary approach of these geographers is too vast to cover its
entirety here, but we highlight a few of these examples in the following section.

More and more, critical race geographers are making important connections
with the law. Borrowing from critical legal studies, geographers are better able to
understand how the law works to demark boundaries to exclude people, define social
institutions, and control public discourse (Peake & Kobayashi, 2002). For these
geographers, then, the law becomes crucial to defining racialized social relationships
within space because it has and continues to serve as a major mechanism for expanding, controlling, and constricting space, often along racialized lines. Educational
spaces are a prime example for understanding the role of law in conditioning spaces
based on race. Using a spatial lens to analyze the 1954 *Brown v. Board of Education* decision, for example, illuminates the social construction of educational spaces

for Students of Color, made possible by the law. It helps us better understand the consequential spaces that resulted, both within and outside of schools, from specific legal strategies aimed at racial integration. Affirmative action policies that additionally emerged from legal battles illuminate how and why access to educational spaces expands the effects such spatial change has on students who inhabit these spaces, and how new educational barriers connected to race are erected within space as a result.

Another important disciplinary connection being made by critical geographers is with immigration studies (Peake & Kobayashi, 2002). According to Peake and Kobayashi (2002), "Immigration inevitably results in a reimagining of the boundaries and meanings of places, a respatialization of both arriving and receiving groups" (p. 53). As a result, immigration studies, which benefits from a transdisciplinary approach already, naturally lends itself to an alliance with a critical geographical approach on space. By illuminating how migration affects racialization, particularly how race and racism intersect with forms of nativism (De Genova, 2005), immigration studies aids geographers in understanding the profound implications of space for the identity formation, civil status, and civic participation of Immigrants of Color. Extending this lens to educational spaces, the combined approach of CRT, geography, and immigration studies can help us examine the racialized dynamics of the often marginal spaces occupied by Immigrant Students of Color in schools.

As demonstrated previously, the transdisciplinary connections that link several modes and fields of study in the quest to understand the sociospatial dynamics of society offer important insights for investigating the connection among space, race, and schools. Schools, and the environments they occupy and are connected to, form crucial places in society. Few would deny their importance. Their definition as and relationship to political, economic, cultural, and racialized spaces make schools and other educational spaces important locales for spatial inquiry, not just for geographers, but for researchers in other fields as well. Consequently, critical race scholars in education could benefit enormously by incorporating this transdisciplinary approach to study the role of race and racism in shaping spaces within schools as well as the spatial relationship between schools and their larger contexts. In the remainder of this chapter, we outline an approach that incorporates spatial analysis, specifically using GIS technologies, within the broader framework of CRT in education. Before addressing the nuts and bolts of a CRSA for educational research and practice, however, we first turn to a discussion of one of the most important methods for examining, analyzing, and visualizing space: the map.

GIS: Its Uses, Purpose, Limitations, and Potential for Critical Race Scholarship in Education

> Maps are active; they actively construct knowledge, they exercise power and they can be a powerful means of promoting social change. (Crampton & Krygier, 2006, p. 15)

As mentioned earlier, mapmaking is one of the most important tools geographers use to study space. In the last 30 years, the construction of maps has been greatly facilitated by the use of computerized GIS. GIS software has made it easier to visualize data on a map and conduct certain analyses to reveal patterns and concentrations of spatial phenomena. It does this by constructing maps through layers of information, thereby helping to reveal spatial relationships among different sets of data. According to Elwood and Leitner (2003), "GIS is a computer technology that enables storage, analysis, and mapping of a wide range of geographic information, including demographic, socio-economic, housing, crime, environmental, and land-use data" (p. 140). This capacity to analyze and display a large variety of data has made GIS useful for many institutions, from the military to community organizations to city planning departments and even the health industry, and benefits academics and non-academics alike. Much of the reason its use is so broad is that GIS is able to quickly analyze and display spatial data in the form of maps, which often make complex data accessible to multiple audiences. Though other statistical tools that analyze space can provide the what, how, and why of research questions, they often fall short of adequately answering and conveying the where. In addition, GIS has become more and more accessible to "non-GIScientists," such as nongovernmental, grassroots, and community groups, who are finding that the technology enables them to design their own maps with alternative knowledge that is often missing in more dominant representations of space (Elwood, 2002a). In fact, the growth of GIS use in these spaces has prompted a field of inquiry, known as public participation geographic information science (PPGIS), that explores the power of GIS, both its empowering and marginalizing effects, for use by so-called nontraditional users (Kellogg, 1999; Ghose, 2001; Elwood, 2002b).

Despite the many uses of GIS, it has been heavily critiqued by feminist geographers and critical cartographers. Summing these critiques, Kwan (2002a) states that GIS has been challenged "for its inadequate representation of space and subjectivity, its positivist epistemology, its instrumental rationality, its technique-driven and data-led methods, and its role as surveillance . . . technology deployed by the state" (p. 645). Knigge and Cope (2006) further add that social theorists are concerned with how GIS is "used in ways that rigidify power structures while simultaneously *masking*—through the legitimizing strength of 'science' and gee-whiz displays—the possibility of multiple versions of reality or 'truth,' socially constructed knowledges, and other sources of subjectivity that are inherent in all social research" (p. 2022). Most of these critiques are based in the often exclusive association between GIS and quantitative spatial analysis and the politics of representation inherent in maps, a concern that stems from the use of early maps whose generalizations of the world drove imperialist and colonial efforts. The emerging field of critical cartography also cautions GIS mapmakers referring to the power of maps not just in representing reality but also in actively creating it (Crampton & Krygier, 2006).

Using these critiques as a basis for their own work, many critical geographers, mostly feminists, are beginning to reimagine and employ innovative techniques that can further GIS as a critical practice (Kwan, 2002a, 2002b; Knigge & Cope, 2006). Their work is opening an emerging field known as *critical GIS*. Citing the practices of critical, feminist, and postcolonial cartographers, Kwan (2002a) argues that GIS can be renegotiated as a discursive tactic to create *counter-maps*, or what Crampton and Krygier refer to as *subversive cartographies* that challenge dominant representations of the world. Kwan (2002a) refuses to accept the *technological determinism* of associating GIS with a particular positivist epistemology, asserting that the very subjectivities and agency of GIS users can help illuminate the meaningful aspects of everyday life. As an approach to critical GIS work, Kwan (2002a) offers a form of GIS *feminist visualization*, which she defines as "the material practice of critical visual methods in feminist research" (p. 656). Through this approach, GIS technologies are used to analyze both quantitative and qualitative data to create what are termed *cartographic narratives* that establish connections between large-scale phenomena and the everyday lives of people, particularly women. Kwan (2002a, 2002b) challenges GIS users to complement their quantitative data with other contextual information, and uses primary sources from individuals to complement secondary sources that can often overgeneralize communities, such as census data. Similarly, Knigge and Cope (2006) suggest using *grounded visualization*, an approach that combines grounded theory and GIS visualization, as a way of representing multiple interpretations of the world and diverse views of reality. Both *grounded visualization* and *feminist visualization* honor the concept of "situated knowledges" by acknowledging the positionality of the GIS mapmaker in constructing knowledge and recognizing that the GIS mapmaking process is created from a particular political, social, and historical subjectivity. Kwan (2002b) also suggests that GIS users need to practice reflexivity when using GIS methods by reflecting on what we want to "produce" through maps; the actual image of the map to examine the possible exclusions, silences, and marginalizing power of our representations; and the audience to whom we hope to convey our representations as a way of thinking ahead about how our maps may be contested and renegotiated by different people. What this suggests is that that critical work using GIS shouldn't just rest on interpreting maps for counterhegemonic ends, but should also be deeply attentive to the actual process, or methodology, of creating them.

Given the critiques by feminist and other critical geographers concerning GIS technologies, how can we use GIS in conducting educational research on space, particularly in investigating the role of race and racism in place and spatial location in the relationship between schools and their larger contexts? One powerful way is by exploring the spatial dimensions of educational inequality on a GIS map that shows the availability of educational opportunities in schools within segregated communities, by race, class, immigration status, and so forth. Although using GIS in educational research and practice is rare, work conducted by Horng and colleagues (2004) is beginning to lay the groundwork for the use of GIS in this way, namely to spatially analyze the unequal distribution of educational resources based on race and class. This work could be additionally extended to using a critical GIS approach by including qualitative data, like photographs of the schools under investigation, as a way of further comparing schools that have differential access to resources. Current functions in GIS allow users to attach photographs and even link video to certain spatial locations on a map. This enables critical approaches to GIS, like those suggested by Kwan (2002a, 2002b) and Knigge and Cope (2006), to powerfully include qualitative data as a visual representation on a map. This type of approach lends itself to another possible study that could involve the use of GIS technologies to examine how youth define *culturally wealthy*[11] spaces in their communities and the proximity of these spaces to schools.

Laying the groundwork for a theoretical and methodological approach that critically utilizes GIS technologies to investigate educational research questions on schools and space, particularly the role of race and racism in shaping these spaces, we introduce a new approach that we are calling, for now, CRSA. Although the implications of this approach extend beyond just using GIS as a tool for educational inquiry on space, we focus our attention here on describing how GIS can be used to address spatial inquiries within a critical race education framework.

Mapping Race and Racism in School Contexts: Toward a Working Definition of *CRSA*

As we described previously, critical race geographers have much to offer critical race educational researchers, but rarely are their tools, such as GIS mapmaking, being used in ways that further the goals of CRT in education. Although we have provided a conceptual argument for the importance of centering a spatial lens in educational research on race, little is being done to integrate these two approaches—critical race geography and CRT in education—despite their shared goals and perspectives.

As a way of making a connection, we provide the following working definition for *CRSA*[12] in education:

> Critical race spatial analysis (CRSA) is an explanatory framework and methodological approach that accounts for the role of race, racism, and white supremacy in examining geographic and social spaces and that works toward identifying and challenging racism and white supremacy within these spaces as part of a larger goal of identifying and challenging all forms of subordination. CRSA goes beyond description to spatially examine how structural and institutional factors influence and shape racial dynamics and the power associated with those dynamics over time. Within educational research, CRSA is particularly interested in how structural and institutional factors divide, constrict, and construct space to impact the educational experiences and opportunities available to students based on race.

Drawing from the tenets of CRT in education, employing CRSA in educational research requires

- foregrounding the color-line, underscoring the relationship among race, racism, history, and space; its intersection with other forms of subordination; and its material and perceived impact on the daily lives of Students of Color, their families, and their communities;
- challenging race-neutral representations of space by exposing how racism operates to construct space in ways that limit educational opportunity for Students of Color, their families, and their communities;
- focusing research, curriculum, practice, and activism on mapping the spatial expression of the lived experiences of Students of Color, their families, and their communities and constructing a sociospatial narrative that portrays these experiences as sources of strength;
- centering a transformative solution by investing in and often reimagining "spatial" research and teaching tools that work for racial justice, and expanding the reach and use of these tools to eliminate subordination in and beyond the academy;
- utilizing the transdisciplinary knowledge base of critical race studies in education (ethnic studies, women's studies, sociology, feminist geography, history, humanities, and the law) as well as visual sociology, critical geography, and radical/tactical cartography to inform praxis; and
- emphasizing maps and mapmaking as a point of departure for analyzing the sociospatial relationship between race and space and refusing to allow maps to speak for themselves.

Although one could imagine a CRSA approach utilizing several qualitative and quantitative techniques to study racialized spaces within and connected to schools, maps and mapmaking are key to CRSA. It is important to acknowledge that CRSA, and the GIS technologies it may use, is a *conceptual* and *methodological* approach and not simply a spatial analytical technique. The epistemological and ontological implications of geographical research tools, especially GIS, as many feminist geographers have pointed out, require that we frame CRSA in this way. Based on this working definition, then, *how can critical race education scholars use CRSA in their work? How can it be utilized as a transformative, antiracist practice?*

Borrowing from the work of Knigge and Cope (2006) on grounded visualization, one way is to merge grounded theory with GIS.[13] Based on the work of Strauss and Corbin (1998), Silverman (2001), Creswell (1997), and others, grounded theory involves multiple stages of the collection and analysis of various forms of qualitative data in a way that allows themes to emerge through "iterations of 'constant comparison'" (Knigge & Cope, 2006, p. 2024). By working to allow theories to emerge from data, grounded theory, in effect, grounds itself in people's everyday experiences. As Knigge and Cope (2006) point out, grounded theory merges nicely with critical GIS because they both attend to small-scale and large-scale social phenomena, as well as specific instances and broader trends in an effort to highlight subjectivity, differences, partial knowledges, and power. They highlight five specific ways in which critical GIS and grounded theory merge:

1. They are both exploratory by enabling researchers to investigate data from multiple angles, including using visual techniques in their explorations.
2. They both involve several stages of data collection, display, and analysis.
3. They both pay simultaneous attention to the particular and the general.
4. They both accommodate and represent several interpretations and diverse versions of reality.
5. They both recognize and accept "partial" and "situated" knowledges.

The merging of GIS and grounded theory works well within a critical race education framework. We argue that it maintains a critical awareness of the research process as a political, and potentially transformative, act, embedded in particular social, political, and historical moments. Furthermore, it aims to conceptualize and theorize about the social world from the basis of the lived experiences of Students of Color and their communities.

Merging grounded theory with GIS through a CRSA approach allows us to reimagine particular GIS techniques, such as ground-truthing.[14] *Ground-truthing* is traditionally defined as a process whereby GIS technicians are sent to gather data in the field that either complement or dispute airborne remote-sensing data collected by aerial photography, satellite sidescan radar, or infrared images. From these data, scientists are able to identify land use or cover of the location and compare it to what is shown on the image. Maps are then verified and updated based on this comparison. Adapting this definition for use within CRSA, ground-truthing can be reimagined as the process of sending community members, particularly those at the margins, to gather data in the field that either complement or dispute information portrayed in maps. Ground-truthers, employing their expertise as community members, define and verify neighborhood boundaries, color-lines, the uses of certain spaces, and the perceptions of those spaces. From these data, critical cartographers are able to identify sociospatial characteristics of a particular area and compare it to what is shown on the image. They then verify and update existing data and maps. Ground-truthing in CRSA is a way of looking at an entire neighborhood, school district, or public transit system; park access and placement; or any number of resources (or lack thereof) in a community and understanding many of the realities involved. With critical community expertise, we can measure an entire system of distribution of educational and community resources and understand its impact on a region. Without verification via ground-truthing, data from supposedly accurate or objective sources are hypothetical at best.

Another tool to apply GIS within a CSRA frame is portraiture—a qualitative research technique introduced by Lawrence-Lightfoot and Hoffman Davis (1997) originally within the field of education. *Portraiture* is a transdisciplinary methodological approach that seeks to bridge aesthetics and empiricism in order to create a narrative or "portrait" of a particular group of people within a particular setting. In this process of creating the portrait, the portraitist or researcher is actively involved not only in documenting and interpreting the content of his or her portrait but also in creating it and intervening with the subject(s) in an effort to create a more authentic and compelling narrative and work collectively to transform oppressive realities. In this way the researcher is a central part and intervening component of the narrative. Similar to grounded theory, portraiture seeks to capture the nuances of the social world through rich, textured, detailed descriptions of specific social phenomena as a way of illuminating more universal patterns. It also involves an iterative process by which the "portraitist is active in selecting the themes that will be used to tell the story, strategic in deciding on points of focus and emphasis, and creative in defining the sequence and rhythm of the narrative" (Lawrence-Lightfoot & Hoffman Davis, 1997, p. 34). By ensuring that the portraitist is visible throughout the research process and product, portraiture addresses similar critiques to those posed by feminist geographers who criticize the ability of GIS to mask the subjectivity of its users. By calling for a more intentional approach to embed the mapmaker within the GIS products created, portraiture aligns with the recommendations put forth by critical geographers concerning GIS use. Additionally, the combined central interest in context for understanding social phenomena makes portraiture and critical GIS highly compatible. Finally, the ability of both to challenge deficit thinking as a way to transform oppressive realities makes evident the utility of this joint approach under a CRSA framework. By seeking to build spatial models and understandings of the world from the lived experiences of People of Color and through its explicit attempt to reach a larger audience through the portrait of a map, the merger of portraiture and critical GIS can powerfully serve critical race scholars.

In keeping with the emerging perspectives of critical GIS and critical race geography, particularly work that seeks to merge GIS with qualitative research techniques, as we have outlined previously, CRSA can help illuminate how specific spatial features or markers, like a street or freeway, can become inscribed with important racial meaning that has particular consequences for the schools that coexist near these spatial features or are affected by how these features are used. To illustrate this, some of our recent work on South Los Angeles high schools explores how the Alameda Corridor served as a demarcation boundary that racially segregated residential communities and the student populations that attended schools on either side of the corridor. Using GIS, we have been able to establish the robustness of the Alameda Corridor as a racially dividing boundary by examining the demographic changes that occurred along the corridor in South Los Angeles over the course of a 30-year period. Using a CRSA lens, we can use GIS to investigate how certain spatial markers, like the Alameda Corridor, can operate to facilitate racism and perpetuate racial divides that have important consequences for schools. By collecting qualitative data—in the form of photographs, written district policies that established the Alameda Corridor as a boundary between school attendance zones, and student interviews—CRSA becomes a tool for telling *contextualized countercartographic narratives* (Knigge & Cope, 2006) about the importance of race and racism in South Los Angeles, its high schools, and its relationship to the Alameda Corridor. This type of narrative aligns with the counterstorytelling approach of critical race scholars in education. Solórzano and Yosso (2002a) define a *counterstory* as a "method of telling the stories of those people whose experiences are not often told [and] . . . for challenging the majoritarian stories of racial privilege" (p. 32). GIS technologies within a CRSA approach could also be used to examine how certain spaces that are defined by city and real estate institutions as "safe" or "marketable" are racialized and how this impacts the ways schools, and the students who attend them, are viewed within these spaces.

Learning from the lessons produced by feminist geographers on the uses of GIS, it is important to highlight a few cautions for employing CRSA that if heeded can serve to strengthen it as a conceptual and methodological framework. The first is a recognition that varied meanings are attached to race and racism in different spaces and places and over different geographic contexts. Because GIS has been criticized for generalizing the spatial realities of one locale to another, it is important to keep in mind that racial meanings are geographically and historically specific. By taking a critical GIS approach within CRSA, we can "highlight the complexity, the historical contingency, the fluidity and the richness of even the most extreme, and therefore painful racialized circumstances" (Kobayashi & Peake, 2000, p. 399). Additionally, as education scholars using CRSA, we need to take into account and problematize the empty spaces that result from the normalization of "whiteness" that occurs in a racist society.

Although still in its formative stages, CRSA nonetheless provides a much-needed approach to the study of race and racism by critical race educational scholars. We argue that it forms part of what Kobayashi and Peake (2000) call an *antiracist land-scape analysis*. In this way, it supports the social justice aims of critical race scholars who use CRT not just as a theory but as a standpoint from which to engage in radical social change. We conclude with a few final thoughts about how CRSA, particularly its use of GIS, can be used as an antiracist practice by educational researchers and practitioners.

GIS as an Antiracist Practice in Education

It is important that we are able to as activist geographers disrupt those established attributes of place and the confining boundaries that have literally allowed whiteness to take place. Such disruption depends on an analysis informed by practice—as critical race scholars we not only want to understand the processes constructing white-ness but establish a means of resisting its effects. (Kobayashi & Peake, 2000, p. 400)

Beyond the importance of GIS for critical race research, it can serve as an important pedagogical tool for teaching about race and racism at all levels of schooling. Through a CRSA framework we can use GIS to construct maps as teaching devices that high-light the importance of geographical or spatial features for maintaining racial divides that often lead to residential segregation, limited access to educational and social services, and so forth. By showing how racism becomes inscribed in space, GIS maps can become important devices for teaching students about the structural and institutional aspects of race and racism that challenge deficit framings of Communities of

Color (Solórzano & Solórzano, 1995; Valencia, 1997). In addition, with the availability of GIS technologies to a larger audience, it holds great potential for use by students in constructing their own meaningful maps of their environments. This is in line with a critical GIS approach that argues for using GIS to represent multiple realities and local knowledges. As mentioned earlier, the emerging field of PPGIS is hoping to make GIS more accessible and user friendly to nontraditional audiences. By helping to equip students, teachers, and local community members with this tool in the critical ways that we have described, we, as critical race scholars, move from "participant observation" to active participation *with* local communities to achieve an antiracist agenda. This, Peake and Kobayashi (2002) argue, is a fundamental method of antiracist research.

We end this chapter in much the same way that we began, with Lorena and her experience in Barrio Rosas. After her university class ended, we sent her the maps of her community. She asked permission to share them with a community organization she was working with as a way to initiate critical dialogue about inequitable educational outcomes for students in Barrio Rosas. We happily accepted her request. We had always envisioned utilizing GIS beyond the boundaries of academic research and into the arena of community organizing and activism. A few months later Lorena recounted her experiences sharing the maps with parents and local community organizers, who were both astonished and excited by the maps. Immediately the maps began to spread as different community groups asked for copies to share with their constituents. In one community, Lorena shares, children in an after-school program have begun using the maps to study their neighborhoods and create their own maps to reflect a much more local reality that includes sites of community cultural wealth (Yosso, 2005).

We begin and end with Lorena's story because layering her narrative onto the map breaks the invisible shell of neutrality that often covers the map. Maps don't reflect facts as much as they reflect one way of approaching and organizing space. Lorena's first experience with GIS exposes the degree to which a conversation between the map and an individual experience can emerge and grow. In Lorena's case we argue that the map gave her evidence, documentation to affirm that her feelings as a young girl were not trite or superficial. They were a sophisticated way of knowing that can be visually displayed through GIS. This conversation then blossomed into a larger community dialogue in which many parents, organizers, and residents began sharing similar and contrasting interpretations of their lived experiences in the regions shown. The map assists Lorena and her community in translating enfleshed experiences into theory, contributing to the formation of new eyes through which they can return to the map and look again at their experiences. There is the potential to gain a new understanding of how the spaces that define individuals' lives, such as a freeway that both enables travel and distinguishes white from non-white, are not arbitrary, but rather concrete manifestations of the complexity of social life. And finally, as Lorena shared with us in relation to the elementary school students who are studying maps, GIS can begin to transform how youth imagine, understand, and interact with different spaces in their lives.[15] In her experience, maps can be used to intently document places of hope, possibility, and creativity in areas often defined and dismissed as "lost, drug-infested ghettos."

Although the notion of GIS mapmaking is still relatively new in educational research, we believe in its potential to create powerful and accessible displays of spatially related data for multiple audiences. Applied together with CRT through a critical space analysis approach, GIS becomes more than just a research tool; it has the power to transform oppressive spaces and become an antiracist practice.

Notes

1. Barrio Rosas is a pseudonym to reflect real neighborhoods throughout southern California.

2. "People of Color" is intentionally capitalized to reject the standard grammatical norm. Capitalization here represents a grammatical move toward social and racial justice. This rule also applies to "Students of Color," "Communities of Color," and similar instances.

3. In her discussion of the Black home as a site of resistance, bell hooks (1990) describes the *feeling* of a space and how racism can be physically and emotionally experienced. For hooks there is a visceral, embodied reaction that comes from walking through an area where it is clearly understood that one is not welcomed.

4. A pseudonym is used here to protect the anonymity of the student.

5. The Alameda Corridor is a street that travels from downtown Los Angeles to the Los Angeles harbor. It has been a rail, industrial, and community corridor for well over 100 years. It has also served as a color-line during various parts of Los Angeles history, with whites on the eastern and African Americans on the western side of the Alameda.

6. For our purposes here, we use *place* and *space* interchangeably but acknowledge their distinct, albeit related, meanings as several scholars have noted and theorized. For example, according to Friedland (1992), "place is the fusion of space and experience, a space filled with meaning, a source of identity" (p. 14). For Patel (2015), "the interactions [that] take place and are experienced by the beings in those places, that is space. Space is contoured, collapsed, made abrasive, and molded through lived experience in specific places. . . . Places become spaces through interactions, imbued with dynamics of power, and, more often than not, inequity." These definitions underscore the multifaceted dimensions of both *space* and *place*. They also highlight very different understandings of the two concepts, which points to both their complexity and the range of interpretations.

7. We use *color-evasive* (Stubblefield, 2005) in lieu of *color-blind*, the more traditional term for this ideology to (a) problematize an assumption that equates blindness with ignorance that, by extension from the figurative to the literal, inaccurately conveys and distorts the unique way blind individuals interact with the world; and, (b) rethink and remove ableist language from critical race discourse as core to our explicit efforts toward social justice in all aspects of our work, particularly in research and scholarship (Annamma, Morrison, & Jackson, 2014).

8. For a more complete analysis of the elusiveness of desegregation and the promise of *Brown v. Board of Education*, refer to Oakes & Lipton (1999).

9. Here we define *white supremacy* as "a system of racial domination and exploitation where power and resources are unequally distributed to privilege whites and oppress People of Color" (Pérez Huber, Benavides Lopez, Malagón, Vélez, & Solórzano, 2008, p. 41).

10. In 1925 Du Bois reaffirmed his views of the color-line: "And thus again in 1925, as in 1899, I seem to see the problem of the Twentieth Century as the Problem of the Color-Line" (Du Bois, 1925, p. 444).

11. Yosso (2005) defines *cultural wealth* as "an array of knowledge, skills, abilities and networks possessed and utilized by Communities of Color to survive and resist racism and other forms of oppression" (p. 77). Yosso's (2005) model of cultural wealth, situated within CRT, challenges traditional interpretations of cultural and social capital. It shifts the lens away from a deficit view of Communities of Color as places full of cultural poverty disadvantages, and instead highlights the unrecognized array of cultural knowledge, skills, abilities, and contacts held by racially marginalized groups.

12. This working definition originally emerged from collaborative work that explores the role of race and racism in shaping the historic, evolving spatial relationship between South Los Angeles high schools near the Alameda Corridor and their surrounding communities. Our initial work in CRSA was presented at the 2007 American Education Research Association annual conference in Chicago, Illinois (Solórzano & Vélez, 2007).

13. For the merging of CRT and grounded theory, see Malagón, Pérez Huber, & Vélez, 2009.

14. For a concise, technical definition of *ground-truthing*, see support.esri.com/en/knowledgebase/GISDictionary/term/ground%20truth and wiki.gis.com/wiki/index.php/Ground_truth

15. For example, students in the ethnic studies program at Roosevelt High School in the community of Boyle Heights in East Los Angeles are using GIS to study the gentrification of their community.

References

Annamma, S., Morrison, D., & Jackson, D. (2014). Disproportionality fills in the gaps: Connections between achievement, discipline, and special education in the school-to-prison pipeline. *Berkeley Review of Education, 5*(1), 53–87.

Bell, D. (2004). *Silent covenants: Brown v. Board of Education and the unfulfilled hopes for racial reform.* Oxford: Oxford University Press.

Bonilla-Silva, E. (2001). *White supremacy and racism in the post–civil rights era.* Boulder, CO: L. Rienner.

Bonnet, A. (1997). Geography, "race," and whiteness: Invisible traditions and current challenges. *Area, 29*, 193–199.

Bonnet, A. (2000). *Antiracism.* New York, NY: Routledge.

Bronars, S., & Jansen, D. (1987). The geographic distribution of unemployment rates in the U.S. *Journal of Econometrics, 36*, 251–279.

Brown, P., & Lauder, H. (2006). Globalization, knowledge, and the myth of the magnet economy. In H. Lauder, P. Brown, J. Dillabough, & A. H. Halsey (Eds.), *Education, globalization, and social change* (pp. 317–340). Oxford, UK: Oxford University Press.

Caughey, J. (1967). *Segregation blights our schools.* Los Angeles, CA: Quail Books.

Crampton, J. W., & Krygier, J. (2006). An introduction to critical cartography. *An International E-Journal for Critical Geographies, 4*(1), 11–33.

Creswell, J. (1997). *Research design: Qualitative, quantitative, and mixed method approaches.* Thousand Oaks, CA: Sage.

De Genova, N. (2005). *Working the boundaries: Race, space, and "illegality" in Mexican Chicago*. Durham, NC: Duke University Press.

Delaney, D. (2002). The space that race makes. *The Professional Geographer, 54*(1), 6–14.

Delgado, R., & Stefancic, J. (2001). *Critical race theory: An introduction*. New York, NY: New York University Press.

Du Bois, W. E. B. (1903/1999). *Souls of Black Folk*. New York, NY: W.W. Norton and Company.

Du Bois, W. E. B. (1925). Worlds of color. *Foreign Affairs, 3*, 423–444.

Dubin, R. A. (1992). Spatial autocorrelation and neighborhood quality. *Regional Science and Urban Economics, 22*, 433–452.

Dwyer, O., & Jones, J. P., III (2000). White sociospatial epistemology. *Social and Cultural Geography, 1*(2), 209–221.

Elwood, S. (2002a). GIS use in community planning: A multidimensional analysis of empowerment. *Environment and Planning A, 34*(5), 905–922.

Elwood, S. (2002b). GIS and collaborative urban governance: Understanding their implication for community action and power. *Urban Geography, 22*(8), 737–759.

Elwood, S., & Leitner, H. (2003). GIS and spatial knowledge production for neighborhood revitalization: Negotiating state priorities and neighborhood visions. *Journal of Urban Affairs, 25*(2), 139–157.

Friedland, R. (1992). Space, place, and modernity: The geographical moment. *Contemporary Sociology, 21*(1), 11–15.

Ghose, R. (2001). Use of information technology for community empowerment: Transforming geographic information system into community information systems. *Transactions in GIS, 5*(2), 141–163.

Harvey, D. (1990). Between space and time: Reflections on the geographical imagination. *Annals of the Association of American Geographers, 80*(3), 418–434.

Haymes, S. N. (2003). Toward a pedagogy of place for black urban struggle. In A. Darder, M. Baltodano, & R. D. Torres (Eds.), *The Critical Pedagogy Reader* (pp. 211–237). New York, NY: RoutledgeFalmer.

Hogrebe, M., & Tate, W. F. (2012). Research and geospatial perspective: Toward a visual political project in education, health, and human services. *Review of Research in Education, 36*, 67–94.

hooks, b. (1990). Homeplace: A site of resistance. In *Yearning: Race, gender, and cultural politics* (pp. 41–49). Boston, MA: South End Press.

Horng, E., Renee, M., Silver, D., & Goode, J. (2004). *The education gap in Los Angeles County*. Los Angeles, CA: UCLA, The Institute for Democracy, Education, and Access.

Jackson, P. (1998). Constructions of "whiteness" in the geographical imagination. *Area, 30*, 99–106.

Jones, J. P., III, Nast, H. J., & Roberts, S. M. (1997). *Thresholds in feminist geography: Difference, methodology, representation*. Lanham, MD: Rowman and Littlefield.

Kellogg, W. (1999). From the field: Observations on using GIS to develop a neighborhood environmental information system for community-based organizations. *URISA Journal, 11*(1), 15–32.

Knigge, L., & Cope, M. (2006). Grounded visualization: Integrating the analysis of qualitative and quantitative data through grounded theory and visualization. *Environment and Planning, 38*, 2021–2037.

Kobayashi, A., & Peake, L. (2000). Racism out of place: Thoughts on whiteness and an anti-racist geography in the new millennium. *Annals of the Association of American Geographers, 90*(2), 392–403.

Kwan, M. (2002a). Feminist visualization: Re-envisioning GIS as a method in feminist geographic research. *Annals of the Association of American Geographers, 92*(4), 645–661.

Kwan, M. (2002b). Is GIS for women? Reflection on the critical discourse in the 1990s. *Gender, Place and Culture 9*(3), 271–279.

Ladson-Billings, G., & Tate, W. (1995). Toward a critical race theory of education. *Teachers College Record, 97,* 47–68.

Lawrence-Lightfoot, S., & Hoffman Davis, J. (1997). *The art and science of portraiture.* San Francisco, CA: Jossey-Bass.

Lefebvre. (1975). The state in the modern world. In H. Lefebvre, (2009). *State, space, world: selected essays* (pp. 95–123). Minneapolis, MN: University of Minnesota Press.

Lefebvre, H. (1991). *The production of space.* Oxford, UK: Blackwell.

Malagón, M., Pérez Huber, L., & Vélez, V. (2009). Our experiences, our methods: Using grounded theory to inform a critical race theory methodology. *Seattle Journal for Social Justice, 8,* 253–272.

Matsuda, M. (1991). Voices of America: Accent, antidiscrimination law, and a jurisprudence for the last reconstruction. *Yale Law Journal, 100,* 1329–1407.

McDowell, L., & Sharp, J. P. (1997). *Space, gender, knowledge: Feminist readings.* London, UK: Arnold.

Monroy, D. (1999). Our children get so different here: Children and parents in Mexico de afuera. In D. Monroy (Ed.), *Rebirth: Mexican Los Angeles from the Great Migration to the Great Depression.* Berkeley, CA: University of California Press.

Moraga, C., & Anzaldúa, G. (eds.). (1983). *This bridge called my back: Writings by radical Women of Color.* (2nd ed.). New York, NY: Kitchen Table Women of Color Press.

Neely, B., & Samura, M. (2011). Social geographies of race: Connecting race and space, *Ethnic and Racial Studies, 34,* 1933–1952.

O'Loughlin, J., & Anselin, L. (1992). Geography of international conflict and cooperation: theory and methods. In M. D. Ward (Ed.), *The new geopolitics* (pp. 11–38). London, UK: Gordon and Breach.

Oakes, J. & Lipton, M. (1999). *Teaching to change the world.* Boston: McGraw-Hill College.

Omi, M., & Winant, H. (1994). *Racial formation in the United States from the 1960s to the 1990s.* New York, NY: Routledge.

Patel, L. (2015, July 17). Places become space: Structural oppression in situ. [Web log comment]. *Decolonizing Educational Research.* Retrieved from https://decolonizing.wordpress.com/2015/07/17/place-becomes-space-structural-oppression-in-situ/

Pattillo, M. (2007). *Black on the block: The politics of race and class in the city.* Chicago, IL: University of Chicago Press.

Peake, L., & Kobayashi, A. (2002). Policies and practices for an antiracist geography at the millennium. *The Professional Geographer, 54*(1), 50–61.

Peake, L., & Schein, R. H. (2000). Racing geography into the new millennium: Studies of "race" and North American geographies. *Social and Cultural Geography, 1*(2), 133–142.

Pérez Huber, L., Benavides Lopez, C., Malagon, M., Vélez, V., & Solórzano, D. (2008). Getting beyond the "symptom," acknowledging the "disease": Theorizing racist nativism. *Contemporary Justice Review, 11*(1), 39–51.

Price, P. (2010). At the crossroads: Critical race theory and critical geographies of race. *Progress in Human Geography, 34*, 147–174.

Price, P. (in press). Race and ethnicity: Geographies of diversity. *Progress in Human Geography.*

Pulido, L. (2000). Rethinking environmental racism: White privilege and urban development in Southern California. *Annals of the Association of American Geographers, 90*, 12–40.

Riles, W. (1966). *Racial and ethnic survey of California public schools.* Sacramento, CA: California Office of Compensatory Education, Bureau of Intergroup Relations.

Rose, H. M. (1970). The development of an urban subsystem: The case of the Negro ghetto. *Annals of the Association of American Geographers, 60*(1), 1–17.

Silverman, D. (2001). *Interpreting qualitative data: Methods for analyzing talk, text, and interaction.* Thousand Oaks, CA: Sage.

Silvern, S. (1995). Nature, territory, and identity in the Wisconsin treaty rights controversy. *Ecumene, 2*, 267–292.

Soja, E. W. (1989). *Postmodern Geographies.* London, UK: Verso.

Soja, E. W. (1996). *Thirdspace: Journeys to Los Angeles and other real and imagines places.* Cambridge, MA: Blackwell.

Soja, E. W. (2000). *Postmetropolis: Critical studies of cities and regions.* Cambridge, MA: Blackwell.

Soja, E. W. (2010). *Seeking spatial justice.* Minneapolis, MN: University of Minnesota Press.

Soja, E. W. (2014). *My Los Angeles: From urban restructuring to regional urbanization.* Berkeley, CA: University of California Press.

Solórzano, D. (1997). Images and words that wound: Critical race theory, racial stereotyping, and teacher education. *Teacher Education Quarterly, 24*, 5–19.

Solórzano, D. G. (1998). Critical race theory, race and gender microaggressions, and the experience of Chicana and Chicano scholars. *Qualitative Studies in Education, 11*(1), 121–136.

Solórzano, D. (2013). Critical race theory's intellectual roots: My email epistolary with Derrick Bell. In M. Lynn & A. Dixson (Eds.), *Critical race theory in education handbook* (pp. 48–68). New York, NY: Routledge.

Solórzano, D. G., & Delgado Bernal, D. (2001) Examining transformational resistance through a critical race and LatCrit theory framework: Chicana and Chicano students in an urban context. *Urban Education, 36*(3), 308–342.

Solórzano, D., & Solórzano, R. (1995). The Chicano educational experience: A proposed framework for effective schools in Chicano communities. *Educational Policy, 9*, 293–314.

Solórzano, D., & Vélez, V. (2007). *Critical race spatial analysis along the Alameda Corridor in Los Angeles.* Presented to the American Education Research Association Conference, Chicago, Illinois.

Solórzano, D. G., & Yosso, T. (2001a). Critical race and LatCrit theory and method: Counter-storytelling. *International Journal of Qualitative Studies in Education, 14*(4), 471–495.

Solórzano, D. G., & Yosso, T. (2001b). Maintaining social justice hopes within academic realities: A Freirean approach to critical race/LatCrit pedagogy. *Denver University Law Review, 78*(4), 595–621.

Solórzano, D. G., & Yosso, T. (2002a). Critical race methodology: Counterstorytelling as an analytical framework for education research. *Qualitative Inquiry, 8*(1), 23–44.

Solórzano, D. G., & Yosso, T. (2002b). A critical race counterstory of race, racism, and affirmative action. *Equity and Excellence in Education, 35*(2), 155–168.

Strauss, A., & Corbin, J. (1998). *Basics of qualitative research: Techniques and procedures for developing grounded theory.* (2nd ed.). Thousand Oaks, CA: Sage.

Stubblefield, A. (2005). *Ethics along the color line*. Ithaca, NY: Cornell University Press.

Tate, W. F. (2008). "Geography of opportunity": Poverty, place, and educational outcomes. *Educational Researcher, 37*(7), 397–411.

Valencia, R. R. (1997). *The evolution of deficit thinking: Educational thought and practice*. London, UK: Falmer Press.

Wild. M. (2002). "So many children at one and so many kinds": Schools and ethno-racial boundaries in early-twentieth-century Los Angeles. *Western Historical Quarterly, 33*(4), 453–476.

Wilson, W. J. (1996). *When work disappears: The world of the new urban poor*. New York, NY: Knopf.

Yosso, T. J. (2005). Whose culture has capital? A critical race theory discussion of community cultural wealth. *Race, Ethnicity, and Education, 8*(1), 69–91.

Zavella, P. (2000). Latinos in the USA: Changing socioeconomic patterns. *Social and Cultural Geography, 1*(2), 155–167.

PART TWO

CASE METHODOLOGIES AND TOOLS

3

DISRUPTING CARTOGRAPHIES OF INEQUITY

Education Journey Mapping as a Qualitative Methodology

Subini Ancy Annamma

Education inequities are often both a social and spatial phenomenon. This notion of a *sociospatial dialectic*, wherein geography impacts social relations while, simultaneously, social processes shape spatiality, is an essential dimension of understanding systemic injustices (Soja, 2010). However, much education research surrounding inequity has focused mainly on the ways social processes result in uneven outcomes. This sole focus on the social relationships has ignored the ways "the spatiality of (in)justice . . . affects society and social life just as much as social processes shape the . . . specific geography of (in)justice" (Soja, 2010, p. 5). In this chapter, therefore, I address a qualitative methodology for equity-focused educational research from a sociospatial dialectic: the creation and application of education journey maps. I begin by situating my work within an explicitly critical conceptual framing, one that addresses racism and its intersections with other systemic inequities, disability critical race theory. Next I explore education journey mapping as a qualitative methodology. Finally, I discuss the potential for using education journey mapping in future research.

Exploring Inequities Through Disability Critical Race Theory

Critical race theory (CRT) and disability critical race theory (DisCrit) allowed for an intersectional framing and therefore a more comprehensive analysis of educational inequities than unidimensional perspectives provided (Annamma, Connor, & Ferri, 2013; Crenshaw, Gotanda, Peller, & Thomas, 1995). In this section, I begin with foundations of CRT, then shift into the branch of DisCrit, and finally illuminate the affordances of this intersectional framework within a sociospatial dialectic.

CRT

Officially, CRT was born out of the critical legal studies (CLS) movement when CLS scholars engaged in a class analysis of the law but left out any recognition of race and racism. However, the intellectual lineage of CRT began much further back historically. Ida B. Wells, Frederick Douglass, Mary Church Terrell, and W. E. B. Du Bois were some of the brilliant scholars and activists who laid the foundations for CRT, centering race in analyses of injustice and listening to the historically oppressed (Lynn, 1999; Rabaka, 2007). Continuing in their footsteps were thinkers and activists such as Yuri Kochiyama, Bayard Rustin, Angela Davis, and Audre Lourde, who considered life at the intersections of race, gender, and sexual fluidity. Some of the foundational scholars developing CRT in law were Derrick Bell (1976), Mari Matsuda (1987), Kimberlé Crenshaw (1991), Richard Delgado (1987), and Neil Gotanda (1991). Gloria Ladson-Billings and William Tate (1995) were the founding principal scholars who expanded CRT into education. Other prominent scholars in CRT in education included Marvin Lynn (1999), Adrienne Dixson (2006), Larry Parker (1998), and Dave Stovall (2004), who have addressed the centrality of race and racism in education. Zeus Leonardo (2004), David Gillborn (2005), and Cheryl Matias (2013) problematized whiteness within the system of white supremacy. Octavio Villapando (2003), and Daniel Solórzano and Dolores Delgado Bernal (2001) considered intersections with language and immigration status in LatCrit. Keith Aoki (1997) and Brian Brayboy (2005) addressed the needs of specific racial groups. No one set of tenets makes up CRT. However, this list, though not exhaustive by any means, reflects scholars in CRT who continued to center race and racism and recognized the ways intersections with other marginalized identities socially construct particular bodies as unwanted in public space.

DisCrit

DisCrit is a branch of CRT that addresses the mutually constitutive nature of racism and ableism. DisCrit recognizes "that racism and ableism are normalizing processes that are interconnected and collusive. In other words, racism and ableism often work in ways that are unspoken, yet racism validates and reinforces ableism, and ableism validates and reinforces racism" (Annamma et al., 2013, p. 6). DisCrit sought to make clear ways in which racism and ableism functioned interdependently; these processes positioned unwanted bodies as deviant in order to justify their removal, isolation, and even execution. This process of dis-abling and targeting of raced bodies in a system of white supremacy meant those who have been constructed as furthest from the margins of ideal norms (e.g., white, male, able, upper class, heterosexual) were most susceptible to educational injustices.

The Affordances of DisCrit for Space Invaders

CRT and DisCrit continued to center race and recognized the ways that intersections with other marginalized identities made particular bodies most susceptible to educational injustice through uneven distribution of resources based on race in a system of white supremacy. As a CRT scholar, I situated myself as a space invader, an outside scholar who brings new epistemologies to the academy (Aoki, 2000). Here, I emulated the mission of other space invaders by connecting the spatial location of students and the way in which youth experienced racial inequity within schooling.

The intersectional framework, which offers an understanding of how bodies at the intersections of race and disability are susceptible to the mutually constitutive racism and ableism and how those bodies are then targeted for removal from public space, provides several affordances. First, beginning with the concept that racism and ableism are normal, not aberrant, DisCrit framing highlights how bodies different from the ideal are immediately identified as problematic. Second, this conceptual framework recognizes how, once identified, those differences are more likely to be pathologized and labeled as a deficit and disabled. Third, this framework acknowledges that these socially constructed disabilities (i.e., as the person becomes equated with the disability) are viewed as needing to be removed from public space and cured through containment in spaces less visible. Fourth, a DisCrit framework reminds us that the only way to resist this master narrative, the everyday, commonsense ideas that favor the privileged, is to juxtapose it against the counternarratives, stories from those without access to culturally valued forms of capital and power. Fifth, a DisCrit framework considered the spatial distribution of privilege and power within a system of white supremacy through critical race spatial analysis (CRSA; Vélez, Solórzano, & Pacheco, 2007). CRSA deliberates "how structural and institutional factors divide, constrict, and construct space to impact the educational experiences and opportunities available to students based on race" (Pacheco & Vélez, 2009, p. 293). Space invaders—scholars who have connected the importance of spatial analysis to highlight how inequities are enacted over geographies—have always existed in CRT (Aoki, 2000; Bell, 1992).

This initial framing allows me to bring different theories, processes, and questions to bear on the issues of educational injustice. A DisCrit framework requires me to focus on students positioned furthest from the desired norms, closest to the margins. The sociospatial dialectic supports this framing and allows me to explore how to best elucidate ways that historically oppressed students are both socially and spatially positioned, as well as ways in which they resist the structural violence education institutions impose. Therefore, my purpose in this chapter is to share a qualitative methodology informed by DisCrit, critical race spatial analysis, and a sociospatial dialectic—a methodology I term *education journey maps*.

Mapping the Margins

The methods researchers choose convey how we view the world and imagine ourselves in it (Paris & Winn, 2014). Our methods also influence and are influenced by the theories in which we situate ourselves, the studies we undertake, and the interactions that we have with and the ways we represent the communities in which we work (Solórzano & Yosso, 2002). My framing requires me to accentuate my participants' expertise in their own lives, situating them as knowledge generators in my conceptual framework, which includes theory, methods, and analysis (Chesney-Lind & Jones, 2010).

Education journey mapping as a qualitative methodology reflects my critical commitment to exploring the individual spatial and temporal journeys of students while situating them in the larger social reality of racism and white supremacy. Education journey maps cannot stand in isolation, but should be part of a larger corpus of data. A commitment to methodological pluralism includes the collection and analysis of textual narratives (e.g., interviews) and visual narratives (e.g., education journey maps; Katsiaficas, Futch, Fine, & Sirin, 2011).

Mapping is often considered a quantitative methodology and linked with geographic information systems (GIS). However, there exists a long history of using mapping in qualitative work as well (Brennan-Horley & Gibson, 2009; Kwan & Knigge, 2006). In geography, mapping of social spaces has been used to illustrate traditional knowledge (Rambaldi & Callosa, 2000) and to better understand individuals' sense of place in a physical space (Elwood & Leitner, 1998). These maps supported understanding of "hidden spatial preferences, cultural meanings, and everyday navigations of the city" (Brennan-Horley & Gibson, 2009, p. 2602). From geography, qualitative mapping expanded to include conceptual, social, and cognitive relationships in various fields and disciplines (Lynch, 1960; Milgram & Jodelet, 1976; Powell, 2010).

Michelle Fine, Valerie Futch, and Selcuk Sirin used mapping as a mediational methodology, one that connects the theories utilized and the stories people tell about themselves across time and space, in multiple empirical research projects, including studies of journeys from home countries to the United States of immigrant students, hyphenated identities of Muslim American youth, and lessons lived in the bodies of teen theater group participants (Futch & Fine, 2014; Katsiaficas, Futch, Fine, & Sirin, 2011; Sirin & Fine, 2008).

As I began to understand the benefits of mapping, I soon learned that maps could provide more than "a sense of the physical spaces that we traverse through, maps can shed light on the ways in which we traverse, encounter, and construct racial, ethnic, gendered, and political boundaries" (Powell, 2010, p. 553). Maps also had the potential to interrogate the space between individuals and social structures, linking the micro/singular embodied experiences with macro/systemic social inequities. Furthermore, as the color-line represented the internal components that were affected by the external settings African Americans could not access, maps could allow for a Du Boisian exploration between internal spaces and external environments (Du Bois, 1903). Maps could be used to critique the racialization of space (Krueger, 2010). Finally, maps may permit for both spatial and temporal representations of selves without reifying developmental stages of individuals (Futch & Fine, 2014).

Creating the Education Journey Maps

With the benefits of mapping in mind and with Fine's support, I adapted identity-mapping techniques to create education journey mapping (Sirin & Fine, 2008). I used these maps in several empirical research projects studying different inequities in education with a variety of students; this chapter describes the general qualitative methodology instead of one specific example. By sharing the process of creating the maps, I hope to illustrate that this is not a mere exercise that can be thrown together. Education journey mapping is a purposeful and rigorous methodological tool with concrete elements in which one can privilege the interactions, voice, and knowledge of participants as an act of "humanizing research" (Paris, 2011, p. 139).

Education journey maps are meant to capture trajectories throughout a student's education, so the prompt was written to allow for shifts of time and space:

> Map your education journey from when you started school to now. Include people, places, obstacles, and opportunities on the way. Draw your relationship with school. You can include what works for you and/or what doesn't. You can use different colors to show different feelings, use symbols like lines and arrows or words. These are just suggestions. Be as creative as you like and, if you don't want to draw, you can make more of a flow-chart. Afterward, you will get a chance to explain it to me.

During map creation, the prompt was displayed the entire time and I often reread it out loud for students when they requested. Materials were simple drawing supplies that varied by setting. In incarceration settings, pencils had to be meticulously counted before and after every meeting with students. The students did all the counting of materials themselves and were kind enough to help me keep track of things. In an environment where pencils were considered weapons, we had to be very diligent because I had what staff considered to be a bag of ammunition with me at all times. In public schools, these materials included a larger array of instruments, including markers, colored pencils, crayons, rulers, and paper.

Each time a student created and shared an education journey map, I created and shared my own for multiple reasons. As a model, I wanted students to understand that I also have a narrative to share, which was not to be interpreted by someone else, but to be discussed. Together we had a conversation about our trajectories, and participants were allowed to ask questions about my education journey map, just as I would about theirs. Students often asked if I would tell them what their maps meant. By creating my own map while students created theirs, I limited my gaze on their process, reassuring them that I was not there to monitor them in any way. Finally, sharing my education trajectory was an attempt to be as transparent with students about my own positionality as I asked them to be with me. There was a time in my life when a doctorate was not even a consideration; as a first-generation college student and an immigrant, it was not simply something I could not achieve, it was something I never contemplated. Additionally, my education trajectory has not been traditional, and I wanted them to know there are many roads to the future. Many students specifically thank me for that transparency during the process and mention in follow-up discussions that it helps them be open with me. Some students share that my map also helps them imagine more expansive futures than they originally had contemplated.

As a Woman of Color I had particular social locations in common with the students, particularly being a Person of Color, and sometimes gender. However, I was also a much more privileged person as I possessed social, economic, and cultural capital that is valued by society, such as being middle class, cis-gendered, and highly educated. The maps cannot eliminate the power differentials between the students and myself, or among students, but they allow for us to make visible those power issues and explicitly discuss where our lives intersected and diverged.

Sharing personal experiences with inequities is deeply intimate, and education journeys of Students of Color are often filled with state violence. Therefore, I found that one of the most important elements of creating the maps was expressing gratitude. In education journey mapping, gratitude was beyond just saying, "Thank you." It was in the listening and speaking, which created a dialogic spiral,

> whereby the dialogic process of listening and speaking co-creates an area of trust between speakers—and the space between. In this between space, the speakers' discourse reveals vulnerabilities and feelings. The conversation moves back and forth when the speaker becomes the listener and the listener becomes the speaker. In order for the conversation to continue, we must see or hear that the other is listening to what we are saying . . . ; by seeing them nod their head, by verbal callbacks like "Mm-hmmm" and "Exactly," and by hearing the other person extend our ideas by adding their own thoughts. . . . According to Bahktin (1981), when we speak, we hope those we are speaking to—our audience—will listen and reciprocate our words by answering them genuinely. (Kinloch & San Pedro, 2014, p. 30)

In education journey mapping, this dialogic spiral used the maps as a launching point for descriptions about trajectories that built trust. Utilizing verbal callbacks, asking questions about particular components of the maps, and requesting clarification about phrases and statements, the process allowed for the expression of gratitude in multiple ways in both data collection and analysis.

Data Analysis in the Cartographer's Clinic

To further situate students as the experts in their own lives, capable of generating knowledge, I included them in the data analysis. Fine originally suggested a gallery walk, and I built that idea into "The Cartographer's Clinic." Positioning the students as emerging expert cartographers, I provided a handout on what the field of cartography is and how maps are created. We began by discussing this cartographic information and then examined what themes and outliers were in relation to mapmaking and research. Next, students did a silent gallery walk of all the maps. They had a place to take notes, which included the following prompts and questions; however, they were not required to take notes if they did not find it useful.

> Start with a silent walk through. Note what you see throughout the education journey maps. Just write them down or make a mental note quietly for now.
> Themes between maps: What are the similarities you see? What do you love? What questions do you have? What does it make you think about your own life? What would you like to be in the map in five years/next year? What part of these maps would benefit younger girls?

Outliers: Ask yourself: What stands out? What is different? Remember that being an outlier takes the courage to say something. It may be something we are all thinking but many of us are too scared to say.

After the silent walk, we discussed the potential to share the maps voluntarily. I opened the conversation with why I created education journey maps, which I have told the individual participants before: every person has a story to tell and it is that person's story to tell. The students and I then set norms of participation together, such as the following: (a) no one is required to share, but we can all learn from each other's stories; (b) we may inquire but not interrupt; and (c) if there are converging or contrasting experiences, we can talk about them in the language of themes and outliers. Students then volunteered to share individual maps while the other participants listened and asked questions, and some continued to take notes. Though no one was forced to share, students were often eager to, as they were rarely asked about their own knowledge and understanding of the world. During this time, the cartographers explicitly discussed outliers and themes between maps. Students who were at first hesitant to share often became more willing as they began to see the similarities and differences between their journey and others. This analysis provided an opportunity for the students to make connections across their journeys and locate their own individual experiences within larger narratives around education. This data analysis illustrated the importance of allowing participants to be an authentic part of the research process. In every instance, students were able to make connections and identify themes and outliers that I had not. Moreover, the Cartographer's Clinic centered participants' perspectives, permitting them to critique their own accounts as well as my representation, a process of in-depth member checking as well as data analysis (Caelli, Ray, & Mill, 2003). They were able to clarify and therefore coconstruct the meaning of my findings. Ultimately, education journey mapping and the Cartographer's Clinic allowed for a sense of the larger inequities students face, ones that are both embodied and resisted.

Education Journey Mapping as Multidimensional

Education journey maps were more than geographic representations of spatial relationships. The sociospatial dialectic in the students' education journey maps was revealed to be multidimensional including topographical, physical, and political dimensions. In the following sections, I use the education journey maps of the three editors[1] of this book to briefly explore each of these dimensions.

Topographical Dimensions

Topographical dimensions of maps illustrate relief, including elevations and depressions. In education journey maps, relief was texture and content, which demonstrated participants' high and low points in their education journeys and their relationships with education. This topography allowed for a multilayered presentation of selves in motion throughout the education trajectory. Moreover it provided for a sense of embodiment, as students were able to illustrate how they felt injustices in their bodies while moving through education spaces.

This relief was illustrated in my own education journey map (Figure 3.1). In my map, I was able to express the depressions and elevations that impacted my own education trajectory. Depressions, or low points, included my mother's alcoholism, the ways my white teachers consistently attempted to silence my voice as a little Girl of Color, the death of my mother, and the death of my brother. Elevations, or high points, were the way I initially loved school, how my high school diploma allowed me to escape the chaos of my house and my hometown, my love for teaching high school, and the eventual achievement of my doctorate. My resistance was illustrated in the "toeing the line" that my sixth grade teacher complained about but that I kept up for years. It is clear from my map that depressions and elevations were not disconnected events; instead, they were deeply linked. The relief of injustices and resistance was embodied throughout this time, all contributing to my journey.

Many student maps included historical memory, wherein ways of learning were transmitted to the students from family and community members. In other words, many students did not believe that learning stopped when they exited the doors of the school. Sometimes these loved ones were people the students had not actually met but were included in a shared history through family and community lore. These topographical dimensions then were historical, social, and spatial. Education journey maps provided an opportunity for students to place themselves in a lineage of learning and education that both experienced and resisted subjugation.

Physical Maps

Physical dimensions of maps represent features of environments. Education journey maps provided an opportunity for students to draw physical dimensions, which provided a sense of the educational spaces, both internal and external, as well as the space between. It made visible power dynamics and state violence, along with factors that protected against those forces.

The map of my coeditor Darrell D. Jackson illustrates the political dimensions of education journey maps (see Figure 3.2). He shared how capitalism and consumerism impacted his life as he felt less affluent and trendy than his peers in elementary school. Darrell remembered the physical boundaries of school shifting when he attended a school outside of his immediate community for a year in middle school. He illustrated how his internal spaces were impacted in high school when a white teacher told her daughter (who later relayed the information to him) that she could not date Darrell because he was Black. Moreover, Darrell noted that he remembers no Teachers of Color to protect him until high school. During those formative years, Darrell found that his internal spaces of self were deeply affected by the external space of school. However, he also noted protective factors in high school, such as his high school principal being an African American man, as well as the deep impact his most formative high school teacher, an African American woman, had on him. These adults in

Figure 3.1. Subini Ancy Annamma's education journey map.

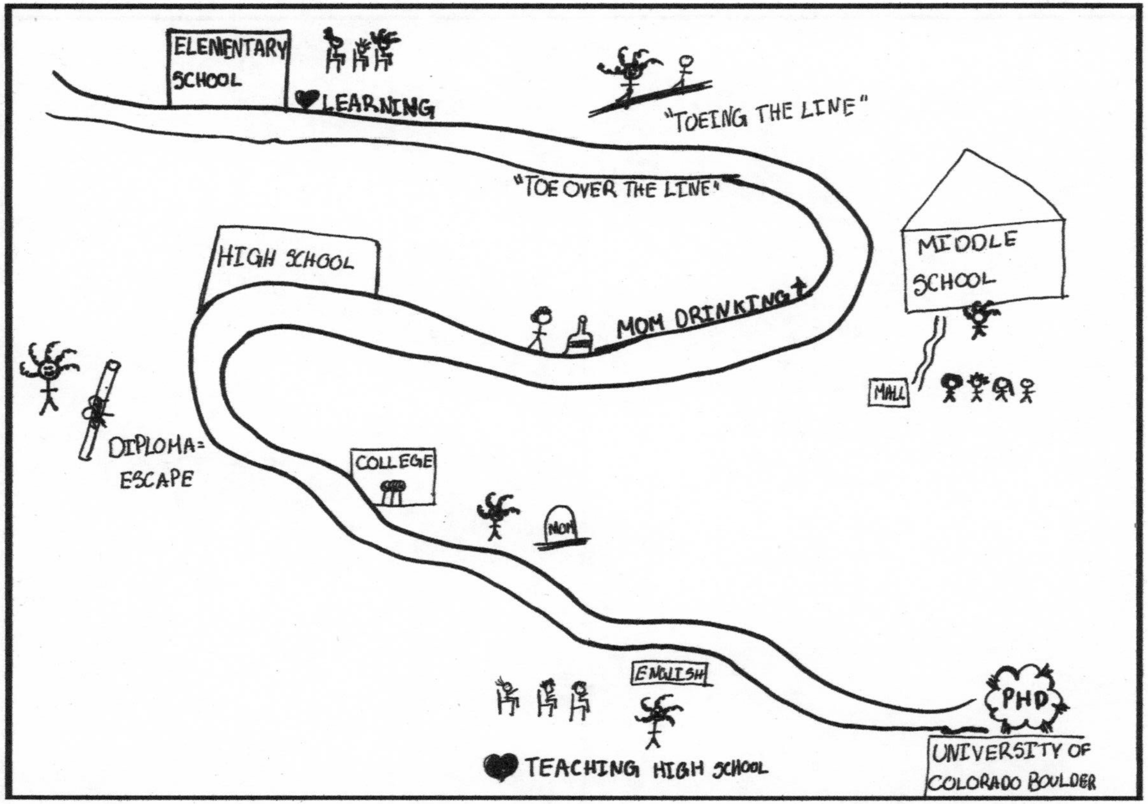

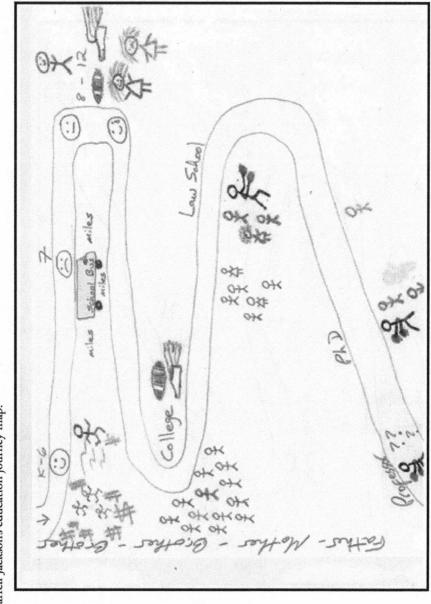

Figure 3.2. Darrell Jackson's education journey map.

positions of power supported and guided him in his internal spaces through affirmation as well as the external spaces of school. As he moved into college and law school, both predominantly white institutions (PWIs), Darrell found a community of People of Color to be his protective factor. First, socially in college, and then politically in law school, Darrell discovered that affinity grouping was necessary to protect him from the micro- and macroaggressions he faced. The affinity groups impacted those physical dimensions of PWIs. Externally, he knew where those safe spaces on campuses were; internally carrying that knowledge of those safe spaces made him feel better protected, even when he was not there. Moreover, when he awoke politically due to socially conscious classmates in law school, Darrell discovered that law could be a method of resistance, bolstering his reclamation of the physical dimensions of the law school.

Elijah Anderson (2015) notes that spaces are often conceived of as white (e.g., city's public spaces such as parks; middle-class or white-collar workplaces; middle- to upper-class neighborhoods, often gated) or Black (e.g., the most difficult service professions, such as stocking shelves in retail or kitchen staff in restaurants; jails; urban ghettos). The physicality of the maps illustrated how schools were considered white spaces in the minds of school personnel, which was communicated to students by continued attempts to force them out of view of this public space. This is despite the fact that Students of Color were given the legal right to occupy the space of public schools in the 1954 *Brown v. Board of Education* decision (Bell, 1976). However, this right to attend racially integrated schools did not mean that racialized students were welcomed into a white space. Students of Color were often assumed to carry the ghetto with them and therefore did not belong in the space of schools (Anderson, 2015). Maps revealed the mechanisms (e.g., labeling and segregating via special education, applying exclusionary discipline, policing through scrutiny and ticketing) through which the racialized space of schools was constructed and maintained within and across schools (Annamma, 2014). Yet these landscapes were not permanent fixtures in students' lives. Education journey maps provided a sense of change over time, allowing individuals dynamic representations throughout a variety of physical spaces. The physical dimensions of education journey maps provided an opportunity to see ways that racism was mutually constituted through spatial and social processes.

Political Maps

Political dimensions of maps tend to reflect boundaries (e.g., national, state, regional, city). Through education journey maps, historically marginalized children were able to represent the social and spatial impacts of the boundaried color-line (Du Bois, 1903). In other words, they were able to make visible the ways that race and racism affected their worlds, through barriers, both constructed and maintained. These barriers limited access to social, political, and economic justice. Yet education journey maps also allowed for a reboundaried cartography. Boundaries were drawn, torn down, and reimagined in the education journey maps.

The map of my coeditor Deb Morrison (see Figure 3.3) demonstrates this sense of both fixed boundaries and those that could be reimagined. Fixed boundaries

Figure 3.3. Deb Morrison's education journey map.

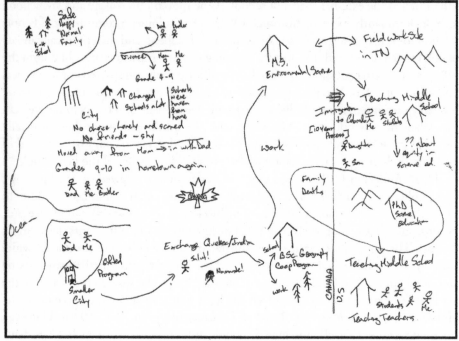

included the international boundaries she traversed traveling to India and immigrating to the United States from Canada. She was able to draw boundaries around certain significant episodes in her life that were meaningful and impacted the way she experienced access to justice. Deb also was able to share instances of reboundaried cartography. When confronted by a student who said, "I don't know what right you have to teach us. You don't know anything about our lives," Deb responded, "You're right." This unexpected answer opened a dialogue between them and provided Deb the opportunity to see the deeply critical and scientific minds her students had, allowing her and her students to tear down a boundary between them. Deb also found that in response to that move, new boundaries were erected between herself and her coworkers. Many teachers possessed narratives about the kids as problems, and Deb's sense of her students as brilliant did not align with those deficit-laden narratives.

This sense of shifting boundaries provided students a chance to identify not only boundaries created by the state, its institutions, and its agents, but also ways that students subverted those boundaries in order that their needs could be met. Many of the students' maps illustrated how they navigated state violence and injustice with savvy and ingenuity.

In creating and analyzing the maps, the students and I unearthed the topographical, physical, and political dimensions of education journey mapping. This tool provided an opportunity to deeply mine the participants' narratives. To that point, the dimensions located here are not the only ones that mapping will reveal. As other researchers and participants cocreate knowledge within a sociospatial dialectic, I believe they will find many more dimensions to add to what education journey maps uncover.

Mapping and Resisting Cartographies of Inequity

Education journey mapping provides an opportunity to explore the terrain between embodied experiences and social realities (Futch & Fine, 2014). This qualitative method informed by DisCrit, CRSA, and a sociospatial dialectic allows for historically marginalized students to uncover cartographies of inequity, the physical and social spaces in their education trajectories that transmit injustice. Most importantly, students are able to articulate how they recognized, confronted, and resisted these cartographies of inequity. Said differently, nondominant students were not simply victims of the state institutions that perpetuated injustice. Instead they were resilient actors within these problematic environments, not only surviving but also thriving.

Education journey mapping is a qualitative methodology useful for exploring the cartographies of inequities that students experience in education as well as the ways they resist those narrow definitions of their lives. However, I believe that a potential use of education journey mapping is to link the students' individual education journey maps more closely with mapping inequities in students' neighborhoods, schools, and communities. Spatially, there are macro- (global), meso- (regional), and microgeographical (local) scales. These scales are not isolated layers with no relationship to each other; instead, they are deeply interconnected (Soja, 2010). In terms of mapping and space, placing students' individual education journey maps in conversation with inequities would allow them to understand how these social and spatial inequities are a multiscalular phenomenon. That is, injustices do not simply occur on the individual level but also within community and global contexts. Education journey mapping has the potential to be part of larger study on mapping, helping students understand how their own journeys are linked to other individuals, communities, and the world. The Cartographer's Clinic allowed the students to understand how inequities played out in their peers' lives, but could be expanded to have students map inequities on multiple scales with different tools, such as GIS. This type of project would move education journey mapping from a qualitative methodology to a potentially discursive liberating tool wherein they connect spatial and social injustices across the macro- (global), meso- (regional), and microgeographical (local) scales more explicitly (Vélez & Solórzano, this volume).

Education journey mapping, a qualitative methodology informed by a sociospatial dialectic, provides an opportunity to collaborate with students to socially and spatially study the injustice that occurs in their lives and, also, how they resist those cartographies of inequity. These countercartographies allow for students from historically marginalized backgrounds to mediate power relations with researchers.

Moreover, they allow for new epistemologies and methodologies to be brought to bear on entrenched inequities, positioning Students of Color as knowledge generators. As Paris and Winn (2014) write, "Our work here, then, joins what we view as a trajectory toward a stance and methodology of research that acts against the histories and continuing practices, ideologies, and accompanying dehumanizing policies of discrimination and unequal treatment of particular bodies" (p. xvi). I hope that with continued applications, education journey mapping—like the research and methodologies that Paris and Winn (2014) refer to—can develop into a widely utilized tool for a variety of purposes, all of which are rooted in a critical commitment to address inequities in the lives of the historically marginalized.

Note

1. I want to express my deepest thanks to coeditors Deb Morrison and Darrell D. Jackson. Both took the time to create the maps and share their journeys with me. Like students before them, I am in deep debt to them and hope that I shared that gratitude during the dialogic spiral we created and afterward.

References

Anderson, E. (2015). The white space. *Sociology of Race and Ethnicity, 1*(1), 10–21.

Annamma, S. (2014). Disabling juvenile justice: Engaging the stories of incarcerated young women of color with disabilities. *Remedial and Special Education, 35*(5), 313–324. doi: 0741932514526785

Annamma, S. A., Connor, D., & Ferri, B. (2013). Dis/ability critical race studies (DisCrit): Theorizing at the intersections of race and dis/ability. *Race, Ethnicity and Education, 16*, 1–31. doi:10.1080/13613324.2012.730511

Aoki, K. (1997). Critical legal studies, Asian Americans in US law and culture, Neil Gotanda, and me. *Asian Law Journal, 4*(19), 19–38

Aoki, K. (2000). Space invaders: Critical geography, the third world in international law, and critical race theory. *Villanova Law Review, 45*(5), 913–958.

Bell, D. A. (1976). Serving two masters: Integration ideals and client interests in school desegregation litigation. *Yale Law Journal, 85*(4), 470–516.

Bell, D. A. (1992). *Faces at the bottom of the well: The permanence of racism.* New York, NY: Basic Books.

Brayboy, B. M. J. (2005). Toward a tribal critical race theory in education. *Urban Review, 37*(5), 425–446.

Brennan-Horley, C., & Gibson, C. R. (2009). Where is creativity in the city? Integrating qualitative and GIS methods. *Environment and Planning, 41*, 2595–2614.

Caelli, K., Ray, L. & Mill, J. (2003). "Clear as mud": Toward greater clarity in generic qualitative research. *International Journal of Qualitative Methods, 2*(2), 1-13.

Chesney-Lind, M., & Jones, N. (2010). *Fighting for girls: New perspectives on gender and violence.* Albany, NY: SUNY Press.

Crenshaw, K. (1991). Mapping the margins: Intersectionality, identity politics, and violence against women of color. *Stanford Law Review, 43*(6), 1241–1299.

Crenshaw, K., Gotanda, N., Peller, G., & Thomas, K. (1995). *Critical race theory: The key writings that formed the movement.* New York, NY: New Press.

Delgado, R. (1987). Ethereal scholar: Does critical legal studies have what minorities want? *Harvard Civil Rights-Civil Liberties Law Review, 22,* 301.

Dixson, A. D. (2006). What's race got to do with it? Race, racial identity development, and teacher preparation. In *Race, ethnicity, and education: The influences of racial and ethnic identity in education* (pp. 19–36). Westport, CT: Greenwood/Praeger.

Du Bois, W. E. B. (1903). *The souls of Black folk.* Oxford, UK: Oxford University Press.

Elwood, S., & Leitner, H. (1998). GIS and community-based planning: Exploring the diversity of neighborhood perspectives and needs. *Cartography and Geographic Information Systems, 25*(2), 77–88.

Futch, V. A., & Fine, M. (2014). Mapping as a method: History and theoretical commitments. *Qualitative Research in Psychology, 11*(1), 42–59.

Gillborn, D. (2005). Education policy as an act of white supremacy: Whiteness, critical race theory and education reform. *Journal of Education Policy, 20*(4), 485–505.

Gotanda, N. (1991). A critique of "Our Constitution is color-blind." *Stanford Law Review, 44*(1), 1–68.

Katsiaficas, D., Futch, V. A., Fine, M., & Sirin, S. (2011): Everyday hyphens: Exploring youth identities with methodological and analytic pluralism. *Qualitative Research in Psychology, 8*(2), 120–139.

Kinloch, V., & San Pedro, T. (2014). The space between listening and storying: Foundations for projects in humanization. In D. Paris & M. T. Winn (eds.), *Humanizing research: Decolonizing qualitative inquiry with youth and communities,* pp. 21–42.

Krueger, P. (2010). It's not just a method! The epistemic and political work of young people's lifeworlds at the school–prison nexus. *Race Ethnicity and Education, 13*(3), 383–408.

Kwan, M., & Knigge, L. (2006). Doing qualitative research using GIS: An oxymoronic endeavor? *Environment and Planning A, 38*(11), 1999–2002.

Ladson-Billings, G., & Tate, W., IV (1995). Toward a critical race theory of education. *The Teachers College Record, 97*(1), 47–68.

Leonardo, Z. (2004). Critical social theory and transformative knowledge: The functions of criticism in quality education. *Educational Researcher, 33*(6), 11–18.

Lynch, K. (1960). *The image of the city.* Cambridge, MA: MIT Press.

Lynn, M. (1999). Toward a critical race pedagogy: A research note. *Urban Education, 33*(5), 606–626.

Matias, C. E. (2013). Who you callin' white?! A critical counter-story on colouring white identity. *Race, Ethnicity, and Education, 16*(3), 291–315.

Matsuda, M. J. (1987). Looking to the bottom: Critical legal studies and preparations. *Harvard Civil Rights-Civil Liberties Law Review, 22,* 323.

Milgram, S., & Jodelet, D. (1976). Psychological maps of Paris. In H. M. Proshansky, W. H. Ittelson, & L. G. Rivlin (Eds.), *Environmental psychology: People and their physical settings* (2nd ed., pp. 104–125). New York, NY: Holt Rinehart and Winston.

Pacheco, D., & Vélez, V. N. (2009). Maps, mapmaking, and a critical pedagogy: Exploring GIs and maps as a teaching tool for social change. *Seattle Journal For Social Justice, 8*(1), 273-302.

Parker, L. (1998). "Race is race ain't": An exploration of the utility of critical race theory in qualitative research in education. *International Journal of Qualitative Studies in Education, 11*(1), 43–55.

Paris, D. (2011). "A friend who understand fully": Notes on humanizing research in a multi-ethnic youth community. *International Journal of Qualitative Studies in Education, 24*(2), 137–149.

Paris, D., & Winn, M. T. (2014). *Humanizing research: Decolonizing qualitative inquiry with youth and communities.* Los Angeles, CA: Sage.

Powell, K. (2010). Making sense of place: Mapping as a multisensory research method. *Qualitative Inquiry, 16*(7), 539–555.

Rabaka, R. (2007). *W. E. B. Du Bois and the problems of the twenty-first century: An essay on Africana critical theory.* Lanham, MD. Lexington Books.

Rambaldi G., & Callosa J. (2000). *Manual on Participatory 3-Dimensional Modeling for Natural Resource Management.* Essentials of Protected Area Management in the Philippines, Vol. 7. NIPAP, PAWB-DENR, Philippines.

Sirin, S. R., & Fine, M. (2008). *Muslim American youth: Understanding hyphenated identities through multiple methods.* New York, NY: New York University Press.

Soja, E. W. (2010). *Seeking spatial justice.* Minneapolis, MN: University of Minnesota Press.

Solórzano, D. G., & Delgado Bernal, D. (2001). Examining transformational resistance through a critical race and LatCrit theory framework: Chicana and Chicano students in an urban context. *Urban Education, 36*(3), 308–342.

Solórzano, D. G., & Yosso, T. J. (2002). Critical race methodology: Counter-storytelling as an analytical framework for education research. *Qualitative Inquiry, 8*(1), 23–44.

Stovall, D. (2004). School leader as negotiator: Critical race theory, praxis, and the creation of productive space. *Multicultural Education, 12*(2), 8–12.

Vélez, V., Solórzano, D., & Pacheco, D. (2007). *A critical race spatial analysis along the Alameda Corridor in Los Angeles.* Presented at the American Education Research Association Annual Conference, April 9–13, Chicago, IL.

Villalpando, O. (2003). Self-segregation or self-preservation? A critical race theory and Latina/o critical theory analysis of a study of Chicana/o college students. *Qualitative Studies in Education, 16*(5), 619–646.

4

REFRAMING TRADITIONAL GEOSPATIAL METHODS AND TOOLS FOR USE IN EDUCATIONAL INEQUITY RESEARCH AND PRAXIS

Deb Morrison and Graham S. Garlick

As researchers engage with the complexity of social contexts influencing education, our ability to gain insight and propose solutions to contemporary challenges is dictated, to some degree, by the critical analytic methods we employ. Spatial analysis, prevalent in many fields, has been taken up to a lesser degree in education for several reasons. First, tools of spatial analysis (e.g., geographic information systems [GIS]) have historically been complex instruments with which to learn and gain proficiency. In addition, such tools have been prohibitively expensive for often meagerly funded educational researchers, particularly those working on educational inequity. This has led to the current situation, where educational researchers, activists, and educators may often not be trained in the use of spatial analysis tools or even in understanding how to consider spatial dimensions of the phenomena they are examining.

With advances in technology in the past few decades, access to inexpensive yet effective spatial analysis tools has improved. In working with spatial data, we have used a range of inexpensive or free tools to construct spatial data representations (e.g., maps, tables, charts) and conduct spatial analyses. This work has allowed us to examine our data in ways that have often provided new and interesting insight. In this chapter we share our current thinking on the types and uses of spatial analysis tools in order to facilitate the use of this type of analysis and visualization with other critically minded educational scholars, activists, and educators. We have found such work improves students' critical geospatial thinking, allowing them to connect physical space with the way humans interact with and racialize such space. The critical use of such tools and analysis by students also helps them develop computational thinking skills that can open up opportunities in careers involving science, technology, engineering, and mathematics (STEM), a goal we have as critical science educators. However, even if students do not choose a STEM career, learning mapping skills in a critical context will allow them to situate themselves in a wider world, understanding systemic inequities and ways to resist those structural imbalances.

Framing

Before engaging in a discussion of possible tools useful for geospatial visualization and analysis of educational inequity, we feel the need to stress that all tools are socially constructed and thus are subject to oppressive ideologies. From this understanding we can see that all tools are constructed within a particular social perspective and with the accompanying assumptions and biases, whether explicitly called out or not, and as a result can be subject to oppressive use; however, such tools can also be reclaimed for liberatory praxis (Soja, 2010; Vélez & Solórzano, 2016).

The idea that tools are value-free or that data analysis is objective is absurd. Harding (2006) argues that it is not just the application of science or in the actions of a single scientist where ideological assumptions enter in but rather that these political philosophies

> help to determine the kinds of scientific questions that will be asked, the ways good scientific method is conceptualized and practiced, and for whom the results of research will be especially useful. Philosophies of science shape and are shaped by social relations, though usually "behind the backs" of the philosophers and scientists who take themselves to be conducting value-free research and argument. (p. 113)

The idea that the creators and users of tools are unconscious of the bias within their methodologies does not excuse them from the oppressive impacts of their application. As critical methodologists, we are deeply committed to raising researchers' awareness about the unintended consequences of their methodologies in an effort to reduce injustice resulting from unjust research practices.

In examining racial oppression as an example of the broader ideas of oppressive methodology, it is important to consider how the tools you use may themselves contain racial bias. Zuberi and Bonilla-Silva (2008) highlight the racial bias of tools in their book *White Logic, White Methods: Racism and Methodology*, stating,

> *White logic*, then, refers to a context in which white supremacy has defined the techniques and process of reasoning about social facts. White logic assumes a historical posture that grants external objectivity to the views of elite whites and condemns the views of non-whites to perceptual subjectivity; it is the anchor of the Western imagination, which grants centrality to the knowledge, history, science, and culture of elite white men and classifies "others" as people without knowledge, history, or science, as people with folklore but not culture. (p. 17)

It is perhaps easier to see how some qualitative methods could be influenced by oppressive social structures and ideologies; however, quantitative methods are equally affected. For example, one of the key ideas within quantitative statistics is probability, often based on the normal curve. We like to talk about variances from the mean and confidence intervals. In doing so we are obscuring a number of important biases in our data analysis. For example, the normal curve holds the average of a phenomena as one possible center of the data against which other data can be compared. While this is helpful for understanding variation in a phenomena, it cannot be decontextualized from the reality that the lived experiences of humans are radically different depending on their social positioning due to current and historical power structures. Inferences we make about such variation have to be situated in this complex sociohistoric context. As Austin (2008) suggested in her analysis of crime statistics, "When racial statistics are interpreted or discussed, race is very often treated as if it were *a cause of*, rather than merely a *factor associated with*, social phenomena" (p. 307). In examining this type of data analysis in the context of white logic we can see that the construction of race categories within our data collection and analysis practices may result in these categories being seen as objective bins into which people can be classified and about which we can assign characteristics. However, in reality the bins themselves are social constructs and, like all classification (in "pure science" as well), there are challenges to delineating such boundaries.

As critical scholars we should ask questions about racial categories used in data collection and analysis, such as:

- Who named the categories? And with what understanding of the impact of naming?[1]
- What happens when an individual could logically be assigned to more than one category? Who decides which one they are put in or how analysis is handled if they are put in two categories?[2] Who is left out of a category?
- How are categories used in ways that may make white a normative comparison instead of holding each group in its own sociohistoric context and not assigning power to one group over another?
- What is the advantage of using existing categorizations that you recognize as oppressive?[3]

Other critical scholars (e.g., of gender, sexual orientation, class) also have examples of how methods in their contexts are biased or oppressive (de Saxe, 2012; Jaggar, 2013; Naples, 2012). Researchers should also be aware that they are positioned in particular ways that influence data collection and analysis. For example, it is well documented that white researchers interviewing People of Color garner different responses than would a researcher positioned as an "insider" within a particular Community of Color (Ritchie & Rigano, 2001; Rhodes, 1994; Song & Parker, 1995).

In the field of geospatial methodologies, critical geographers have expressed concerns with the use of spatial tools developed within dominant ideologies. In

Chapter 1 Vélez and Solórzano provide a more comprehensive review of the work of critical geographers in their theorizing of critical race spatial analysis than we engage in here; however, we wish to briefly highlight this link between critical methodologies as discussed previously and critical spatial analysis, of which critical race spatial analysis is a subset. We draw on scholars examining space in critical ways, where power differences are a central component of research in both choice of the tools employed and ways data are analyzed (Soja, 2010; Solórzano & Vélez, 2007). This critical spatial perspective allows us to consider ways educational equity scholars may identify and analyze spatial components of the phenomena they study. From this perspective, we seek to integrate the social, historical, and spatial factors impacting educational equity in an effort to understand how to improve the experiences and opportunities of those who have historically been marginalized within educational structures. Soja (2010) states,

> Human spatiality in all its forms and expressions is socially produced. We make our geographies, for good or bad, just or unjust, in much the same way it can be said that we make our histories, under conditions not of our own choosing but in real-world contexts already shaped by socio-spatial processes in the past and the enveloping historically and socially constituted geographies of the present. This profoundly displaces the idea of space merely as external environment or container, a naturalized or neutral stage for life's seemingly time-driven social drama. (p. 103)

Thus, in critical analyses of educational phenomena it is relevant to consider not only time (history) and social interactions but also the spaces in and across which these events occur. Furthermore, space itself can be seen as both physical space (external) and the way in which such space is mediated by human interaction with it (internal; Soja, 2012).

Finally, it is important to note that we are deeply committed as critical scholars to the idea of praxis. We draw on Freire's (1970/2000) notion of praxis, which links the ideas of reflection and action and allows us to think about the ways in which we explore phenomena and analyze data with the goal of making some kind of change to disrupt inequity. In addition, Freire clearly highlights the need to work not only with the oppressed but also with oppressors who are caged in their minds by their own structures of supremacy. Our work is both for those who are engaged in liberatory work within Communities of the Oppressed as well as for those who are oppressing and may not even be aware. We want all to be responsible for the deconstruction of oppression. Work in social justice, therefore, is important not simply because it makes visible particular inequities but because of a deeply held commitment those engaged in this work have for *action* against oppression and inequities (Bell, 1997; Chapman & Hobbel, 2010; Nieto & Bode, 2012). Part of that action is in developing skills for GIS analysis within the communities with which one works.

In this chapter, we center our discussion on GIS tools of geospatial analysis, exploring what is currently available, examining tools' potentially oppressive assumptions, and suggesting ways these tools can be used in liberatory praxis. Thus, we are not suggesting that we throw away all tools constructed within oppressive ideologies; we are actually saying the opposite, that we need to be explicit about the limitations of these methods, reclaim responsibility about their use, and find liberatory projects in which such transformative use can be enacted. In taking a praxis stance toward this discussion of geospatial visualization and analysis tools we examine only instruments that are easily and equitably available to researchers, community activists, educators, and students. Our goal here is to provide people interested in engaging in critical spatial analysis work in education with the entry knowledge and resources they need to pragmatically take steps for their own work, constantly iterating between critical reflection and action. While we focus in this chapter on existing geospatial tools, often constructed within normative spaces, we are excited to see an increasing number of methods authored by critical methodologists themselves (Annamma, 2016; Blaisdell, 2016; Hidalgo, 2015; Kellogg, 1999; Kwan, 2002; Malagón, Perez Huber, & Vélez, 2009; Pacheco & Vélez, 2009; Soja, 2010; Tate, 2008; Vélez & Solórzano, 2016) and wish to encourage readers to explore these methods more, as they offer exciting ways to engage in critical methodology.

In this chapter we use our own experiences and those drawn from the research to address the following questions:

- How can researchers determine the nature of the spatial component of their research?
- How can researchers inexpensively examine the spatial components of their data to help inform analysis or guide visual interpretation?

The Challenge of Dynamic Critical Spatial Analysis Methods

In thinking about how best to share our experiences and resources on using geospatial methods and tools in critical projects we found ourselves with a conundrum: the field is expanding so fast that by the time this book is published much more work will be done in this area, thus making our work less relevant. To address this issue we decided to create a webspace (yes, we love spaces of all kinds!), which we have named the Investigating Spatial Equity and Education Hub (ISEE Hub[4]), where we could continue to share new resources for engaging in critical geospatial work. In addition, we created a virtual work and discussion space that could facilitate networking and mentoring among those engaged in this work; however, in order to share work in progress (which may require a degree of risk with those sharing) and copyrighted materials, we have made this a closed work group but welcome people involved in this area of activity to join through our collaborative group, the Investigating Spatial Equity and Education Collaborative (ISEE Collaborative).[5]

As the ISEE Hub has developed over the years, we have attempted to include geospatial resources that are readily available to use in the work of examining spatial components of educationally related phenomena. This effort developed out of a series of conversations with people we knew about tools and resources for spatial analysis.

Other conversations resulted from peer-to-peer referencing; one person would tell us of others we should also talk with or resources we should explore. As such, we make no claims about the extent of our work as representative of available resources; rather, we position this work as an initial attempt to explore the terrain of tools and resources available for scholars interested in examining educational equity. In addition, we have drawn upon our own expertise and the literature in spatial analysis to outline useful types of data displays, which may be helpful in analysis and reporting of educational equity research. All of our ongoing work in this area is available at the ISEE Hub, and we encourage people to suggest further resources or methodologies that this space should include.

Finally, in thinking about the boundaries of this chapter, we would like to differentiate our definitions of geospatial methods from geospatial tools, as we explore both. *Geospatial methods* include a wide variety of ways to organize for and conduct analysis on spatial phenomena. In contrast, *geospatial tools* are the specific artifacts with which people conduct research. For example, a method is data visualization (see later in this chapter for more detail on this topic) of a set of points across space, while possible tools for creating such visualizations include paper and pencil, GIS, or spreadsheets. Thus, a method is a process of theorizing how you will gain spatial understanding of a phenomena and identifying assumptions and engaging in the use of particular tools, whereas a tool is the actual object or software you use to conduct this work. In this chapter, we talk generally about some methods and introduce some tools for use in geospatial analysis (e.g., spreadsheets, web-based maps, or GIS systems) that may be helpful. It is important to restate here that all methods and tools for geospatial research are socially situated in culture and history and thus mediate our understanding of physical space in ways that are also deeply socially situated.

Methods for Determining the Spatial Nature of a Research Interest

People interested in engaging in a critical spatial analysis of educational phenomena need to determine the nature of the spatial component of their research interest. Understanding the spatial nature of a phenomena is usually done before engaging with spatial tools and methods; however, in some situations you may want to engage with critical spatial tools and methods as a way of determining the nature of the spatial component of your research interest. As there are various ways to engage with critical tools and methods, the organization of the remainder of this chapter is somewhat arbitrary and does not reflect a linear path of research or even a singular path, as many methods may be combined in new and interesting ways in your own contexts. Instead, we have simply decided to begin by stating some things to consider about understanding the spatial nature of your research interest. Often, this is where we begin; then we iterate with various methods to refine and possibly redirect our understandings as we progress on a particular path of research.

To begin, we felt it would be helpful to provide novice participants in critical spatial analysis with a set of guidelines for determining the spatial nature of educational equity research. These guidelines are our initial attempt at putting into practice the work of many of the theory and casework researchers mentioned in our "Framing" section. When beginning to work on a project it can often be worthwhile to ask yourselves and all participants in the project a series of questions to help identify, map, and analyze the spatial components of research. Such questions may include, but are not limited to, the following:

- How do your research participants vary across space and time?
- Are there particular corridors of significance, physical features that afford or constrain movement, common community spatial references, or other interesting spatial phenomena that arise in discussions with participants or observations?
- What types of visual or technological methods of data collection may bridge cultural boundaries within your community, allowing for previously unheard data to be documented?
- What spatial referencing is available for you to display your data? How could you use your community to provide alternative georeferencing for your data?
- How can you involve your community in the analysis of data? Who is participating in data analysis with particular tools? How are you organizing for data analysis and GIS skill development among research participants?
- What other factors have covaried over time and space or may have instigated particular shifts, specifically with relation to differential power dynamics?
- What other factors, not currently available in existing data, might be needed to understand your research interest? How could your community be involved in the collection of this data?
- Is the knowledge of tool use being equitably shared with and among the research participants?

To answer some of these questions, in the following section we provide some thoughts to consider.

Spatial Data

Spatial data are any data with a spatial component. Within the realm of equity studies, this will usually be a location (e.g., classroom desk location, public service locations, or school address) or an area (e.g., school district, county, zip code, or state). However, it could also be a line such as a road or path. An example of location data could be the latitude and longitude of a school with the associated data about the percentage of Students of Color attending that school or the proportion of the student population suspended or expelled. Each of the latitude/longitude pairs represents a location on the Earth while the percentage value is the measurement made or observed at that location. An example of area data could be state boundaries with the percentage of women in STEM careers employed in the state. Each state is an area, and the associated value applies to the entire state. Since *state* is a well-understood concept, the geographic location is only implied and the complex description of the boundary of each area is not necessary. Most phenomena have a spatial component. It is very likely that your data measure something at some place (e.g., school, business, community service) or in some area (e.g., community, school district, county, state, or country). In addition, the way in which these points or boundaries are drawn or labeled has implications for the way in which sociohistoric processes or you in your research process—or both—have mediated the internal space, the meaning, of the external physical space.

Spatial data can be examined through two primary methods: visualizations and spatial analysis. However, the division between these methods is not absolute, and some novel critical approaches to spatial data collection and analysis merge these two ways of examining spatial data (e.g., educational journey maps, see Annamma, 2016; augmented fotonovelas, see Hidalgo, Chapter 5, in this volume). Visualization is the transformation of data into a graphical or visual form (Dykes, MacEachren, & Kraak, 2005). Whenever you create a chart or diagram of some data you are doing visualization. For the purpose of discovering whether your data has an interesting spatial component, visualization transforms a dataset from raw words and numbers into a picture that can be checked for patterns of interest.

Spatial analysis is the use of various analytic techniques to ask a question of a set of spatial data. This type of analysis can be done using simple data processing tools such as formulas within spreadsheets that are then mapped, or by using more complex spatial analysis tools such as geographic information systems (GIS), which do both the numerical analysis and the mapping. Once you have determined that your data have an interesting spatial component, using spatial analysis tools will help you investigate the spatial questions you may have.

Spatial Visualizations

In order to visualize data you need to follow a series of steps. To start, you need to recognize what type of spatial data you have: location or area (as mentioned previously). Location data, also known as point data, are generally easier to deal with and require no deep knowledge of GIS for visualization or analysis. Rendering—the creation of a meaningful image from data—is more complex for area data than it is for location data, but the good news is that for the purposes of checking to see if your data have a spatial component, you will be able to use simple points to represent the areas in early stages of analysis.

After identifying your data type you need to geocode your data. *Geocoding* is the process of taking a location description like "5500 Aspen Drive, Broomfield, Colorado," and converting it into a set of spatial coordinates that represents the location using numbers. These coordinates usually end up being in decimal degrees of latitude and longitude. For the example address, the geocoded location is: 39.5052795, -105.5246166 (latitude, longitude). A simple method for geocoding data when you have street addresses, zip codes, municipalities, counties, and states can be found at the ISEE Hub site under Background Information/Visualizing Spatial Data/2) Geocode Your Data.

After geocoding, you need to think about ways to display your data. There are numerous ways to display data, depending on if it is location or area data. For example, with location data you could use Google's Fusion Tables, which have easy-to-read tutorials and guides for rendering your data.[6] If you want or need to keep your data locally on your computer, then GIS software, described more fully in the following sections, is an option. Regardless of the tools used, adding color or symbols to your data based on some attribute will reveal much about the spatial contribution to almost any dataset.

The following example of a data visualization process can help to make these steps more concrete. Suppose we have the small dataset found in Table 4.1. By geocoding the first column we can calculate a specific location (longitude and latitude) with the data values in the last column (Table 4.2). Now that we have coordinates for the data we can visualize them in several ways: plot in a simple chart using a simple spreadsheet charting tool (Figure 4.1), use a desktop GIS system to view the data (Figure 4.2), or upload the data to Google Fusion Tables and see the data on top of a standard map backdrop (Figure 4.3).

While these three techniques produce similar results, they have different advantages and disadvantages. A chart (Figure 4.1) is quick and easy to produce, and the data can stay on your local system. However, you will not have access to GIS analysis tools, which you may want to use in more complex analyses. The primary advantage of spreadsheet charts is that they are a good tool for a quick check for spatial patterns

TABLE 4.1
Initial Example Dataset

Address	Category
123 Pearl St., Boulder, CO	1
80305	2
Boulder County	3
5500 Arapahoe Rd., Boulder, CO	4
Boulder Valley School District, Colorado	5

TABLE 4.2
Example Dataset With Geocoding

Address	Latitude	Longitude	Category
123 Pearl St., Boulder, CO	-105.26230	40.02156	1
80305	-105.25212	39.98052	2
Boulder County	-105.36321	40.10256	3
5500 Arapahoe Rd., Boulder, CO	-105.17571	40.01470	4
Boulder Valley School District, Colorado	-105.20200	40.01420	5

Figure 4.1. Simple chart using a simple spreadsheet charting tool.

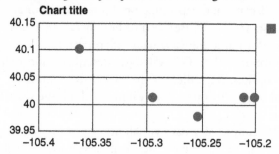

Figure 4.2. Example desktop GIS system used to view the data.

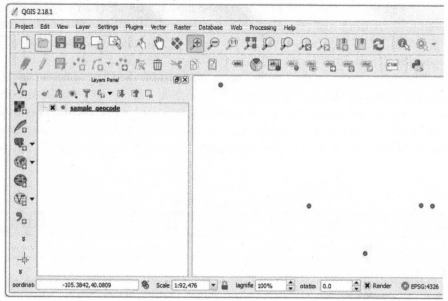

within your data. A desktop GIS system (free or licensed) provides access to all the GIS tools you could need while allowing you to keep your data local (not online); however, these systems can take longer to configure for data import and require more advanced expertise. The main advantage of a desktop GIS system is the complex analyses you can conduct once a spatial curiosity has been uncovered. Google Fusion Tables are fairly simple to use, geocoding can be done during the upload, and a backdrop map will lend immediate relevance to your data. This tool is good at generating aesthetically pleasing location data maps which, with the background map, assist viewers in understanding the data context. An advantage of this technique is that you will be able to see your data on top of the Google road and aerial photo layer, providing spatial context. However, you will have to upload data to do this and will therefore have to think about how to maintain your data privacy when using such online tools.[7] Desktop GIS systems often allow background layers (e.g., road networks) to be rendered, but the GIS configuration can be difficult.

Figure 4.3. A standard map backdrop with data overlaid using Google Fusion tables.

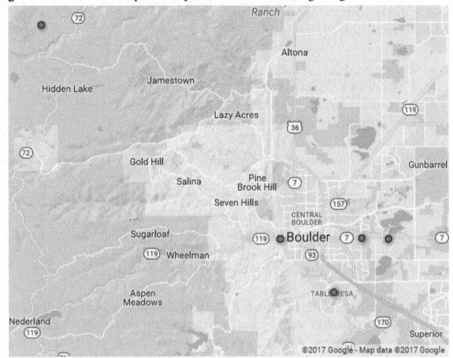

Spatial Analysis

Beyond spatial visualization of educational phenomena, one may also want to engage in some type of spatial analysis. The acronym "GIS" applies to the technology (geographic information systems[8]), as well as the career of working with the technology (geographic information science) or studying the technology (geographic information studies). They can be more generally considered parts of geoinformatics. For the purposes of this chapter, we concentrate on the following two fundamental questions that a GIS can answer:

1. Where is something with particular characteristics?
2. What things are at a particular location?

As you become more skilled with the technology or work with specialists in this area you can ask more elaborate questions. The first of these fundamental questions asks for the location(s) of data in the GIS that fit a particular criteria. Common examples could include the following:

- Which schools have a student population greater than 700?
- Which roads have a name containing the text string "main"?
- Where are the five largest school districts?
- Where is the road called Main Street?

The second question is the digital version of pulling out a map, stabbing your finger down, and examining the location. Common questions you might ask at this stage of analysis include the following:

- Where are the nearest coffee shops to latitude = 39.9 and longitude = -103.5?
- What school is closest to latitude = 25.8 and longitude = -113.6?
- What street is closest to latitude = 15.8 and longitude = -103.3?
- What county is at latitude = 24.2 and longitude = -123.4?

Combining these types of questions we can ask the following very general questions:

- What hospitals are within 1,000 meters of Interstate 25?
- What is the nearest coffee shop to my current location?
- What is the shortest walking route between a public library and a secondary school?
- Is there a grocery store at the corner of Main and First?

Although a multitude of combinations of these fundamental types of spatial analysis questions can be asked of any dataset, it is important as critical scholars to ask questions that may reveal power differentials in the situation you are examining. For example, Hoegrebe and Tate (2016) use spatial analysis to ask about the quantity of advanced math courses offered within different school districts in Missouri. This initial query of their data is then combined with other queries, such as, "What are the characteristics of the various school districts in terms of spending, student demographics, and so on?" The combination of such analyses allows these scholars to make inferences about the opportunities of students in poverty and Students of Color to participate in advanced mathematics, a foundational need for those going into STEM careers.

Spatial Dependency

Also interesting within both spatial visualization work and spatial analysis is the identification of spatial dependency within data, patterns of data characteristics across space. In order to determine spatial dependencies within your data, you can ask the following types of questions:

- Are the the data randomly located or clumped?
- Do the data occur along some land feature (e.g., mountains, valleys, or roads) or have some sociohistoric reason for their location?
- Is there a spatial reason for the locations of your data? How could you use your community to examine possible explanations for data locations?
- Does the value of the location data seem be related to their location?
- Does the spatial pattern of one value seem similar to the spatial pattern of another value?[9]

Once the data are visualized it is often easy to determine if the data have spatial dependencies, as our eyes are fantastic at recognizing patterns. Some examples of common spatial dependencies are found on the ISEE Hub Background Information/ Perceiving Spatial Dependency page. Once you have a visualization or some kind of analysis that speaks to you about your data, you will be in a better position to investigate the source of the apparent spatial aspect of your data.

Tools and Resources for Examining the Spatial Component of Educational Phenomena

While the previous discussion has provided some initial guidance for the process of understanding the spatial nature of your data, this section addresses tools you can use during this process. Specifically, we want to explore tools that allow researchers to inexpensively examine the spatial components of their data to help inform analysis or guide visual interpretation. We have already discussed a few simple visualization tools, such as spreadsheet charts and Google Fusion Tables, so here we limit our discussion to the more complex GIS technologies that are available and lay out some ideas for how educational researchers may begin to engage with these tools.

GIS Software

Of the dozens of GIS applications available through a web search, we list here our favorite two: QGIS and ArcGIS. These tools both have affordances and constraints. QGIS[10] is a not-for-profit, open-source software available free to anyone. As such there are also abundant resources that users and developers have created for new users of this software.[11] ArcGIS is produced by ESRI[12] for profit. While we are reluctant in an educational equity context to highlight any profit-seeking resource, we note the ArcGIS software because it is now free to all K–12 educators and students,[13] it has abundant free online training resources,[14] and using this software with your research participants can help develop valuable skills that are likely to be immediately beneficial in the context of GIS employment due to the extensive use of this software in a variety of contexts.

GIS Education and Training

There are numerous ways in which to learn about GIS. For example, there are "What Is GIS?" web pages; however, many of these may be more technical than you desire. Collaboration with colleagues in geography departments of local universities can provide immediate access to more complex GIS techniques and student experts who will most likely be happy to show you the cool potential of GIS tools. The Data Center,[15] a nonprofit that assists communities with research on justice issues, is also expanding work into the area of geospatial analysis and thus is also a possible collaborator. Finally, an increasing number of online courses or massive open online courses (MOOCs) are available for those interested in playing with GIS. For example, ENet Colorado has

GIS courses available in their professional development area,[16] including ESRI-specific courses.[17] Other training, networking, mentoring, and different types of resources can often be located more locally through state geographic alliances or collaborations.[18]

Conclusion

We believe that taking a critical geospatial analysis lens can deepen the work of many scholars in understanding issues of inequity and finding ways forward in our complex sociohistorical landscape. While we have addressed more of the quantitative aspects of data collection (e.g., statistics and the mechanics of data visualizations), we would like to highlight that the methods and tools discussed here are not to be used to the exclusion of other critical geospatial methods and tools but instead in conjunction with these approaches.

We encourage people engaged in educational research, community activism, teaching and learning, and GIS, often working across the wide variety of nonprofit and for-profit settings, to collaborate in efforts to improve work in the field of critical geospatial analysis. We hope to continue to provide the space for collaborations in this work through this basic primer and through our ongoing work on the ISEE Hub and ISEE Collaborative.

Notes

1. An interesting example here is the term *Hispanic* used in the U.S. Census for many years. This term is offensive to many people who would be assigned to this category as it means "little Spaniard" and is thus derogatory.

2. If you are both "Hispanic" and "Black," where are you assigned in such a classification structure? Where there are multiple racial categories to which you could be assigned, how does analysis prioritize your assignment to one category over another?

3. As we frame our work in critical theory to outline structural factors resulting in racial disproportionality, we may work from existing statistical categories of ability and race, not because we believe they are biological realities, but because these categories highlight socially constructed inequalities. We feel this is important to state as we in no way wish to reproduce these classifications or impose naming on any one individual or group of people; instead we want to highlight how the process of structural racism externally imposes identities on individuals by applying socially constructed labels and associating specific actions and subsequent consequences to those so labeled. We thus acknowledge that while ability and racial categories are socially constructed, they do have real outcomes for the lived experiences of Youth of Color. (Adapted footnote from Annamma, Morrison, & Jackson, 2014, p. 56, for use in calling out assumptions of race category use.)

4. The ISEE Hub is found at https://sites.google.com/site/spatialequityandeducation/spatial-data

5. Membership can be requested at https://groups.google.com/d/forum/spatial-equity-and-education

6. More information on Google Fusion Tables can be found at www.google.com/drive/apps.html#fusiontables

7. A simple way to maintain data privacy is to numerically code data prior to uploading so that the actual meaning of your data is obscured. The numerical categories can then be plotted in different colors or with different symbols, and when writing about your image you can discuss these categories with their real-world labels and meanings.

8. See https://en.wikipedia.org/wiki/Geographic_information_system for more detailed information on this topic.

9. This question is a little more complex. An example here could be the similar patterns found by Annamma, Morrison, and Jackson (2014) in regard to Colorado school district disciplinary practices and juvenile justice incarceration when viewed through a lens of critical race analysis.

10. www.qgis.org

11. For example, introductory video tutorials found at http://qgis-tutorials.mangomap com/post/79334660226/qgis-video-tutorials-module-1-the-interface

12. www.esri.com

13. A recent agreement between ESRI and the U.S. government through the Connected Education initiative provides free ArcInfo access for "any US K–12 school"—public, nonpublic, or home school, in the U.S. states, districts, and territories, and U.S. schools in foreign lands (e.g., Department of Defense schools on military bases or embassies). The form at http://www.esri.com/connected includes a link to Terms and Conditions. While there are currently no parallel programs in other countries, they may come soon as the need for this type of education continues to grow (C. Fitzpatrick, personal communication, June 19, 2015, ESRI).

14. For example, www.esri.com/landing-pages/story-maps/contest-winners or http://learn.arcgis.com/en/arcgis-book

15. www.datacenter.org

16. www.enetcolorado.org/professional-development/online-course-catalog

17. https://sites.google.com/a/enetcolorado.org/esri

18. http://alliances.nationalgeographic.com

References

Annamma, S. (2016). Disrupting the carceral state through education journey mapping. *International Journal of Qualitative Studies in Education, 29*(9), 1210–1230.

Annamma, S., Morrison, D., & Jackson, D. (2014). Disproportionality fills in the gaps: Connections between achievement, discipline, and special education in the school-to-prison pipeline. *Berkeley Review of Education, 5*(1), 53–87.

Austin, R. (2008). Crime statistics, disparate impact analysis, and the economic disenfranchisement of minority ex-offenders. In T. Zuberi & E. Bonilla-Silva (Eds.), *White logic, white methods: Racism and methodology* (pp. 307–326). Lanham, MD: Rowman & Littlefield.

Bell, L. A. (1997). Theoretical foundations and frameworks. In M. Adams, L. A. Bell, & P. Griffin (Eds.), *Teaching for diversity and social justice: A sourcebook* (pp. 3–15). New York, NY: Routledge.

Blaisdell, B. (2016). Schools as racial spaces: Understanding and resisting structural racism. *International Journal of Qualitative Studies in Education, 29*(2), 248–272

Chapman, T. K., & Hobbel, N. (2010). Introduction: Conversations, problems, and action. In T. K. Chapman & N. Hobbel (Eds.), *Social justice pedagogy across the curriculum: The practice of freedom* (pp. 1–6). New York, NY: Routledge.

de Saxe, J. (2012). Conceptualizing critical feminist theory and emancipatory education. *Journal for Critical Education Policy Studies, 10*(2), 183–201.

Dykes, J., MacEachren, A. M., & Kraak, M. J. (2005). *Exploring geovisualization.* San Diego, CA: Elsevier.

Freire, P. (1970/2000). *Pedagogy of the oppressed.* New York, NY: Continuum.

Harding, S. (2006). *Science and social inequality: Feminist and postcolonial issues.* Chicago, IL: University of Illinois Press.

Hidalgo, L. (2015). Augmented fotonovelas: Creating new media as pedagogical tools and social justice tools. *Qualitative Inquiry, 21*(3), 223–238.

Jaggar, A. (2013). *Just methods: An interdisciplinary reader.* New York, NY: Routledge.

Kellogg, W. (1999). From the field: Observations on using GIS to develop a neighborhood environmental information system for community-based organizations. *URISA Journal, 11*(1), 15–32.

Kwan, M. (2002). Feminist visualization: Re-envisioning GIS as a method in feminist geographic research. *Annals of the Association of American Geographers, 92*(4), 645–661.

Malagón, M., Perez Huber, L., & Vélez, V. (2009). Our experiences, our methods: Using grounded theory to inform a critical race theory methodology. *Seattle Journal for Social Justice, 8*, 253–272.

Naples, N. A. (2012). Queer methods and methodologies: Intersecting queer theories and social science research. *Contemporary Sociology: A Journal of Reviews, 41*(4), 477–479.

Nieto, S., & Bode, P. (2012). *Affirming diversity: The sociopolitical context of multicultural education.* Boston, MA: Pearson.

Pacheco, D., & Vélez, V. N. (2009). Maps, mapmaking, and a critical pedagogy: Exploring GIS and maps as a teaching tool for social change. *Seattle Journal for Social Justice, 8*, 273–302.

Rhodes, P. J. (1994). Race-of-interviewer effects: A brief comment. *Sociology, 28*(2), 547–558.

Ritchie, S. M., & Rigano, D. L. (2001). Researcher-participant positioning in classroom research. *International Journal of Qualitative Studies in Education, 14*(6), 741–756.

Soja, E. W. (2010). *Seeking spatial justice.* Minneapolis, MN: University of Minnesota Press.

Solórzano, D., & Vélez, V. (2007). *Critical race spatial analysis along the Alameda Corridor in Los Angeles.* Presented at the American Education Research Association Conference, April 9-13, Chicago, Illinois.

Song, M., & Parker, D. (1995). Commonality, difference, and the dynamics of disclosure in in-depth interviewing. *Sociology, 29*(2), 241–256.

Tate, W. F. (2008). "Geography of opportunity": Poverty, place, and educational outcomes. *Educational Researcher, 37*(7), 397–411.

Vélez, V. N. (2013). *Furthering a spatial consciousness in critical race educational research: GIS, counter-cartographic narratives, and the pursuit of spatial justice.* Presented at the Critical Race Studies in Education Association (CRSEA) conference, May 29–June 1, Nashville, TN.

Zuberi, T., & Bonilla-Silva, E. (Eds.). (2008). *White logic, white methods: Racism and methodology.* Lanham, MD: Rowman & Littlefield.

5

PREDATORY LANDSCAPES

Pedagogical and Social Justice Tools to Uncover the Racist
Nativism in the Spatial Dimensions of Economic Exclusion

Leigh Anna Hidalgo

M y mom worked full-time, and my dad held multiple occupations as a jani-
tor and newspaper deliverer, as well as his entrepreneurial endeavors as a
CD salesman. We had lived in Guatemala and migrated to the United
States five years before, but, despite my parents' best efforts, they were struggling to
make ends meet. With four young daughters to raise, my dad did what any father in
his situation would do; he got an auto-title loan, a loan against our family car. He
hoped our economic situation would improve soon and this loan would help keep us
afloat. However, the economic strain continued. My dad defaulted on the small loan,
and then the vehicle was gone. My dad kept us in the dark, not wanting to worry us,
but it was impossible to hide the secret. I wished that I could take back all the times
I had asked my parents for materialistic things that in hindsight we could not afford.
I felt full of rage and wanted to march to the auto-title loan company, raise my voice,
and shout, "Leave my family alone!"

Ten years after my devastating first encounter with an auto-title lender, I became
an undergraduate student at Arizona State University (ASU), working as a bilingual student researcher as part of an undergraduate Chicana/o and Latina/o research
team in South Mountain Village (SMV).[1] We were investigating household coping
strategies for staying healthy despite the uncertainty of the economic downturn and
changing immigration and employment laws. While working on the research project,
I noticed a familiar pattern: a Latina/o neighborhood with a high proliferation of
fringe financial services and a marked absence of traditional financial services, such as
banks and investment firms.[2] On the job, I met several families whose second family
vehicle was in the process of repossession by an auto-title lender. These families now
faced the dilemma of transporting all the members of their family with only one vehicle. These stories hit a raw nerve for me, given my intimate knowledge of the financial and family stress in such situations, and I was moved to take action. With the
extraordinary support of one of the lead researchers from the project, I independently

researched the phenomenon of payday lending in South Phoenix between 2010 and 2012.

In recounting the story of my study, I provide background information, expand on fotonovela methods, and provide some insight into my findings and action steps. The first section, "Economic Structures of Spatial Oppression," sets out the existing empirical studies on fringe financial services and predatory lending practices from the fields of geography and economics, providing a descriptive grounding for my intervention based on a critical race theory (CRT) methodology I call *augmented fotonovelas*. Second, the "Methods" section provides a description of the location of the study, the participants, and an explication for the idea of an augmented fotonovela. Finally, the third section "Raising Our Voices and Taking Back Our Streets" presents the findings of my own community-based case study of fringe financial services through a visual project called *Predatory Financial, Legal, and Political Landscapes in Phoenix, Arizona: A Fotonovela* (Hidalgo, 2011; also referred to as *predatory landscapes*). Throughout the case study I present the collaborative process of augmented fotonovelas and the synergies between this visual method and the CRT conceptual frameworks of racist nativism, visual microaggressions, and community cultural wealth, as well as the methodological framework of critical race spatial analysis (CRSA; Pérez Huber et al., 2008; Pérez Huber & Solórzano, 2015; Pacheco & Vélez, 2009).[3] I conclude my case discussion by examining what I term *geographies of hope*.

Economic Structures of Spatial Oppression

As I began reviewing the literature on fringe financial services, studies by economists and geographers helped to contextualize the payday lending phenomenon that families in SMV were experiencing. The Depository Institutions Deregulation and Monetary Control Act of 1980 (H.R. 4986, Pub.L. 96–221) began the consolidation of U.S. banks into megabanks and the propensity toward hypercompetition in financial markets and light market regulation (Dymski, 2010). The radically transformed financial markets of the 1980s and 1990s negatively affected families in urban low-income neighborhoods as mainstream banks began disinvesting and retreating further into Anglo suburban neighborhoods (Graves, 2003). According to Gary Dymski (2010), racial inequality in access to credit and banking services has several primary forms:

- Redlining—systematic denial of home mortgages to [ethnic minorities] in urban areas;
- Racial discrimination—higher denial rates for home mortgage [credit] to minority applicants; [and]
- Unbanked areas and people—the tendency of banks and savings and loans to avoid opening branches in areas with [high] concentrations of minorities. (p.8)[4]

In this review, I focus on the literature on traditional financial services, the unbanked and underbanked, and fringe financial services.

The absence of mainstream banks in the 1990s provided fertile soil for fringe financial services to move in and multiply by meeting the needs of those neglected by traditional financial services.[5] In 1993, the first payday lender outlet opened its doors for business. Since then the industry has expanded to between 15,000 and 22,000 outlets nationwide (Gallmeyer & Roberts, 2009). In 2007, payday lending was reportedly a $50 billion industry, and currently the United States has more payday lending outlets than McDonald's restaurants (Gallmeyer & Roberts, 2009).[6]

Over the last decade, geographers began drawing on geographic information systems (GIS) to develop ways of analyzing place-based social inequality and testing environmental equity hypotheses to show the racial bias in the spatial patterning of payday lending. Recent empirical studies conducted in Massachussets, North Carolina, Colorado, Louisiana, and Illinois emerged to show the spatial association of fringe financial services with neighborhoods that have specific sociodemographic characteristics (Burkey & Simkins, 2004; Graves, 2003; Joassart & Stephens, 2009; Gallmeyer & Roberts, 2009). Geographers demonstrate that neighborhoods targeted by payday lenders have the following characteristics: low median incomes; high mean poverty rates; and large proportions of ethnic/racial minorities and migrants, young adults, the elderly, and active duty military (Graves, 2003; Burkey & Simkins, 2004; Gallmeyer & Roberts, 2009).

In a spatial study on the location of fringe financial services, researchers found that immigrants were particularly vulnerable to these services. Immigrants were severely unbanked or underbanked; for example, 32% of foreign-born households in the United States do not have a transaction account, compared to only 18% of U.S.-born households (Joassart & Stephens, 2009). Scholars argue that sociocultural factors draw immigrant groups to fringe financial services. For example, Mexican immigrants demonstrated a high level of mistrust of banks because of inflation, fraud, and the banking crises in Mexico (Joassart & Stephens, 2009). Due to mistrust, many Latino migrants preferred to send remittances (money to friends and relatives in their native countries) through smaller banks, credit unions, private money-transfer services, and personal networks rather than traditional banks (Joassart & Stephens, 2009). Traditional financial services were unaccommodating to immigrant customers with linguistic and educational barriers to accessing banking services (Joassart & Stephens, 2009). The high cost of traditional banking and the limited hours of operation were additional deterrents for immigrant financial consumers (Joassart & Stephens, 2009).

While geographers compellingly argue that the structural predation of fringe financial services signified the structural neglect of mainstream banks, the deficit framing of Communities of Color presented residents as victims with little or no agency (Graves, 2003).[7] The following quote demonstrates how scholars focus on the predation with very little consideration for the ways in which these communities resist economic subordination:

> My guess is that payday lenders are quickly becoming signifiers of "the system" that, by hook or by crook, keeps the downtrodden down. The success of payday lending is very likely underwritten by inner-city cultures that have, over generations, come

begrudgingly—or perhaps even passively—to accept perpetual indebtedness as a way of life. (Graves, 2003, p. 315)

This statement highlights the researchers' uninformed assumptions about Communities of Color and the framing of these communities as "passive" victims. While the quantitative data illuminate structural predation, the methodological approach does not engage in an emancipatory project of centering the voices of Communities of Color who daily experience and actively resist economic subordination.

The financial and sociospatial studies previously outlined identify the symptom by providing examples of the class bias and racial bias that exist in banking, access to credit, and exposure to fringe financial services without explaining this phenomenon. Scholars accurately frame the symptom with phrases like *predatory landscapes* and *hazardous environments*, but fail to move beyond description to interrogate how their empirical findings are shaped by racist nativism.[8] In this chapter the metaphors of illness geographers draw on to describe payday lenders, auto-title loans, and pawnshops as *predatory*, *hazardous*, and *toxic* are expanded on through a CRT and Latino critical theory (LatCrit) framework that argues that the overrepresentation of fringe financial services are symptoms of an epidemic brought about by the disease of white supremacy (Pérez Huber et al., 2008).[9] Prior to expanding on the themes found in my research, I provide a description of my methods.

Methods

I have framed my qualitative approach to data collection and analysis in CRT and LatCrit with the goal of not only highlighting structural predation but also, with an activist stance, providing a space that centers in the research study the voices of participants who daily experience and actively resist economic subordination (Hidalgo, 2015). Here I describe a new method I have contributed to this area of research, the augmented fotonovela; the location of my research; and the process of interviews.

Augmented Fotonovelas

To stop the victimization of Communities of Color, researchers must employ new methodologies. During my time as a graduate student living in California, I began to develop a new way of working with Communities of Color born from my desire to force audiences to see and hear my community and fully recognize Latina/o immigrants in Arizona as the dignified and resilient people they are. I call the new visual methodology I have developed *augmented fotonovelas*. Augmented fotonovelas have much to offer CRT and LatCrit scholars, specifically in the way that the form facilitates the critical agenda of putting theory into practice to democratize the research and artistic processes through the cocreation of new media objects that address the concerns of Communities of Color. The augmented fotonovela project described in the following case study is grounded in CRT and places the voices and concerns of Communities of Color at the center of the work itself.

Augmented fotonovelas draw upon the aesthetic of traditional fotonovelas but incorporate new technologies, such as video interviews, interactive mapping, smartphone technology, and augmented reality (AR).[10] Augmented fotonovelas also make the most of the classic form, utilizing photographs, text, and bubble captions. Through this methodology, new and old come together to produce augmented scholarship (Hidalgo, 2015), scholarship as knowledge production bridging the gap between Communities of Color and the academy, where researchers and communities draw on creative research and traditional research methods to produce alternative narratives that reveal erased histories. As a CRT tool, augmented fotonovelas privilege the voices of the community, thus amplifying their knowledge and experiences in ways that are accessible to both the community and the academy. CRT scholars can draw on this method to produce augmented scholarship with the power to inform, educate, raise public consciousness, elicit community action, and effect social change (Hidalgo, 2015).

This is a unique time, one where smartphone applications and access to the Internet allow researchers to reinvent the fotonovela to expand the aesthetic into the digital age. The augmented fotonovela is designed to be multimodal—existing in print and online, and accessible through a variety of media. Once an augmented fotonovela approaches a final draft, online and print versions are designed with a separate set of navigational instructions (Hidalgo, 2015). The online augmented fotonovela is created through a free publishing platform called Calameo, which enables video to be embedded and audio interviews to be featured. Figure 5.1 shows the print version of the augmented fotonovela that is created using a free web platform called Aurasma Lite, which relies on AR technology to superimpose video interviews onto corresponding trigger images that bring audiovisual stories to life. AR allows the fotonovela to be layered with "multimedia that enhances the real world through the

Figure 5.1. Photograph of video tutorial walking viewer through the process of interacting with augmented reality (AR) embedded in an augmented fotonovela.

addition of virtual information" so that select images throughout the fotonovela can trigger the corresponding video to begin playing on your smartphone (Liarokapis & Anderson, 2010, p. 1).

Within the augmented fotonovelas, I have also drawn on a CRSA methodological framework. *Predatory, Financial, Legal, and Political Landscapes in Phoenix, AZ: A Fotonovela* (Hidalgo, 2011) engages CRSA using GIS to demonstrate the spatial dimensions of race, racism, and the intersection of immigration (Pacheco & Vélez, 2009). The goal of CRSA in the augmented fotonovela is to both identify and challenge racism by revealing how white supremacy operates to construct space in ways that subordinate the financial, credit, and economic opportunities for Neighborhoods of Color in South Phoenix, Arizona (Pacheco & Vélez, 2009; Hidalgo, 2015).

Site and Interviews

In the spring of 2010, we collaboratively obtained information about active locations of payday lending, auto-title lending, and pawnshop outlets, using multiple methods of data collection. My colleagues and I physically canvassed the neighborhoods, recorded outlets listed on the government website of the Arizona Department of Financial Institutions, and researched advertising sites with listings of outlets.[11] The use of multiple data sources helped to create a comprehensive database to compare SMV to Awhatukee Foothills Village (AFV).

This case study shows the process by which *predatory landscapes* (Hidalgo, 2011) create a space where the everyday experiences, stories, and voices of Latinas/os are at the center of the visual project. A CRT and LatCrit lens allow scholars to "analyze, subvert, and intervene in the dominant conceptual frameworks that mask the oppressive experiences of Communities of Color" and in particular the intersection of race, immigrant status, and financial exclusion and economic subordination (Pérez Huber et al., 2008, p. 47). Through augmented fotonovelas, researchers, community members, activists, architects, designers, photographers, and artists contest the social, spatial, and historical ways that white supremacy produces *geographies of despair*, defined as where Neighborhoods of Color are economically, politically, and legally marginalized, while highlighting *geographies of hope*, a term describing where People of Color resist the hegemony by establishing counterspaces where community flourishes (Yosso, Smith, Ceja, & Solórzano, 2009, p. 677).

This study is set in a complex social, political, and economic terrain. To understand this complexity, I turned to the Latina/o grassroots group Puente Arizona, which "successfully mobilized a coalition of immigrants, students, religious believers, artists and others to hold Dignity Marches" in order to "consistently be a vocal presence at the Arizona Capitol demanding the repeal of SB 1070" (Szkupinski Quiroga, 2013, p. 584).[12] I recruited members of this organization to collaboratively interrogate racist nativism and produce content for the augmented fotonovela. The epistemological foundation of augmented fotonovelas centers participants' narratives, along with my own observations, research, and collection of documents. The fruits of this labor became *Predatory, Financial, Legal, and Political Landscapes in Phoenix, AZ: A Fotonovela* (Hidalgo, 2011), an augmented fotonovela in which participants and

myself explore the ways racist nativism creates *geographies of predation* that disproportionately expose Immigrants of Color to hazardous financial services.

In order to address the experiences of undocumented communities, I highlight
the current political climate in Arizona. Since 2002, Arizona has been a state partner
with the Homeland Security program known as ICE 287(g), which granted state,
county, and city law enforcement the authority to ask for papers and detain immigrants without criminal charges. Research on Arizona migrants is crucial due to the
radical changes they have experienced in their social status in the last decade (as Arizona has become ground zero for anti-immigrant and anti-Latino legislation). Table
5.1 outlines the anti-immigrant laws crafted to constrain and restrict the lives of
undocumented Latinas/os. Combined, these laws create a landscape where Latinos in
Arizona are discriminated against and segregated politically, legally, and economically.

TABLE 5.1
Anti-Immigrant Legislation in Arizona

Legislation (Yr)	Description
Prop. 200 (2004)	Requires proof of citizenship to vote or apply for public benefits
Prop. 103 (2007)	Makes English official language
Prop. 300 (2007)	Requires proof of citizenship for in-state tuition and financial aid
Prop. 208 (2007)	Penalizes employers who knowingly employ undocumented workers
HB 2008 (2009)	Requires public workers to report illegal (im)migrants who apply for public benefits
SB 1070 (2010)	Fines those "transporting, harboring, or concealing unlawful aliens" Makes it a crime for undocumented (im)migrants to seek or accept work Mandates police to investigate the immigration status of anyone suspected of being illegal Criminalizes (im)migrants failing to carry federal registration papers are guilty of a crime
SB 1490 (2011)	Requires food workers to provide proof of citizenship to obtain a food workers permit

Source. Szkupinski Quiroga, Medina, & Glick, 2014.

Raising Our Voices and Taking Back Our Streets

The results of talking and working with community members in South Phoenix over
the course of my study are described in the following case study under three themes:
militarized spaces, geographies of despair, and geographies of hope. Within each of
these emergent themes, the voices of the Communities of Color are heard, and the
images of their stories within the augmented fotonovela are shared, depicting their
experiences with the economic structures affecting their lives.

Militarized Spaces

In interviews, participants and myself interrogated white supremacy as a system of racial domination and exploitation that places the white race as superordinate to People of Color (Solórzano, 1998; Solórzano & Yosso, 2002b; Pérez Huber et al., 2009). Together we theorized on how racist nativism, a racial ideology of white supremacy, creates and maintains highly militarized spaces and the criminalization of Latinas/os. This criminalization plays a role in increasing undocumented Latinas/os' economic vulnerability to fringe financial services. As Caleb Alvarado, a resident of SMV, explained, undocumented Latino migrants are particularly economically vulnerable because they have little mobility; lacking the proper documentation to acquire a driver's license, they are afraid of deportation if they are pulled over by police:

> Immigration has played a role in people using pawnshops or payday loans. A certain fear has been created within the community. There have been families in our church that have been forced out. Or someone's been deported. Say the husband is deported, and that was the only source of income for the family, then the wife is selling goods to people or pawnshops or taking out payday loans. (personal communication, C. Alvarado, May 16, 2012)

Carlos Garcia from Puente, Arizona, described how the limited mobility of undocumented immigrants and the proximity and density of fringe financial outlets are factors that make the consumption of fringe financial products a viable option:

> Our communities are fond of something smaller [payday loan outlets] that's near them because of their fears. Whether it's fear of driving long distances because they are afraid they are going to get pulled over or just going into a larger institution [bank] that is straight up intimidating. (personal communication, C. Garcia, May 16, 2012)

In another interview, community organizer Sandra Castro identified how the signage hanging outside of payday loan outlets are daily "racial microaggressions" that function to keep Immigrants of Color economically subordinated (Pérez Huber & Solórzano, 2015):

> In Phoenix and South Phoenix, where there are Latino and migrant communities, you see [signage] automatically pre-approved, auto-title loans, mortgage loans, you don't need an I.D., you don't need social security, and they do little pitches and by their pitches you automatically know they are targeting the undocumented community. (personal communication, S. Castro, May 16, 2012)

These visual assaults "reinforce institutional racism and perpetuate the ideologies of white supremacy that justify the subordination of People of Color" (Pérez Huber & Solórzano, 2015, p. 225). Figure 5.2 shows a layout of the augmented fotonovela

Figure 5.2. Visual microaggressions targeting Latinas/os in SMV.

Source. Copyright 2011 by Jeff Newton. Reprinted with permission.

with photographs I commissioned of payday loan outlets and signage demonstrating the visual microaggressions specifically targeting Latinas/os in SMV. As community resident Caleb Alvarado stated, "Me, personally, I hate payday lending because it is associated with poverty" (personal communication, C. Alvarado, May 16, 2012).

During this interview, Caleb further articulated his frustration with living in a neighborhood that is neglected and stigmatized as poor, when there is so much talent and intelligence and many good things happening that are not recognized by people outside the community. The overwhelming prevalence of payday lenders in the community is a symbolic reminder to Caleb of the low status ascribed to residents of SMV. He shared his experience of living in a neighborhood where banks continue to disinvest, leaving families vulnerable to predatory lending:

> My parents have lived in South Phoenix for 28 years, in the same house. One of the biggest complaints my mom has is there aren't enough banks. She was with one bank and had to switch with another because the bank she used to use shut down. (personal communication, C. Alvarado, May 16, 2012)

Geographies of Despair

Since the days of residential segregation, South Phoenix has remained an area with low land value. The area is known as a place where Latina/o migrants have settled for generations. South Phoenix continues to be a predominantly low-income Latina/o community. While driving through the area, I saw empty lots, foreclosure signs, broken sidewalks, adult shops, liquor stores, and payday loan outlets overwhelming residential neighborhoods. In contrast, AFV is a quickly growing urban neighborhood south of SMV that lies directly at the northeastern border of South Mountain Park. AFV continues to be a predominantly white and affluent neighborhood.[13] The differences in demographic data indicate that the barriers between these two communities extend much further than the natural, physical barrier of South Mountain. These communities are divided by the economic and social benefits marked by the symbolic meanings ascribed to the spatial divides. SMV and AFV are polar opposites socioeconomically and are bound in a paradoxical relationship.

These two neighborhoods were chosen as they are located in South Phoenix and border each other. Another reason for choosing these neighborhoods was the stark juxtaposition of their conditions: the contradictions of the city are laid bare as white supremacy plays a role in shaping the quality of life of residents in each neighborhood. On the basis of white supremacy, power and privilege are unequally distributed in order to privilege whites to the detriment of People of Color (Bonilla-Silva, 2001; Pérez Huber et al., 2009). Under white supremacy, the superiority of whites is normalized and white beliefs and values are upheld as dominant (Delgado & Stefancic, 2012; Pérez Huber et al., 2009). While uncovering the social injustice of spatial disadvantage is an absolute necessity, too often spatial analysis studies focus solely on the spaces inhabited by People of Color (Gallmeyer & Roberts, 2009; Joassart-Marcelli & Stephens, 2009; Bolin et al., 2005; Graves, 2003). I argue that to fully grasp an accurate picture of economic and financial inequality in Phoenix, researchers need to take spatial analysis studies further—by examining not only the disadvantages of space for People of Color, but also the advantages of spaces inhabited by white people (Hidalgo, 2015). *White privilege* is defined as "a system of opportunities and benefits conferred upon people simply because they are white" (Delgado & Stefancic, 2012; Solórzano & Yosso, 2001). White privilege has economic implications as it contributes to a system of white supremacy built on generations of sociospatial relations and spatial arrangements that manifest themselves in higher property values, better schools, or the ability to exclude others from the workplace (Pulido, 2000). White supremacy as a system retains economic, material, and social advantages for whites, while systematically disadvantaging People of Color, specifically Immigrants of Color.

The GIS maps generated in Figure 5.3 show the boundaries of SMV and AFV. Dark gray circles represent traditional financial services, with the symbol for a building in the center, and light gray circles represent fringe financial services, with the symbol of cash in the center. Figure 5.3 shows more fringe financial outlets than traditional banks in SMV. Conversely, in AFV there were more traditional bank outlets than fringe financial outlets. In SMV there were 27 payday loan and check cashing outlets and only 6 banks. In AFV, there were only 2 payday loan and check cashing outlets and 14 banks. Thus, there were 13.5 times more fringe financial services in SMV than in AFV. Further, there were more than twice as many traditional financial services in AFV than in SMV.

The data convey how residents of SMV were exposed to a proliferation of economically hazardous fringe financial services. Likewise, the results showcase the economic advantages for residents of AFV, who benefited from increased access to traditional financial services and decreased access to fringe financial services. These predatory landscapes are symptoms of the disease of white supremacy, and, when unchallenged, these hazardous outlets crop up to devastate Latina/o families by trapping them into mounting debt that drains the wealth and economic assets of the community and further exacerbates their financial insecurity.

In addition to CRSA, *Predatory, Financial, Legal, and Political Landscapes in Phoenix, AZ: A Fotonovela* (Hidalgo, 2011) drew on archival photographs to locate space in South Phoenix through time, uncovering the legacies of inequality and making visible the erased histories of Arizona. Figure 5.4 highlights my collaboration with Arizona State University librarian Christine Marin, in which archival photographs of Latina/o residents were incorporated into the augmented fotonovela to humanize the experiences of Latinas/os who were historically spatially segregated from the rest of the city. In uncovering the legacy of white supremacy, the augmented fotonovela demonstrates how the disproportionate number of fringe financial services in SMV stems from the ways in which race permeated zoning regulations and influenced urban development and bank lending processes, which enforced housing segregation patterns, racialized employment patterns, and predatory financial practices (Hidalgo, 2015). In describing the geographies of despair in South Phoenix, Bob Bolin, Sara Grineski, and Timothy Collins (2005) wrote about how, as early as 1877, the expansion of the east-west railroad corridor created a physical and symbolic line that

Figure 5.3. The augmented fotonovela features a GIS map of traditional bank outlets and fringe financial outlets in two racially and ethnically diverse bordering neighborhoods.

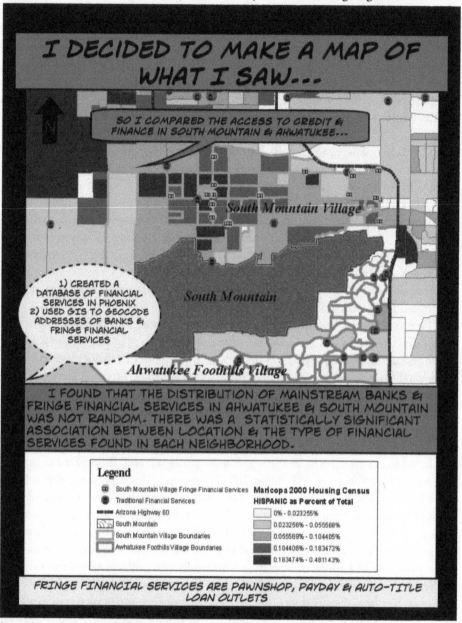

divided Anglo Phoenix from Mexicans in South Phoenix. Mexicans were excluded from the economic sectors, and the Southwest came to rely on low-wage Mexican labor, specifically, agricultural production. In the dominant ideology of the period, Mexicans were primarily relegated to low-wage fieldwork, as it was generally accepted

Figure 5.4. Archival images from 1958 of South Phoenix residents.

PRODUCTION OF SPACE

ANGLO-AMERICANS FOUNDED PHOENIX IN THE 1870S. BY 1877, THE EXPANSION OF THE EAST-WEST RAILROAD CORRIDOR CREATED A PHYSICAL & SYMBOLIC LINE THAT DIVIDED ANGLO-DOMINATED NORTHERN PHOENIX FROM LATINA/OS AND AFRICAN AMERICANS IN SOUTHERN PHOENIX.

IN THE 1890S, WITH A POPULATION OF 5,000, WHITES CONSTRUCTED RACIAL CATEGORIES & SPATIAL PRACTICES THAT WORKED TOGETHER TO "PRODUCE A STIGMATIZED SPACE OF RACIAL EXCLUSION AND ECONOMIC MARGINALITY IN SOUTH PHOENIX" (BOLIN ET AL: 2005).

DURING THIS TIME PERIOD, LATINA/OS & CHICANA/OS WERE PRIMARILY RELEGATED TO LOW-WAGE FIELDWORK AS IT WAS GENERALLY ACCEPTED THAT THEY WERE BETTER ADAPTED TO WITHSTANDING HARD LABOR, LOW WAGES, & POVERTY (BOLIN ET AL: 2005).

TENTS USED FOR DWELLINGS NEAR THE RAILROAD TRACKS. RUSSELL LEE: 1940

HOUSING FOR MEXICAN FIELD LABORERS. DOROTHEA LANGE: 1937

CHILDREN OF MEXICAN COTTON LABORERS. DOROTHEA LANGE: 1937

SPACES OF DOMINATION

TO HENRI LEFEBVRE, THE COMPETITION OVER THE PRODUCTION OF SPACE HAPPENS BETWEEN THOSE WHO PRODUCE SPACE FOR DOMINATION & THOSE WHO PRODUCE SPACE FOR APPROPRIATION (MOLOTCH: 1993).

THE APPARATUS OF OFFICIAL CITY PLANNING PRODUCE SPACES FOR DOMINATION AND CREATES WHAT LEFEBVRE CALLS "ABSTRACT SPACE" (LEFEBVRE: 1991). THE PRODUCTION OF ABSTRACT SPACE IS INHERENTLY VIOLENT BECAUSE IT SEEKS TO GENERATE PROFITS FOR ITSELF REGARDLESS OF THE HUMAN TOLL ON OTHERS (LEFEBVRE: 1991).

JOSE VILLELA COLLECTION

JOSE VILLELA COLLECTION

JOSE VILLELA COLLECTION: 1958

that they were better adapted to withstanding hard labor, low wages, and poverty (Dimas, 1999).

During flood seasons in the 1890s, untreated sewage from white neighborhoods in the north was directed toward the south. A few decades later, this process continued, as waste produced by white neighborhoods was intentionally redirected to South Phoenix's sewage processing facility and landfills, creating stench and contamination in Latino and Black neighborhoods (Bolin, Grineski, & Collins, 2005). Factories dominated South Phoenix neighborhoods, along with stockyards, warehouses, mills, and other unregulated industries that exposed residents to environmental hazards (Bolin, Grineski, & Collins, 2005). As one space was systematically disinvested in and exposed to hazardous chemicals and untreated sewage, with the establishment of white-only spaces in nineteenth-century Phoenix, Arizona, Anglos in white-only neighborhoods continued to expand into middle-class suburbs, away from not only the city center but also the pollution and poverty of South Phoenix. Until the 1960s, public expenditures such as water lines, sewage, paved roads, and urban services were directed toward northern, white-only neighborhoods, while South Phoenix barrios had to do without such amenities (Bolin, Grineski, & Collins, 2005).

The SMV area continues to have low land value and to attract industrialization (Bolin, Grineski, & Collins, 2005). I argue that the legacy of white supremacy in the nineteenth century continued to influence twenty-first-century structures and policies that resulted in the disproportionate exposure of People of Color and Immigrants of Color to hazardous financial services in South Phoenix.

Geographies of Hope

As our discussion of *predatory landscapes* (Hidalgo, 2011) came to an end, Caleb Alvarado and I engaged in a conversation about how Latinas/os resist spatial domination through their creative and inventive appropriation of space (Lefebvre, 1992). I refer to these examples of appropriation by Immigrants of Color as geographies of hope, where informal economies and microenterprises thwart the city's hegemonic domination. These reclaimed spaces are social counterspaces that build community and cultivate a sense of family, home, and belonging (Yosso, Smith, Ceja, & Solórzano, 2009). In my time in SMV, I saw social counterspaces through a network of neighbors who took turns cooking and selling *platos típicos* (traditional foods) from their home countries, transforming if only momentarily their *vecindades* (neighborhoods) into Mexico, El Salvador, and Peru. Another example of a social counterspace was a family who operated a small *tienda* (shop) from inside their home where I frequently went for refreshments and snacks while in SMV. In the augmented fotonovela, Caleb described how the spaces claimed by Latinas/os become social counterspaces of resistance that nurture resilience for the Latina/o community (Yosso, Smith, Ceja, & Solórzano, 2009):

> Street vendors create this, almost this hub of a mobile social network. They are taking whatever space they are in and reappropriating it to create a small community. . . .

The city is a grid and along comes a street vendor, he sells paletas and people come out and the vendor creates these interactions. Now there is no longer a grid, now there's these little hot spots within the community. So this reappropriation of physical space creates a reappropriation of social networking and space. (personal interview C. Alvorado May 16, 2012)

This explanation highlights how the augmented fotonovela provided a space where participants voiced the ways in which SMV residents resisted by appropriating space to serve the community's needs (Lefebvre, 1992; Purcell, 2003). These acts of reappropriation by community members transformed sidewalks into dynamic places where community grew and flourished, in spite of structural predation. Figure 5.5 shows a conversation with Caleb Alvarado where he described his community from an asset-based perspective, identifying street vendors as part of the community cultural wealth within South Phoenix (Yosso, 2005; Pérez Huber, 2009). I call the spaces created by street vendors *geographies of hope* because these Immigrants of Color contested economic and social domination by transforming public space into the *mercados* (marketplaces) from their homelands (Davis, 2000: Muñoz, 2008). In these community-appropriated spaces, multiple forms of capital were circulated within the neighborhood, not only economic but also linguistic, familial, cultural, aspirational, and social (Yosso, 2005).[14] Figure 5.6 features the photography of Diane Ovalle as her lens captures the portrait of a street vendor framed by a low-rider on each side. Through an asset-based lens, Diane captured an image of a street vendor as one of the heroes in our community, transforming geographies of despair into geographies of hope for the benefit of the neighborhood.

Augmented fotonovelas themselves can create geographies of hope as they are multimodal pedagogical tools that are not bound to university settings. *Predatory landscapes* (Hidalgo, 2011) exist in public settings, such as community centers, workshops, and events. In addition to being shared with the civil rights and advocacy organization Arizona Hispanic Community Forum and requested by ASU's Morrison Institute for Public Policy, *Predatory, Financial, Legal, and Political Landscapes in Phoenix, AZ: A Fotonovela* (Hidalgo, 2011) has been used as a teaching tool in three workshops and four undergraduate classrooms at Arizona State University and California State University at Long Beach. Augmented scholarship exists on multiple platforms to appeal to many audiences in various settings and is accessible on smartphones and computers by community members living far from the institutional setting. Augmented scholarship can also be enjoyed in private settings, including family households where audiences can interact with the augmented fotonovelas, allowing the audience to see and hear Communities of Color actively addressing the issues affecting them.

Augmented fotonovelas serve as visual critical race tools to demonstrate how racist nativism produces spaces of economic marginalization that continue to be a part of modern-day racism, while also uncovering the legacy of white supremacy. This methodology allows for the augmenting of history, enhancing it by making visible the historical legacy of racism and by reclaiming and retelling stories that have been lost. Augmented fotonovelas serve as visual critical race tools that challenge dominant

Figure 5.5. Photograph of Caleb Alvarado talking about how street vendors in South Phoenix appropriate spaces for the community.

perspectives of Immigrants of Color and demonstrate the everyday experiences of Communities of Color that are resilient in their efforts to resist racist nativism (Pérez Huber et al., 2008). Depending on how this tool is used, augmented fotonovelas have the potential for allowing marginalized communities to regain control and dictate the

Figure 5.6. Photograph of street vendor in South Phoenix.

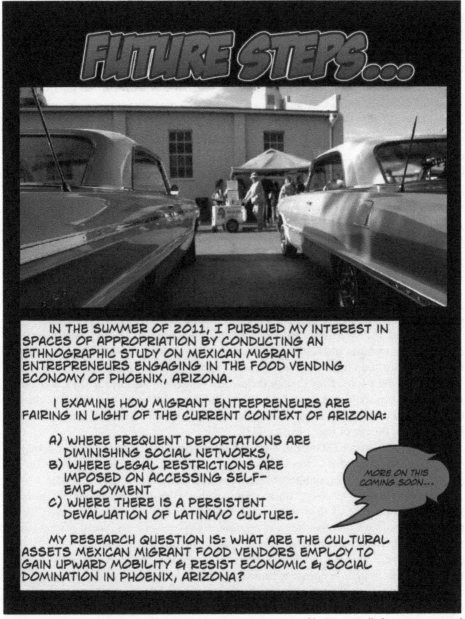

narrative by which they are described, discussed, and analyzed. Augmented foto-novelas provided a space for communities to take an active role in cocreating visual counterstorytelling that presents new narratives (Solórzano & Yosso, 2001; Solórzano & Yosso, 2002a).

Epilogue

After engaging in this work, I was no longer the adolescent who felt alone and power-less in protecting her family from the clutches of an auto-title loan outlet. That experience and so many others like it had molded me into a CRT scholar concerned with the economic inequality in my community. Developing the methodology of aug-mented fotonovelas gave me a space where I could work with participants to create beautiful visual projects that amplify our collective rage, share multiple voices, and celebrate the resilience in our communities. Today, my critical socioeconomic justice work includes supporting a campaign to legalize street vending in Los Angeles, inves-tigating immigrant deportations in the United States connected to Latin American disappearances, and examining elderly Central American retirement strategies in the United States. There is healing, strength, and wholeness in working collaboratively with communities through the augmented fotonovelas to reclaim our silenced voices and make visible our erased stories.

Notes

1. South Mountain Village (SMV), Arizona, is a low-income minority community on the northeastern border of the 16,500-acre South Mountain Park. The demographic composition of SMV is 61.8% Latinos, 18.8% African Americans, and 17.2% whites (U.S. Bureau of the Census, 2003). Despite the national prosperity of the 1990s, in 1999 the median income of an SMV household was in the $25,000 to $35,000 range, and 21.7% were at the poverty level. Even though the median household income for SMV households in 1999 was consistent with that of the greater Phoenix area, which was $41,207, the dra-matically high poverty rate suggests that there is wide economic variation between families in SMV (U.S. Bureau of the Census, 2003).

2. Steven Graves (2003) defines *fringe financial services* as "companies that defer pay-ment and charge an excess of fees for their services, such as payday lenders, check cashing services, rent-to-own stores, sub-prime mortgages, and title/pawn lenders" (p. 303).

3. CRSA is an explanatory framework and methodological approach that recognizes the potential for the use of GIS to investigate and challenge the spatial dimensions of race, racism, and its intersections with other forms of oppression in geographic and social spaces, such as schools and, in this book chapter, neighborhoods (Pacheco & Vélez, 2009).

4. Economists argue that financial discrimination is marked by areas of unbanked peo-ple, which result from the tendency of banks and savings and loans to avoid opening or closing down outlets in areas with concentrations of minorities, which has led to the disproportionate number of minorities who are without checking and savings accounts (Dymski, 2010).

5. Geographer Steven M. Graves draws on the work of the famous economist John Caskey (1994) to define *traditional financial services* as "banks and investment firms" (Graves, 2003, p. 304). When a neighborhood has a scarcity of these institutions, it is classified as being "under-banked" and "unbanked," meaning residents have unmet financial needs (Dymski, 2010).

6. Fringe financial services seem to follow a business model that focuses on popula-tions who are underbanked and unbanked, who have volatile low incomes, and who have less financial equity, savings, and assets, because these customers need recurring credit to close income-expenditure gaps (Dymski, 2010). Thus, the borrower writes a postdated check with

the amount of the loan plus fees and interests in exchange for immediate cash, and in a few weeks the lender cashes the check. If a borrower does not pay in time, they are saddled with more late fees and forced to pay the bank charges for the bounced check. Since many families in low-income communities lack financial stability and the financial safety net of emergency savings funds, low-income families find themselves in need of small and short-term personal loans that fringe financial outlets specialize in and traditional banks do not offer. Because mainstream banks underserve these populations, the fringe financial outlets can exercise market power by charging higher fees and rates than traditional banks. Fringe financial lenders are physically accessible, and the loans they offer can be easily attained with no credit check and only proof of employment required.

7. Steven Graves (2003) introduces the concepts of structural predation and structural neglect, arguing that "the absence of quality schools, parks, banks, and grocery stores all figure into the construction and maintenance of structural restrictions upon residents' ability to make informed life choices" (p. 315). To Graves (2003), "landscapes of predation" are spaces where "opportunities to lower one's quality of life dot the landscape" and "payday loans are but one invitation to make a bad decision" (p. 314).

8. CRT scholars define *racist nativism* as "the assigning of values to real or imagined differences, in order to justify the superiority of the native, who is perceived to be white, over that of the non-native, who is perceived to be People and Immigrants of Color, and thereby defend the right of whites, or the native, to dominance" (Pérez Huber et al., 2008, p. 43).

9. Geographers argue that predatory financial landscapes create hazardous environments that trap racial and ethnic minorities into mounting debt (Gallmeyer & Roberts, 2009).

10. Fotonovelas are a traditional print medium with a long history in Latin America. Essentially, they are photo-based comics combining elements of written text, bubble dialogue captions, sequential photographs, and artistic alterations (Emme, Kirova, Kamau, & Kosanovich, 2006; Hidalgo, 2015). Fotonovelas are a popular adult literature that began with stills from films aimed at retelling the plot of a motion picture in an accessible and affordable medium (Flora & Flora, 1978; Hidalgo, 2015). The fotonovela's long history as a form of popular art in Latin America has made it possible to now use the fotonovela to serve educational purposes for social change and benefit among Latin American immigrants in the United States. Scholars and practitioners in the United States have utilized the fotonovela medium in different ways (Emme et al., 2006; Hidalgo, 2015).

11. My sister Natalie Hidalgo and friend Courtney Peña were my collaborators. Both assisted me in researching the locations of fringe financial services, which allowed me to compile a database of fringe financial services in Phoenix.

12. SB1070 is Arizona's controversial anti-immigrant law, which includes the following provisions: (a) It made it a crime for undocumented immigrants to seek or accept work, (b) it mandated police to investigate the immigration status of anyone suspected of being "illegal," (c) it criminalized immigrants failing to carry federal registration papers, and (d) it made those "transporting, harboring, or concealing unlawful aliens" subject to fines (American Civil Liberties Union, 2011).

13. In 1999 the median household income in AFV was $50,000 to $75,000, and the percentage of families in poverty was 2.1%. This is higher than the median income in 1999 for both SMV and the greater Phoenix region and twice that of SMV.

14. Tara Yosso's (2005) analysis of the cultural capital of Latino students from an asset-driven perspective led to her development of the community cultural wealth (CCW) conceptual model. Yosso (2005) argues that earlier studies have operated under the implicit

logic that Students of Color have cultural deficiencies that prevent them from being successful in school. Moreover, Yosso (2005) criticizes the notion that some communities are labeled
as culturally wealthy, while others are labeled as culturally poor. Yosso (2005) describes the
CCW model as "an array of knowledge, skills, abilities and contacts possessed and utilized by
Communities of Color to 'survive' and 'resist' macro and microforms of oppression" (p. 77).

References

American Civil Liberties Union. (2011). *SB 1070 at the Supreme Court: What's at stake.*
Retrieved from www.aclu.org/files/pdfs/immigrants/sb1070_infographic5.pdf

Bolin, B., Grineski, S., & Collins, T. (2005). The geography of despair: Environmental racism and the making of South Phoenix, Arizona, USA. *Research in Human Ecology, 12*(2),
1–13.

Bonilla-Silva, E. (2001). *White supremacy and racism in the post–civil rights era.* Boulder, CO:
Lynne Rienner Publishers.

Burkey, M. L., & Simkins, S. P. (2004). Factors affecting the location of payday lending and
traditional banking services in North Carolina. *Review of Regional Studies, 34*(2), 191–205.

Caskey, J. P. (1994). *Fringe banking: Check-cashing outlets, pawnshops, and the poor.* New York,
NY: Russell Sage Foundation.

Davis, M. (2000). *Magical urbanism: Latinos reinvent the U.S. big city.* New York, NY: Verso.

Dimas, P. (1999). *Progress and a Mexican American community's struggle for existence: Phoenix's
gold gate barrio.* New York, NY: Peter Lang.

Delgado, R., & Stefancic, J. (2012). *Critical race theory: An introduction.* New York, NY: New
York University Press.

Dymski, G. (2010). *Understanding the subprime crisis: Institutional evolution and theoretical views.* Retrieved from http://kirwaninstitute.osu.edu/FairHousing_FairCredit/gary_
dymski_subprime_crisis_merge.pdf

Emme, M., Kirova, A., Kamau, O., & Kosanovich, S. (2006). Ensemble research: A means
for immigrant children to explore peer relationships through fotonovela. *Alberta Journal of
Educational Research, 52*(3), 160–181.

Flora, C. B., & Flora, J. L. (1978). The fotonovela as a tool for class and cultural domination.
Latin American Perspectives, 5(1), 134–150.

Gallmeyer, A., & Roberts, W. T. (2009). Payday lenders and economically distressed communities: A spatial analysis of financial predation. *Social Science Journal, 46*(3), 521–538.

Graves, S. (2003). Landscapes of predation, landscapes of neglect: A location analysis of payday lenders and banks. *Professional Geographer, 55*(3), 303–317.

Hidalgo, L. (2011). *Predatory, financial, legal, and political landscapes in Phoenix, AZ: A fotonovela.* Retrieved from www.calameo.com/read/000553314050ed3a3eff4

Hidalgo, L. (2015). Augmented fotonovelas: Creating new media as pedagogical tools and
social justice tools. *Qualitative Inquiry, 21*(3), 223–238.

Joassart-Marcelli, P., & Stephens, P. (2009). Immigrant banking and financial exclusion in
greater Boston. *Journal of Economic Geography, 10*(1), 1–30.

Lefebvre, H. (1992). *The production of space.* 1st ed. Cambridge, MA: Wiley-Blackwell.

Muñoz, L. (2008). "Tamales . . . elotes . . . champurado . . .": *The production of Latino vending landscapes in Los Angeles* (Unpublished doctoral dissertation). University of Southern
California, Los Angeles.

Pacheco, D., & Vélez, V. N. (2009). Maps, mapmaking, and a critical pedagogy: Exploring GIS and maps as a teaching tool for social change. *Seattle Journal for Social Justice, 8*, 273-302.

Pérez Huber, L. (2009). Challenging racist nativist framing: Acknowledging the community cultural wealth of undocumented Chicana college students to reframe the immigration debate. *Harvard Educational Review, 79*(4), 704–729.

Pérez Huber, L., Lopez, C. B., Malagon, M. C., Vélez, V., & Solórzano, D. G. (2008). Getting beyond the "symptom," acknowledging the "disease": Theorizing racist nativism. *Contemporary Justice Review, 11*(1), 39–51.

Pérez Huber, L., & Solórzano, D. (2015). Everyday racism, critical race theory, visual microaggressions, and the historical image of Mexican banditry. *Qualitative Inquiry, 21*(3), 223–238.

Pulido, L. (2000). Rethinking environmental racism: White privilege and urban development in Southern California. *Annals of the Association of American Geographers, 90*(1), 12–40.

Purcell, M. (2003). Citizenship and the right to the global city: Reimagining the capitalist world order. *International Journal of Urban and Regional Research, 27*(3), 564–590.

Solórzano, D. G. (1998). Critical race theory, race and gender microaggressions, and the experience of Chicana and Chicano scholars. *Qualitative Studies in Education, 11*, 121–136.

Solórzano, D. G., & Yosso, T. J. (2001). Critical race and LatCrit theory and method: Counterstorytelling. *International Journal of Qualitative Studies in Education, 14*(4), 471–495.

Solórzano, D., & Yosso, T. (2002a). Critical race methodology: Counterstorytelling as an analytical framework for education research. *Qualitative Inquiry, 8*(1), 23–44.

Solórzano, D. G., & Yosso, T. (2002b). A critical race counterstory of race, racism, and affirmative action. *Equity and Excellence in Education, 35*, 155–168.

Szkupinski Quiroga, S. (2013). Vamos a aguantar: Reflections on how Arizona's SB 1070 has affected one community. *Latino Studies, 11*(4), 580–586.

Szkupinski Quiroga, S., Medina, D, & Glick, J. E. (2014). In the belly of the beast: Effects of anti-immigrant policy on Latino community members. *The American Behavioral Scientist, 58*(13), 1723-1742.

U.S. Bureau of the Census. (2003a). *Profile of general demographic characteristics for Ahwatukee Foothills Village planning.* Retrieved from www.phoenix.gov/pddsite/Documents/ pdd_pz_pdf_00220.pdf#search=U%2ES%2E%20summary%20file%20ahwatukee

U.S. Bureau of the Census. (2003b). *Profile of general demographic characteristics for South Mountain Village planning.* Retrieved from www.phoenix.gov/pddsite/Documents/pddp-zpdf00234.pdf#search=U%2ES%2E%20summary%20file

Yosso, T. (2005). Whose culture has capital? A critical race theory discussion of community cultural wealth. *Race, Ethnicity and Education, 8*(1), 69–91.

Yosso, T., Smith, W., Ceja, M., & Solórzano, D. G. (2009). Critical race theory, racial microaggressions, and campus racial climate for Latina/o undergraduates. *Harvard Educational Review, 79*(4), 659–690.

PART THREE

CASE EXAMPLES

6

USING CRITICAL RACE SPATIAL ANALYSIS TO EXAMINE REDLINING IN SOUTHERN CALIFORNIA COMMUNITIES OF COLOR, CIRCA 1939

Daniel G. Solórzano and Verónica N. Vélez

As critical race researchers and pedagogues, we are constantly looking for examples of contemporary everyday racism and their historical corollaries. As an example, we had unsuccessfully been looking for artifacts of racially restrictive covenants[1] in Mexican American[2] communities. This journey to find these illustrations of institutional racism begins with a legal case that went to the U.S. Supreme Court in 1948: *Shelley v. Kraemer* (334 U.S. 1, 1948). The *Shelley* case was trying to answer the question: Does the enforcement of a racially restrictive covenant violate the Equal Protection Clause of the Fourteenth Amendment? We were trying to find other legal cases where Latinas/os were parties in these or similar proceedings (see Chao Romero & Fernandez, 2012; Ramos, 2001). Since the National Association for the Advancement of Colored People (NAACP) served as attorneys for the plaintiffs (i.e., *Shelley*) in the case, our journey took us to the Library of Congress to search the NAACP archives.[3] There we found numerous grant deeds with the language of racial restriction, but none that restricted Latinas or Latinos from buying or leasing property. We were looking for archival materials of formal and informal Jim Crow laws and customs that separated whites from Blacks in all walks of life and emerged in the post–Civil War era (1865–1964) and how they impacted the Mexican American community.[4]

As we moved to other archives in search of racially restrictive covenants toward Mexican Americans, we found a photo in the archives of the Dolph Briscoe Center for American History at the University of Texas.[5] It was part of a project titled *The Study of the Spanish-Speaking People of Texas: A Photo Essay.* It was a sign in a restaurant window in Dimmit, Texas, in 1949 that provided us our first evidence for our

Figure 6.1. Sign in a restaurant window in Dimmit, Texas, in 1949.

archival data search of the spatial segregation of Mexican Americans (Figure 6.1). In 1949 signage of this type could be part of everyday life in this small Texas town. We found racial restrictions in access to restaurants but still couldn't find the racial artifacts of property deeds that applied to Mexican American residents. We knew from our readings that this form of everyday racism was part of the daily life of Mexican Americans in this and other parts of the United States prior to and after this date (see Avila, 2006; Essed, 1991; Lipsitz, 2006; Nicolaides, 2002; Romo, 1983; Sanchez 1993; Weaver, 1948).

How are we to understand the effects of these images, legislation, and other customs and practices on Mexican Americans who come in contact with them, and how do they respond to these forms of everyday racism? This chapter is the story of how we came to answer these questions. In order to organize our journey, we begin by defining the concepts of *race*, *racism*, and *racist nativism*. We then introduce critical race theory (CRT) as an overarching framework and critical race spatial analysis (CRSA) as our tool to understand the documents that were gathered in our journey. Finally, we try to show how these vestiges of racial discrimination have continued to this day in the institutions that serve these communities, such as schools, health care, and social services.

Defining *Race, Racism, Racist Nativism, White Supremacy,* and *Critical Race Theory*

In order to address these questions, we must ask another: Does the discrimination of a nondominant racial group require a rationalizing ideology? In response, one could argue that dominant groups (i.e., those in power) try to legitimate their interests or positions by means of an ideology—a set of beliefs that explains or justifies some actual or potential social arrangement (Pérez Huber & Solórzano, 2015a, 2015b).

Therefore, what ideologies are needed to justify not serving Mexican Americans or the non–English speaking in restaurants? What ideologies are needed to justify restricting Mexican Americans from buying or leasing property in certain communities? We argue that race, racism, racist nativism, and white supremacy are parts of an ideology that justifies the dominance of one racial group (i.e., whites) over others (i.e., Blacks, Native Americans, Asian Americans, and documented and undocumented Mexican Americans).

In order to understand this rationalizing ideology, we begin by defining its elements and start with the concept of *race*. Race is a socially constructed category created to justify racism (see Lorde, 1984; Marable, 1992). That is, race is a socially constructed category used to differentiate racial groups and to show and justify the superiority or dominance of one race over another (i.e., racism). Another element of these ideologies is *racism*, defined as the belief in the inherent superiority of one race over another in order to justify unequal and oppressive social arrangements, and tied to institutional power to enact that superiority (see Lorde, 1984; Solórzano, 1997). Specifically, *institutional racism* can be defined as the formal or informal structural mechanisms, such as policies and processes, that systematically subordinate, marginalize, and exclude nondominant groups. The next element in these ideologies is racist nativism. *Racist nativism* is defined as a form of racism that examines the link between race and immigration status. Specifically, racist nativism (a) occurs within a historical and contemporary context, (b) intersects with other forms of oppression, and (c) is based on real or perceived immigration status (Pérez Huber, Benavides Lopez, Vélez, & Solórzano, 2008). Finally, *white supremacy* is defined as the set of beliefs or ideologies that guides a system of racial domination and exploitation where power and resources are unequally distributed to privilege whites and oppress People of Color (Pérez Huber, Benavides Lopez, Vélez, & Solórzano, 2008; Pérez Huber & Solórzano, 2015a, 2015b). This ideology also justifies actual or potential social arrangements that legitimate the interests or positions of a dominant group (i.e., whites) over nondominant groups (i.e., People of Color).

In order to examine everyday forms of racism that Communities of Color experience, we use an overarching framework in education called CRT. We define *CRT in education* as the work of scholars who are developing an explanatory framework that accounts for the role of race, racism, and white supremacy in education. CRT works toward identifying and challenging racism and white supremacy in its historical and contemporary forms as part of a larger goal of identifying and challenging all forms of subordination. Specifically, for this article we use a tool of CRT called *CRSA* and define it as

> An explanatory framework and methodological approach that accounts for the role of race, racism, and white supremacy in examining geographic and social spaces and that works toward identifying and challenging racism within these spaces as part of a larger goal of identifying and challenging all forms of subordination. CRSA goes beyond description to spatially examine how structural and institutional factors influence and shape racial dynamics and the power associated with those dynamics

over time. Within educational research, CRSA is particularly interested in how structural and institutional factors divide, constrict, and construct space to impact the educational experiences and opportunities available to students based on race. (Solórzano & Vélez, 2007; Pacheco & Vélez, 2009, p. 293).

A precursor to CRSA is W. E. B. Du Bois's (1903/1999) concept of the color-line.[6] Du Bois's often quoted line, "The problem of the twentieth century is the problem of the color-line, the relation of the darker to the lighter races of men in Asia and Africa, in America and the islands of the sea" (p. 17) is a foundational construct in CRSA. In fact, in *The Souls of Black Folk*, Du Bois (1903/1999) referenced the color-line eight times. Two quotes that speak to the work that we are about to present are relevant here. First,

> Since then a new adjustment of relations in economic and political affairs has grown up,—an adjustment subtle and difficult to grasp, yet singularly ingenious, which leaves still that frightful chasm at the *color-line* across which men pass at their peril. (Du Bois, 1903/1999, p. 66, italics added)

Du Bois argued that crossing the color-line is real and can be frightful and have perilous consequences. In the second reference Du Bois stated, "It is usually possible to draw in nearly every Southern community a physical color-line on the map, on the one side of which whites dwell and on the other Negroes" (1903/1999, 106–107).[7] These color-lines could be a street, a highway, a river, railroad tracks, or any other geographic or spatial indicator that separates the racial groups. How did these color-lines play themselves out in the Mexican American community, and what impact might they have today?

Establishing Color-Lines: The Case of Racial Segregation in Southern California

In order to study the color-line in Mexican American communities we want to examine segregated housing patterns and the impact on their everyday lives. Specifically, we seek to find out how Mexican American communities became and remained racially segregated and what impact this had for institutions (i.e., schools, health care, and social services) that serve these communities. How did a color-line emerge that separated Mexican Americans from whites? We examine two tools used for the purpose of racial separation or to establish a color-line: racially restrictive covenants and redlining.

Racially Restrictive Covenants

A *racially restrictive covenant* is a clause in a property deed or lease that restricts the sale or lease to particular racial or ethnic groups. This is a tool that white communities used to keep People of Color and other "undesirables" out of their neighborhoods.

This legal tool was used to erect and maintain color-lines and other Jim Crow laws and customs and was part of everyday racism throughout the United States. As mentioned earlier, we were looking for the actual grant deeds that prohibited Mexican Americans from purchasing or leasing property, or what internal colonial theorists might call "keeping them in their place" (Bonilla & Girling, 1973). Two colleagues[8] shared with us a facsimile of a November 1949 property grant deed from Oxnard, California (see Appendix, Figure 6A.1). The grant deed shows Mildred Nye's transfer of property to Hurshel Keeter in the city of Oxnard in Ventura County, California. The second page of the grant deed states,

> This deed is made and accepted subject to the restrictions and conditions as follows: No part of said premises shall ever be occupied (other than in capacity of servant to the occupant) by any person or persons other than of the white or caucasian race and for the purpose of this paragraph no Japanese, Chinese, Mexican, Hindu, or any other person or persons of the Ethiopian, Indian, or Mongolian races shall be deemed to be Caucasian.

While these racially restrictive covenants were outlawed in the *Shelly v. Kramer* U.S. Supreme Court decision in 1948, the justices ruled that state courts could not constitutionally prevent the sale of real property to Blacks even if that property was covered by a racially restrictive covenant. The court ruled that racially restrictive covenants violated no rights. However, the enforcement of racially restrictive covenants by state courts constituted the state action, and it was that state action that was in violation of the Fourteenth Amendment. To this day, one can go to local county offices where property transactions are recorded and find examples of grant deeds that continue to have the racially restrictive language similar to the language in Figure 6A.1. For generations, racially restrictive covenants were used to keep People of Color out of white communities and are examples of institutional racism and the racial tools used to maintain the color-line. Although we had succeeded in finding the grant deeds that targeted Mexican Americans, we realized that other tools were also used to keep People of Color and the poor out of the more affluent and white neighborhoods, including redlining.

Redlining

Redlining is the practice of denying or limiting financial services to certain neighborhoods based on racial or ethnic composition without regard to the residents' qualifications or creditworthiness. The term *redlining* refers to the practice of using a red line on a map to delineate the area where financial institutions would not lend or invest. In 1933, as part of New Deal legislation, the federal government created the Home Owners Loan Corporation (HOLC)[9] to assist with the refinancing of small home mortgages in foreclosure during and after the Great Depression (see Lipsitz, 2006; Marciano, Goldberg, & Hou, 2011). One of the tools of the HOLC in the late 1930s was the creation of "appraisal maps" or "residential security maps" (Marciano,

Goldberg, & Hou, 2011).[10] These color-coded maps in 239 cities across the United States combined with the Federal Housing Administration's (FHA) strict lending standards, contained in their *Underwriting Handbook*, determined which kinds of properties it would approve for mortgages (see Avila, 2006; Lipsitz, 2006; Marciano, Goldberg, & Hou, 2011; Weaver, 1948). In addition to physical quality standards of the properties, the FHA also based its lending decisions on these residential security maps which indicated the location and the racial and ethnic composition of the neighborhood where the property existed (Avila, 2006; Lipsitz, 2006; Weaver, 1948). These color-coded maps used racial criteria to categorize lending and insurance risks and showed the level of security for real estate investments in these 239 U.S. cities. The color-coded designations on the maps were based on descriptive assumptions about the community and not on the ability of various households to satisfy lending criteria. For instance, using these appraisal maps, the HOLC, the FHA, and private lenders granted the vast majority of loans to the predominantly white suburbs of Los Angeles and not the neediest areas of inner-city Los Angeles (Nicolaides, 2002; Weaver, 1948).

To show how this worked, Figure 6A.2 (Appendix 6) is a 1939 HOLC Los Angeles and vicinity residential security map. This map shows the color-coded classifications (reproduced here in grayscale) that HOLC appraisers developed to differentiate neighborhoods so as to categorize lending and insurance risks. These classifications were determined based in part on the HOLC appraisers' descriptions of the occupation, income, and ethnicity of the inhabitants, along with the physical conditions of the neighborhoods and dwellings. A closer look at the residential security map shows that, in addition to being color-coded, the map has alphanumeric designations attached to these communities (see Appendix 6, Figures 6A.2, 6A.3, 6A.4, and 6A.5; high-resolution and color versions of the maps are available at https://sites.google.com/site/spatialequityandeducation/critical-race-spatial-analysis/chp-6-resources). The following descriptions of the color-coded neighborhoods are hierarchical, with "A" (green) being the most desirable and "D" (red) being the least desirable (see Crossney & Barteltn, 2005):

- A (green): Best; new; homogenous
- B (blue): Still desirable; area has reached peak
- C (yellow): Definitely declining
- D (red): Hazardous

Using the residential security maps as our guide, we journey to communities south and east of downtown Los Angeles (see Appendix 6 Figures 6A.2. 6A.3, 6A.4, and 6A.5). We look at the neighborhoods that, in 1939, had sizeable and growing Mexican American and African American populations and the least desirable or "red" designation. We begin by focusing on four neighborhoods in South Central Los Angeles: Central Avenue District (D-52), Florence Industrial District (D-60), Watts (D-61), and Northwest Compton District (D-65). We then move to communities east of downtown Los Angeles: Elysian Park and Dog Town District (D-35), Lincoln Park (D-38, which is now the community of Lincoln Heights), and Boyle Heights (D-53).

Finally, we explore two other neighborhoods in the San Gabriel Valley that are 10 miles east of downtown Los Angeles: San Gabriel (D-13) and San Gabriel Wash and Whittier Way (D-57).[11] These alphanumeric designations are attached to HOLC appraiser area descriptions (see Figure 6A.6),[12] which provide a one-page description of the community and give the reasons for the designation.

South Central Los Angeles

South Central Los Angeles is one of the oldest African American communities in Southern California. In the 1930s, the heart of the African American community was Central Avenue (see Figure 6A.2). It is situated south of downtown Los Angeles and has been the city's historical center of African American culture and history (Cox, 1996; Smith, 2006). In 1939 the area description of the Central Avenue District (see Figure 6A.6—D-52) depicted it as 50% "Negro" and 40% "foreign families."[13] The other "nationalities" in the district were "Mexicans, Japanese, and low class Italians." The HOLC appraiser goes on to describe the community as the following:

> This is a "melting pot" area of Los Angeles, and has long been thoroughly blighted. The Negro concentration is on the eastern two thirds of the area. . . . Population is uniformly of poor quality and many improvements are in a state of dilapidation. This area is a fit location for a slum clearance project. (Figure 6A.6)

What this residential security map and the appraiser's area description of the Central Avenue District (D-52) show is that the "Negro concentration on the eastern two thirds of the area" could not move east beyond Alameda Avenue[14] and into more "desirable" areas of South Gate or Huntington Park (see Nicolaides, 2002). This was the eastern color-line for African Americans in Los Angeles. The security maps and area descriptions also show that this area was not going to get support from the FHA, HOLC, or private lenders for it was seen as "blighted" and a "fit location for a slum clearance project." The residential security map and area description also provide evidence of why this area of South Central Los Angeles has been and, to this day, continues to be one of the poorest and most segregated areas of Los Angeles.

To continue the story of segregation, we move just south of the Central Avenue District to an area called the Florence Industrial District (D-60; see Figure 6A.2). It is an area with 25% "foreign families," mostly "factory workers, laborers, and WPA [Works Progress Administration] workers." In terms of "nationalities" it is made up of "Mexicans and Italians" and "3% Negro." However, it cautions that there is an "infiltration of more Negroes and subversive racial elements"[15] into the area. In the description and characteristics of the area, the HOLC appraiser states that the "population is largely composed of low income workingmen, with an increasing number of Negroes and Mexican." Indeed, unlike the lack of movement to the east, African Americans did move south into the communities of Watts and Compton and eventually west into the Crenshaw District and the city of Inglewood.

South of the Central Avenue District and the Florence Industrial District is the community of Watts (D-61; see Figure 6A.2). The appraisers describe the community as "25% foreign families" of mostly "Mexican and Japanese" nationalities. At "50% Negro," Watts "contains one of the largest concentrations of Negroes in Los Angeles County." They go on on to claim that "subversive racial elements and encroachment of industry and business [is] increasing" in the area. Finally they state, "while slum conditions do not yet prevail, the trend is definitely in that direction . . . The area is thoroughly blighted."

Just south of the community of Watts, the Northwest Compton District (D-65) is near the southern end of South Central Los Angeles (see Figure 6A.3). The HOLC appraisers describe it as "30% foreign families" of mostly "Mexicans" and "few Negroes." They then state that there is a "threat of negro infiltration from areas to the north" (i.e., the Central Avenue and Florence Industrial Districts, and Watts). They go on to state, "There are no deed restrictions. . . . The prospects for this area are not bright and while a 'medial red' grade is assigned it is believed that its downward trend will continue. If population density increases it may easily develop into a 'slum district.'"

African Americans did migrate south into the community of Compton and into an area where there was little financial support from the FHA, HOLC, and private lenders to keep Compton from becoming a "slum district." These residential security maps and area descriptions of South Central Los Angeles and Compton illustrate how African Americans and Mexican Americans are clearly connected in the community's racial history—at least in the way the HOLC appraisers described and allocated resources to their communities.

East Los Angeles

East Los Angeles is one of the oldest Latina/o communities in Southern California. It is situated east of downtown Los Angeles generally and east of the Los Angeles River in particular (see Avila, 2006; Romo, 1983; Sanchez, 1993; Sanchez & Villa, 2005). It has also been an immigrant port of entry for Jewish, Russian, Japanese, and Mexican Americans (Sanchez, 1993). Viewing the Los Angeles and vicinity residential security map (see Figure 6A.2), we continue the story by moving to a "port of entry" community just east of downtown Los Angeles—the Elysian Park and Dog Town District (D-35). The 1939 area description of this district depicts it as inhabited by "laborers and WPA workers"; "90% foreign families"; and of "Mexican, Japanese, and Chinese" nationalities. The HOLC appraiser described the community as

> within walking distance of [Los Angeles] Civic Center. This is an extremely old area which was never highly regarded and is now thoroughly blighted. A part of it known as "Dog Town" is a typical Mexican peon district. Although there are a few old fairly presentable homes which are still in original ownership, the area as a whole is dilapidated and inhabited by a highly heterogeneous and subversive population. (see Figure 6A.2)

As we move farther east of downtown Los Angeles, we cross the Los Angeles River into another immigrant port of entry community—the Lincoln Park District (now called Lincoln Heights). According to the HOLC appraiser, Lincoln Park is inhabited by "factory workers, railroad men, artisans, laborers, and WPA workers"; about "20% foreign families"; and "Mexican and Italian" nationalities. This was the original "Little Italy" section of Los Angeles. The area description also stated that "subversive racial elements are increasing" in the Lincoln Park District. The HOLC appraiser describes the community as follows: "Parts of area are rapidly approaching 'slum' conditions. The area is definitely 'blighted.'"

As we move south from the Lincoln Park District we enter the community of Boyle Heights (see Figure 6A.2). This community was another immigrant port of entry for Jews, Russians, Japanese, and Mexicans in the 1930s (Sanchez, 1993). The HOLC appraiser described the community as "Jewish professional and business men, Mexican laborers, WPA workers." About "50% are foreign families" made up of "Russians, Polish, and Armenian Jews, Slavs, Greeks, American Mexicans, Japanese and Italians," and "subversive elements are increasing." It was one of the most ethnically diverse communities in Los Angeles and was described as

> a "melting pot" area and is literally honeycombed with diverse and subversive racial elements. It is seriously doubted whether there is a single block in the area which does not contain detrimental racial elements. . . . The federal government, in conjunction with the city government are undertaking a slum clearance project covering 41 areas in the extreme northeast part of the area. (see Figure 6A.2)

Similar to South Central Los Angeles, these descriptions make clear how the HOLC appraiser explicitly racialized neighborhoods for the purpose of assessing which areas were "good" versus "bad," and therefore determining where redevelopment would take place.

San Gabriel Valley

As we move farther east from Boyle Heights we come to two communities in the San Gabriel Valley of Southern California—San Gabriel (D-13) and San Gabriel Wash and Whittier Way (D-57). The first of these San Gabriel Valley communities is found on the San Gabriel residential security map (see Figure 6A.4). In the San Gabriel District (D-13), the HOLC appraiser describes the district as "90% American-born Mexicans." The appraiser goes on the describe the area as

> the original San Gabriel settlement which was established at the time the Mission of that name was built in 1776. . . . With the exception of a few residents occupied by these old families, there is no apparent pride of occupancy or ownership. The vast majority of the population, while American-born, are still "peon Mexicans," and constitute a distinctly subversive racial influence. Many of the Mexican-born inhabitants were repatriated during the depression years and their places in many cases are said to

have been taken by hybrid Mexicans of American birth who are a distinctly less desirable type. . . . This area is considered a menace to this whole section and pressure is being exerted to confine the population and keep it from infiltrating into other districts.

The final community in our story is the San Gabriel Wash and Whittier Way District (D-57; see Figure 6A.5). The HOLC appraiser's report describes it as having "100% foreign families," of Mexican nationality with "many Mexican born—impossible to differentiate." The HOLC appraiser also describes an "infiltration of goats, rabbits, and dark-skinned babies," going on to portray the community as

an extremely old Mexican shack district, which has been "as is" for many generations. Like the "army mule" it has no pride of ancestry nor hope of posterity. It is a typical semitropical countryside "slum."

Once again these descriptions make clear how the HOLC appraiser explicitly racialized neighborhoods and, by extension, the communities within them. These appraisals were intentional and served to reinforce color-lines already in existence in these areas.

Conclusion

Each of the communities we examined received a "D" or red designation on the residential security map. These residential security maps and area descriptions, which separated neighborhoods primarily by race, paved the way for segregation and discrimination in lending and other resources. We argue that the HOLC residential security maps and area descriptions were blatant examples of institutional racism in U.S. housing and lending (Avila, 2006; Lipsitz, 2006; Marciano, Goldberg, & Hou, 2011; Weaver, 1948).

The narratives used by the HOLC appraisers in their area descriptions to describe African American and Mexican populations in Los Angeles and the San Gabriel Valley is the framing language that is part of an ideology that creates and maintains the color-line (see Pérez Huber, 2009). It is a framing language that also reinforces cultural deficit thinking regarding the African American and Mexican communities and is worth repeating (see Solórzano & Yosso, 2001; Valencia & Solórzano, 1997). Here is a sampling of the language used by the HOLC appraiser to describe these communities.

- **Community Descriptions**
  - "Slums"
  - "Slum conditions"
  - "Slum districts"
  - "Semi tropical countryside slums"
  - "Dilapidation"
  - "Blighted"

- **Broad Ethnic Racial Descriptions**

  o "Subversive racial elements"
  o "Subversive racial influences"
  o "Subversive populations"
  o "Detrimental racial elements"

- **Specific Ethnic Racial Descriptions**

  o "Mexican peon district"
  o "Peon Mexicans"
  o "Hybrid Mexicans of American birth"
  o "Distinctly less desirable type"
  o "No pride of ancestry"
  o "Menace to the whole section"
  o "Infiltration of goats, rabbits, and dark-skinned babies"
  o "Infiltration of more Negroes and subversive racial elements"

If an ideology is a set of beliefs that explains or justifies some actual or potential social arrangement, then the residential security maps and the language used in the area descriptions reinforce the belief that African Americans and Mexicans are an inferior people and rationalize keeping them in segregated neighborhoods. This same language and ideology has also been used to justify the inferior schools in these neighborhoods (see Solórzano, 1997; Solórzano & Solórzano, 1995; Solórzano & Yosso, 2001; Valencia & Solórzano, 1997). This language and ideology also justify other substandard social and commercial services for these communities, such as in health care, supermarkets, banking, and social services. It should be noted that similar language was also used to describe Blacks and Mexican Americans as good only for menial work (see Davis, 1997).

The first part of Solórzano and Vélez's (2007) *CRSA* definition states that "it is an explanatory framework that accounts for the role of race and racism in examining social and geographic spaces." The evidence provided in the HOLC security maps and area descriptions are clear examples of how race is both a socially and spatially constructed category used to differentiate racial groups and communities and to show and justify the superiority, dominance, and separation of one race over another (i.e., institutional racism and white supremacy)—in this case, to maintain racial and economically homogeneous neighborhoods. The second part of the definition states that CRSA "works toward identifying and challenging racism within these spaces as part of a larger goal of identifying and challenging all forms of subordination." Sharing this information with others and using it to challenge the dominant deficit narrative of Communities of Color reminds us that CRT generally and CRSA in particular are about moving toward racial justice (Pacheco & Vélez, 2009; Solórzano & Vélez, 2007; Yosso, 2005). We hope the story of these Communities of Color moves us in that direction.

Notes

1. A racially restrictive covenant is a clause in a property deed or lease that restricts the sale or lease to particular racial or ethnic groups.

2. The term *Mexican American* is defined as persons of Mexican ancestry living in the United States regardless of immigration status. This term is also used synonymously with *Chicana* and *Chicano*.

3. The NAACP archive at the Library of Congress starts with a 1,400-plus-page Finding Aid on the artifacts in the collection titled "National Association for the Advancement of Colored People: A Register of Its Records in the Library of Congress."

4. This chapter has an explicit focus on Mexican Americans because they represented the overwhelming majority of Latinas/os in the Los Angeles neighborhoods during the historical period we studied. The data we collected on HOLC appraisers confirms that Mexican Americans were specifically targeted.

5. See www.cah.utexas.edu/ssspot/lesson_plans/lesson_4.php

6. In 1897, W. E. B. Du Bois wrote an article in the *Atlantic Monthly* called the "Strivings of the Negro People" (p. 194) in which he first introduces us to early elements that in *The Souls of Black Folk* (1903/1999) help us understand the concept of the color-line: the veil, second-sight, double-consciousness, two-ness.

7. In 1925 Du Bois reaffirmed his views of the color-line, stating, "And thus again in 1925, as in 1899, I seem to see the problem of the Twentieth Century as the Problem of the Color Line" (Du Bois, 1925, p. 444).

8. The two colleagues are UCLA professor David G. Garcia and UCSB professor Tara Yosso.

9. The HOLC was not an independent agency but functioned under the supervision of the Federal Home Loan Bank Board.

10. The authors thank Richard Marciano and the Testbed for Redlining Archives of California's Exclusionary Spaces (T-RACES) Project for access to maps and records of the Federal Home Loan Bank Board, National Archives (see http://salt.umd.edu/T-RACES/).

11. The names of these districts were created by the HOLC.

12. Appendix 6A.6 is an example of the HOLC appraiser's description for the Central Avenue District (D-52) attached to the HOLC residential security map (Appendix 6A.2). Similar HOLC appraiser's descriptions were used to characterize other communities in this article.

13. Quotes are from Area Descriptions, Security Maps of Los Angeles County, Area No. D-52—Central Avenue District.

14. Alameda Avenue was also referred to as the "Cotton Curtain" or "the Wall" (see Nicolaides, 2002). It was a clear color-line that separated Black from white Los Angeles.

15. According to Nicolaides (2002), "subversive racial elements" were used by the HOLC to describe "Mexicans, Blacks, and Japanese" (p. 193).

References

Avila, E. (2006). *Popular culture in the age of white flight, fear, and fantasy in suburban Los Angeles.* Berkeley, CA: University of California Press.

Bonilla, F., & Girling, R. (Eds.). (1973). *Structures of dependency.* Stanford, CA: Stanford Institute of Politics.

Chao Romero, R., & Fernandez, L. (February 2012). *Doss v. Bernal ending Mexican apartheid in Orange County.* Research Report No. 14. Los Angeles, California. UCLA Chicano Studies Research Center.

Cox, B. (1996). *Central Avenue: Its rise and fall, 1890–1955.* Los Angeles, CA: BEEM Publications.

Crossney, K., & Barteltn, D. (2005). Residential security, risk, and race: The Home Owners' Loan Corporation and mortgage access in two cities. *Urban Geography, 26,* 707–736.

Davis, M. (1997). Sunshine and the open shop: Ford and Darwin in 1920s Los Angeles. *Antipode, 29,* 356–382.

Du Bois, W. E. B. (1925). Worlds of color. *Foreign Affairs, 3,* 423–444.

Du Bois, W. E. B. (1903/1999). *Souls of Black folk.* New York, NY: W.W. Norton and Company.

Essed, P. (1991). *Understanding everyday racism: An interdisciplinary theory.* Newbury Park, CA: Sage.

Home Owners Loan Corporation City Survey Files, Area D-53, Los Angeles, 1939.

Lipsitz, G. (2006). *The possessive investment in whiteness: How white people profit from identity politics.* Philadelphia, PA: Temple University Press.

Lorde, A. (1984). *Sister outsider.* Freedom, CA: Crossing Press.

Marable, M. (1992). *Black America.* Westfield, NJ: Open Media.

Marciano, R., Goldberg, D., & Hou, C. (2011). T-RACES: A testbed for the redlining archives of California's exclusionary spaces. Retrieved from http://salt.umd.edu/T-RACES.

Nicolaides, B. (2002). *My blue heaven: Life and politics in the working-class suburbs of Los Angeles, 1920–1965.* Chicago, IL: University of Chicago Press.

Pacheco, D., & Vélez, V. (2009). Maps, mapmaking, and critical pedagogy: Exploring GIS and maps as a teaching tool for social change. *Seattle Journal for Social Justice, 8,* 273–302.

Pérez Huber, L. (2009). Challenging racist nativist framing: Acknowledging the community cultural wealth of undocumented Chicana college students to reframe the immigration debate. *Harvard Educational Review, 79,* 704–729.

Pérez Huber, L., & Solórzano, D. (2015a). Visualizing everyday racism: Critical race theory, visual microaggressions, and the historical image of Mexican banditry." *Qualitative Inquiry, 21,* 223–238.

Pérez Huber, L., & Solórzano, D. (2015b). Racial microaggressions as a tool for critical race research. *Race, Ethnicity, and Education, 18,* 297–320.

Ramos, C. (2001). The educational legacy of racially restrictive covenants: Their long-term impact on Mexican Americans." *The Scholar, 4:*149–184.

Romo, R. (1983). *History of East Los Angeles: History of a barrio.* Austin, TX: University of Texas Press.

Sanchez, G. (1993). *Becoming Mexican American: Ethnicity, culture, and identity in Chicano Los Angeles, 1900–1945.* New York, NY: Oxford University Press.

Sanchez, G., & Villa, R. (2005). *Los Angeles and the future of urban cultures.* Baltimore, MD: Johns Hopkins University Press.

Smith, R. (2006). *The great Black way: L.A. in the 1940s and the lost African American renaissance.* New York, NY: Public Affairs.

Solórzano, D. (1997). Images and words that wound: Critical race theory, racial stereotyping, and teacher education. *Teacher Education Quarterly, 24,* 5–19.

Solórzano, D., & Solórzano, R. (1995). The Chicano educational experience: A proposed framework for effective schools in Chicano communities. *Educational Policy, 9,* 293–314.

Solórzano, D., & Vélez, V. (2007). *Critical race spatial analysis along the Alameda Corridor in Los Angeles.* Presented at the American Education Research Association Conference, April 7–11, Chicago, IL.

Solórzano, D., & Yosso, T. (2001). From racial stereotyping and deficit discourse toward a critical race theory of teacher education. *Multicultural Education, 9,* 2–8.

Weaver, R. (1948). *The Negro ghetto.* New York, NY: Harcourt, Brace and Company.

Valencia, R., & Solórzano, D. (1997). Contemporary deficit thinking. In R. Valencia (Ed.), *The evolution of deficit thinking in educational thought and practice* (pp. 160–210). The Stanford Series on Education and Public Policy. New York, NY: Falmer Press.

Vélez, V., Pérez Huber, L., Benavides Lopez, C., De La Luz, A., Solórzano, D. (2008). Battling for human rights and social justice: A Latina/o critical race analysis of Latina/o student youth activism in the wake of 2006 anti-immigrant sentiment. *Social Justice: A Journal of Crime, Conflict, and World Order, 35*(1), 7-27.

Yosso, T. (2005). Whose culture has capital? A critical race theory discussion of community cultural wealth. *Race Ethnicity and Education, 8,* 69–91.

APPENDIX 6

All Appendix Figures are available in high-resolution and color formats at https://sites.google.com/site/spatialequityandeducation/critical-race-spatial-analysis/chp-6-resources

Figure 6A.1. Grant Deed, Mildred Nye's Transfer of Property to Hurshel Keeter, Ventura, California, November 1, 1949 (Original Facsimile).

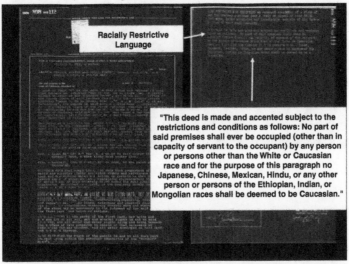

Figure 6A.2. Los Angeles and vicinity residential security map.

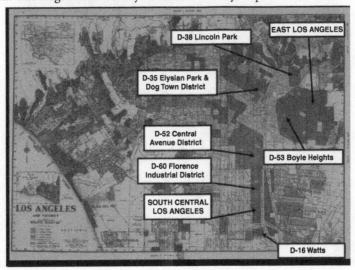

Figure 6A.3. Northwest Compton residential security map.

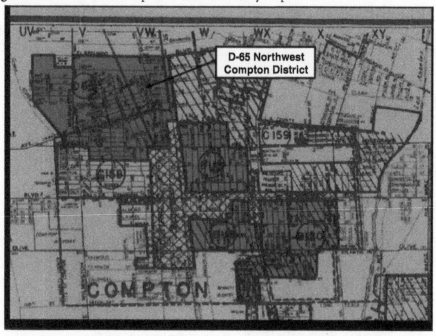

Figure 6A.4. San Gabriel residential security map.

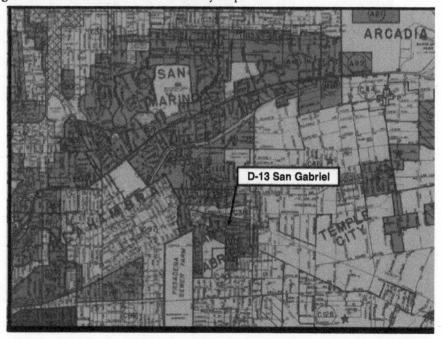

Figure 6A.5. San Gabriel Wash and Whittier Way residential security map.

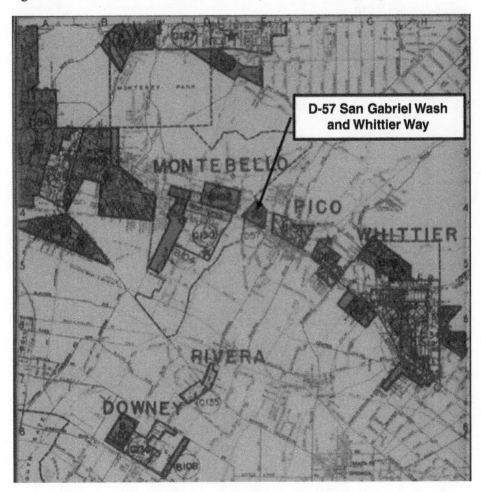

Figure 6A.6. Area description, security map of Los Angeles County, Area No. D-52—Central Avenue District.

AREA DESCRIPTION

Security Map of ___LOS ANGELES COUNTY___

1. POPULATION: a. Increasing ___-___ Decreasing ___-___ Static ___Yes___

   b. Class and Occupation ___WPA workers, laborers, low scale clericals, factory workers,etc___ Income $700 to $1500

   c. Foreign Families ___40 %___ Nationalities ___Mexicans, Japanese and low class Italians___ d. Negro ___50 %___

   e. Shifting or Infiltration ___Encroachment of industry a threat.___

2. BUILDINGS:

	PREDOMINATING ___85 %___	OTHER TYPE ___%___
a. Type and Size	5 rooms	
b. Construction	Frame	
c. Average Age	35 years	
d. Repair	Very poor	
e. Occupancy	97%	
f. Owner-occupied	20%	
g. 1935 Price Bracket	$2000-2750 ___%change___	$ ___%change___
h. 1937 Price Bracket	$2500-3500 ___20 %___	$ ___%___
i. 1939 Price Bracket	$2500-3500 ___- %___	$ ___%___
j. Sales Demand	Fair	
k. Predicted Price Trend (next 6-12 months)	Slowly down	
l. 1935 Rent Bracket	$25.00-30.00 ___%change___	$ ___%change___
m. 1937 Rent Bracket	$27.50-35.00 ___13 %___	$ ___%___
n. 1939 Rent Bracket	$27.50-35.00 ___- %___	$ ___%___
o. Rental Demand	Fair	
p. Predicted Rent Trend (next 6-12 months)	Static	

3. NEW CONSTRUCTION (past yr.) No. ___3___ Type & Price) ___Fr.-$4000___ How Selling ___Slowly___

4. OVERHANG OF HOME PROPERTIES: a. HOLC ___9___ b. Institutions ___Few___

5. SALE OF HOME PROPERTIES (3 yr.) a. HOLC ___74___ b. Institutions ___Few___

6. MORTGAGE FUNDS ___Bank___ 1937-8 7. TOTAL TAX RATE PER $1000 (193__) $ ___52.80___

8. DESCRIPTION AND CHARACTERISTICS OF AREA:

   Terrain: Level. No flood or construction hazards. Land improved 90%. Zoning is mixed, but improvements are largely single family dwellings. Conveniences are all readily available. This is the "melting pot" area of Los Angeles, and has long been thoroughly blighted. The Negro concentration is largely in the eastern two thirds of the area. Original construction was evidently of fair quality but lack of proper maintenance is notable. Population is uniformly of poor quality and many improvements are in a state of dilapidation. This area is a fit location for a slum clearance project.
   The area is accorded a "low red" grade.

9. LOCATION ___Central Ave.Dist.___ SECURITY GRADE ___4th -___ AREA NO. ___D-52___ DATE ___3-3-39___
   400

7

RESISTING REDLINING IN THE CLASSROOM

A Collaborative Approach to Racial Spaces Analysis

Benjamin Blaisdell

In this chapter I use the concept of redlining to describe how teachers contribute to the racialization of space, effectively segregating their Students of Color within supposedly integrated classrooms. Based on ethnographic work at a public elementary school, I also explain how redlining is an analytic tool that can be used collaboratively with teachers. Using this tool, teachers can learn to see their complicity in the racialization of space and create more integrated classroom spaces.

Racial Spaces Analysis

Racial spaces analysis (Blaisdell, 2016b) is a methodology that examines the connection between space, race, and white supremacy. It focuses on the formation of racial spaces, where access and mobility are dictated by white supremacy. Specifically, racial spaces analysis uses analytical tools from critical race theory (CRT)—such as culture of segregation and whiteness as property—in order to uncover how structural racism controls power and access within racial spaces and to illuminate the spatial and racial discourses that normalize that control. It is an approach both similar to and distinct from *critical race spatial analysis* (CRSA), which is a methodology that "accounts for the role of race and racism in examining geographic and social spaces" (Pacheco & Vélez, 2009, p. 293). Both approaches use CRT to examine the connection between race and space, and both seek to challenge how structural racism controls power and access. The difference is that CRSA focuses on using geographic information systems (GIS) "to visually represent the impact of race and racism within Communities of Color" (Pérez Huber, 2008, p. 168). Conversely, racial spaces analysis does not employ GIS or visual representation. Rather, its focus is analyzing how the connections between race and space manifest in teachers' perceptions and treatment of students.[1] For example, Blaisdell (2016b) used racial spaces analysis to show how teachers can contribute to racializing space and how teachers with critical under-standings of race and space can resist that process and create more equitable class-room spaces. What is important is that, like CRSA, racial spaces analysis is not only descriptive but also a critical methodology that works to challenge racism. Key to that effort is an analysis of white supremacy.

White supremacy is "a political, economic, and cultural system in which whites overwhelmingly control power and material resources," one where "white dominance and non-white subordination are daily reenacted" (Ansley, 1997, p. 592). Racial spaces analysis examines how whites secure this system of supremacy via the racializa-tion of space, or "the process by which residential location and community are carried and placed on racial identity" (Calmore, 1995, p. 1235). Space becomes racialized when it is associated with the race of the people who live in it (or occupy it in other ways, such as with schools). Mills (1997) explains, "The norming of space is partially done in terms of the *racing* of space, the depiction of space as dominated by individu-als (whether persons or subpersons) of a certain race" (p. 42, italics in original). This racial status becomes attached to the spaces where people live, leading white spaces to be considered superior and non-white spaces inferior. By linking racial status to space, the racialization of space simultaneously legitimizes and hides the role of white supremacy in governing people's lives.

> Connecting cultural inferiority to those physical spaces (whether real or imagined) legitimates viewing people as inferior—higher crime rates, lower health outcomes, and lack of academic success in those communities can all be used as justifications of deficit viewpoints. Furthermore, the focus on space makes it seem as if these deficit perspectives are not being assigned because of race. (Blaisdell, 2016b, p. 4)

The result is that even though white supremacy governs racial spaces, they are perceived to be spaces of equal opportunity.

In racial spaces, white supremacy is sustained via the property functions of whiteness. Harris (1993) explains that whiteness carries with it a higher social status (compared to other racial categories) and that this status causes whiteness to func-tion as a form of property. As property, whiteness carries a societal value that awards whites additional rights and resources. "Whiteness as property has historically and continues to function as a tool to confer social benefits, from the intangible to the material, on those who possess it and to punish those who do not" (Annamma, 2015, p. 298). These social benefits are regulated via white status, which allows whites to either adhere to or break the norms of a space and, in either case, maintain their right to that space. Therefore, whites have the "right to use and enjoyment" (Harris, 1993, p. 1734) of not just increased freedom within a space but also increased access to the resources that come with it, such as the resource of curriculum in the case of schools (Ladson-Billings & Tate, 1995).

People of Color, on the other hand, do not have the right to use and enjoy the status of whiteness. People of Color, and Black Americans in particular, continue to be segregated into racially isolated neighborhoods, and those segregated spaces are denied access to goods and services (Calmore, 1995; Chang & Smith, 2008; Mandell, 2008). Because those spaces are raced as non-white, they do not carry the status that comes with whiteness. The lack of status justifies the denial of resources to those segregated communities. Harris (1993) calls this the "absolute right to exclude" (p. 1736) based on the lack of whiteness. The right to deny is upheld because non-white spaces are interpreted as having a culture of segregation (Calmore, 1995), a deficit-based argument that blames inferior conditions on the people in those neighborhoods and not on the ongoing segregation those communities face.

Even in white spaces, People of Color are associated with racialized, non-white spaces and are therefore denied access to resources via culture-of-segregation arguments. Mills (1997) explains that people themselves are spaced, or "imprinted with the characteristics of a certain kind of space" (p. 42). When People of Color adhere to non-white norms, they are viewed according to culture-of-segregation perspectives linked with certain spaces. Even if they perform whiteness—that is, code switch to speak like middle-class whites or wear the same clothing or hairstyles as whites—and even if they come from white neighborhoods, People of Color are still not viewed as white because they are associated with non-white space. Mills (1997) explains that "those associated with the jungle will take the jungle with them even when they are brought to more civilized regions" (48). People of Color can never attain white status and thus will always be subject to the right to denial in racialized space.

Redlining in the Classroom

Outside of schools, one of the ways that the denial of access is carried out is through redlining. Originally referring to actual red lines drawn on maps, the term *redlining* now refers more broadly to any "lending (or insurance) discrimination that bases credit decisions on the location of a property to the exclusion of characteristics of the borrower or property" (Hillier, 2003, p. 395). That is to say, it is a practice that bases a person's worth on the value society places on his or her residential location (or assumed residential location). Redlining justifies the divestment of resources away from segregated neighborhoods and is still practiced today (Chang & Smith, 2008; Soja, 2010). Usually referring to a practice that occurs on the neighborhood or municipal level, redlining normalizes the creation and maintenance of racialized space. However, the normalization of racialized space does not occur only at the neighborhood level.

> Space must be normed and raced at the *macro*level (entire countries and continents), the *local* level (city neighborhoods), and ultimately even the *micro*level (the contaminated and contaminating carnal halo of the non-white body). (Mills, 1997, pp. 43–44)

Therefore, individuals are spaced (i.e., they carry their space with them) and can thus be treated like the location from which they come or are perceived to come. When that space is deemed inferior (i.e., not white), the culture-of-segregation discourse can be assigned to them individually. Thus, people can in essence be redlined on an individual level. In schools as racial spaces, teachers use culture of segregation arguments and whiteness as property to draw invisible redlines around their Students of Color (Blaisdell, 2016b). In doing so, teachers divest educational resources from those students, limiting their freedom, mobility, and voice in the classroom.

When they redline their Students of Color, teachers are complicit in *dysconscious racism*, which King (1991) defines as "an uncritical habit of mind (including perceptions, attitudes, assumptions, and beliefs) that justifies inequity and exploitation by accepting the existing order of things as given" (p. 135). Dysconscious racism involves relying on notions of white supremacy to justify the privileging of whites and marginalization of People of Color. King explains that it is not just being unaware of racism but rather a way whites learn to distort the effects of race. The racialization of space facilitates that process of distortion. The result is that the "hidden curriculum of whiteness saturates everyday school life" (Leonardo, 2004, p. 144).

Redlining can be a useful metaphor to help teachers uncover how this hidden curriculum of whiteness governs school space and understand their own complicity in the racialization of space (Blaisdell, 2016b). It is a simple concept that captures the intricate and hidden way that white supremacy is maintained in schools. Racial spaces analysis, when done collaboratively with teachers, can help them counter dysconscious racism and develop racial literacy. Guinier (2004) defines *racial literacy* as "the capacity to decipher the durable racial grammar that structures racialized hierarchies" (p. 100). Guinier also explains that racial literacy involves agency, but an agency that carefully takes into consideration that racial structure. In the rest of this chapter, I discuss my attempt to take up my own call to use the metaphor of redlining in an effort to help teachers develop racial literacy and the agency to challenge white supremacy in their schools.

Setting and Methodology

This chapter is based on an ethnographic study at City Elementary (a pseudonym). City is a new school located in a small, affluent town in the Piedmont region of North Carolina. That affluence is largely due to the presence of several major universities and a large business park with several large technological and medical industries within commuting distance. The school district has 10 elementary schools, with City being the newest. Even with the town's affluence, the district has experienced persistent racial achievement and discipline gaps. These gaps were no different at City. In its second year, the school had 518 students, with a racial breakdown of 44% white, 22% African American, 17% Asian, and 14% Latino. The African American and Latino students faced significant academic and discipline disparity. For instance, in math, almost 89% of white students but only 27% of African American students passed the end-of-grade test. In reading, 86% of white but only 20% of African

American students passed. Furthermore, Students of Color were seven times more likely than white students to be referred to the office for disciplinary reasons.

Based in CRT and racial spaces analyses, my methodology has also been inspired by Duncan-Andrade's (2006, 2007) recommendation for research to foreground the concept of *cariño*—the Spanish word for caring—where the researcher sees the participants not as subjects of the research study but rather as cofacilitators of the work.

> The direct aim is to positively impact on the material conditions of those involved with the study. By focusing more directly on improving the immediate circumstances . . . it seeks to democratize the tools of research and knowledge creation. This way, when researchers leave, there remains left behind a sense of hope and promise, one that is directly tied to the participants' sense of themselves as capable change agents. (Duncan-Andrade, 2007, p. 619)

I have been working with the school as an equity coach since the fall of 2013. As equity coach, I collaborate with the school's equity team to address the school's discipline and achievement gaps. The equity team is a group of 16 teachers and administrators charged with developing and implementing the school's professional development goals on racial equity. The racial makeup of the group is seven African Americans, seven whites, one Latino, and one Indian American. In a cariño-based approach, the equity team and I have been trying to use the research project as a way to help the school build a culture that can consistently challenge white supremacy and to develop a structure that helps them maintain that culture. So far, I have conducted 20 group and individual interviews with about 20 teachers and administrators, observed 15 classes, and led 8 faculty professional development sessions.

To analyze and represent the data from this study, I have also adhered closely to a cariño-based approach and focused on those moments when the research project has led to the results that Duncan-Andrade (2007) highlights—that is, improving immediate conditions, instilling a sense of hope, or inspiring teachers to be change agents. As the next section of this chapter explains, the project has involved working with teachers to develop the tools that can help them sustain change. To present these efforts, I specifically highlight some of the epiphanies of the project. *Epiphanies* are "interactional moments" and "turning point experiences" after which "a person is never quite the same again" (Denzin, 2001, p. 34). These experiences reveal how people come to terms with crises in their understandings of the world and show breaks in the unquestioned patterns of daily life. I emphasize the epiphanies that teachers have had in order to share the immediate effects of this project, and how it has been able to interrupt dominant discourses and practices as they relate to race. With this focus, I hope to show the performative potential of this kind of collaborative work, and how ethnographic research has the power to disrupt the taken-for-granted operations of daily life and the master narratives that sustain them (Madison, 2005).

A Focus on Supremacy

Compared to many schools I have worked with, the equity team at City has been particularly astute in discussing issues of racism. The school is located in the largest historically African American neighborhood in town and has implemented a yearly schoolwide project across all grade levels to celebrate and take advantage of the neighborhood's "community cultural wealth" (Yosso, 2005). In addition, most of the equity team members have undergone racial equity training from a regional antiracist organization and are able to openly discuss race and whiteness with each other and the broader faculty. Despite these strengths, the team has recognized that achievement and discipline gaps have persisted. When we met early on, I wanted to understand what the team believed was causing those gaps, about their attempts to address them, and the ways in which those attempts were both successful and unsuccessful.

An epiphany that came out of these conversations was that the team's focus on whiteness was as privilege rather than as supremacy. For instance, we had a conversation about why it was so hard for the white faculty to talk about race with each other.

Kate: I think that has a lot to do with whiteness. I think that white teachers are really scared to talk about race.

Kerry: Didn't we say we're going to have a training on this?

Zoe: Last year we tried that, about addressing your implicit biases, but I do feel that something people don't want to admit to themselves is that they have a bias.

Helen: With whiteness, I'm wondering if that invisible knapsack article[2] would at least bring a base awareness to everybody.

Many of the team members understood that whiteness existed at a societal level—how it affected implicit bias and controlled how society viewed People of Color. However, when it came to thinking about how to address whiteness with the faculty, they fell back to focusing on white privilege. *White privilege* refers to "the unearned advantages that whites, by virtue of their race, have over people of color" (Leonardo, 2004, p. 138). While analyzing white privilege is important, focusing only on privilege fails to address how whites actively reinforce their own racial advantage on a daily basis. Addressing privilege without supremacy actually allows privilege to continue because "the conditions of white supremacy make white privilege possible" (Leonardo, 2004, p. 137). Leonardo goes on to explain that it is important to analyze whiteness as supremacy—as an ongoing system of racial domination—and argues that focusing only on privilege has the effect of personalizing racism, of focusing on the self. This approach can divert whites from looking at the systemic and dominating nature of whiteness, as seen in Zoe's earlier comment. By focusing only on how whiteness affects bias, the teachers were stuck in discussing their own sense of self rather than on how their actions affect People of Color. I tried to make this point to the team.

Ben: I'll be tackling [whiteness] not from the perspective of privilege but from the perspective of supremacy. . . . Because, with privilege, the response often is, "Well, I'm not like that." A lot of whites like myself might say, "I'm an exceptional white. I'm the exception to the rule."

Zoe: The other response that I've heard in response to that is, "Why are you holding that against me? I can't *help* that I'm white."

Ben: Right. If we stick to the personalizing, it ends up actually recentering whiteness. The discussion is, "Am I or am I not a bad person?" which is unproductive.

Zoe showed that she understood how the focus on privilege could lead to whites personalizing racism. Then, drawing on the work of Leonardo (2004), I was able to further clarify the difference between white privilege and white supremacy.

Ben: Privilege is by and large talking about whiteness in a passive sense. It's just something whites have that we don't continually reconstruct and re-create. With supremacy, it becomes a system that we're all complicit in rather than it just being our biases. Biases are important, but they're important because they're connected to a structure that's already set up.

Jackie: Biases are more personalized as opposed to the system that you're talking about. You're going for a more institutional approach.

Ben: It's even more than institutional, it's what we call a structural understanding. . . . The personal is important, but the personal is only one part of it. If we only personalize it, we think if we work on the personal that we've solved the structural part, and that's not true because that structural part remains.

At this point, the team members expressed needing help in understanding more specifically how whiteness functioned as a system of domination at the school level. In response, I directly presented to them my work on racial spaces analysis, giving us a common language to talk about complicity in white supremacy. I specifically used my own work on racial spaces analysis because—in addition to helping me understand the specific nature of white supremacy in the district—it can be useful for developing teachers' racial literacy (Blaisdell, 2016b).

The more I worked with the equity team, the more we realized the need for them to develop the ability to see and counter specific instances of complicity in white supremacy. As one team member explained, a key goal of the project was for them to "build the capacity" to sustain a challenge to whiteness. Therefore, we decided to use the project to train the team members to be equity coaches who could walk their faculty though critical analyses of whiteness. We spent our monthly team meetings developing an understanding of whiteness as supremacy and used the monthly schoolwide meetings to train the entire faculty on racial spaces analysis. I also began following up on how the analysis was being used throughout the school by meeting with the grade-level professional learning communities (PLCs). In the next section, I explain the faculty-wide trainings in more detail, focusing on how we gave the faculty practice in conducting racial spaces analysis on a series of real school examples. As I present these examples, I also explain how we analyzed them and highlight how the redlining concept was useful.

Building Capacity

To train the faculty, I first used Omi and Winant's (1994) work on racial projects to define *race* and *racism* and Ansley's (1997) and Leonardo's (2004) work to help the faculty distinguish between white privilege and white supremacy. Then I presented my work on racial spaces, which included introducing the faculty to the concepts of the culture of segregation (Calmore, 1995) and whiteness as property (Harris, 1993). To help make this analysis wieldy for the teachers, I centered on the concept of redlining. To explain how redlining leads to divestment, I shared a map (Figure 7.1) from an educational website showing how redlining occurred in the 1930s in Durham, North Carolina, a city familiar to many of the teachers.

This map shows how the Home Owners' Loan Corporation (HOLC) appraised Durham's real estate. While it is debated if the HOLC itself directly restricted loans from redlined areas, redlining was practiced both prior to and after the creation of the HOLC maps, and a variety of other institutions (e.g., newspapers and insurance

Figure 7.1. Redlining in Durham, North Carolina.

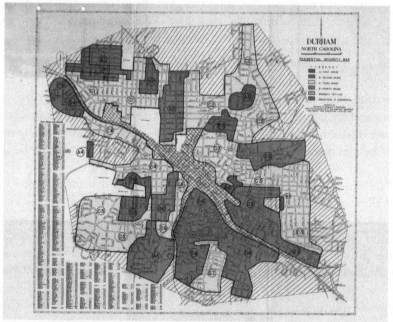

Note. This map is based on HOLC data and is a product of "Main Street Carolina software, which overlays a georeferenced version of the Durham City Survey Map over Google Maps" (Dividing Durham, n.d.).
Source. Dividing Durham, n.d.

agencies) created their own maps to assess and redline neighborhoods (Hillier, 2003). In its broader definition, a *redlined area* is "where local savings and residential income are drained away to other areas and to external interest, based largely on the perception that the affected area is dangerous, unsettled, or simply an unattractive place to do business" (Soja, 2010, p. 58). The map in Figure 7.1 shows how race was used to justify this divestment of resources. In color on the website, it shows the city's neighborhoods shaded in four different colors, each signifying a different set of grades with red representing the lowest grades (those marked as D1 to D6). On the website, the map is interactive. Viewers could click on a section, and a page would open that included the actual forms used by lenders to describe and determine the value of the neighborhood. Those forms included data on the percentage of African Americans in the neighborhood (the percentages of other racial groups were not listed). The red-shaded areas had the highest percentage of African Americans, and those forms contained clarifying remarks such as, "Northwest part occupied by Negroes," or "This was formerly a good white residential area but negroes [*sic*] are gradually taking over" (Dividing Durham, n.d.). This map shows, therefore, how beliefs about the value of space were linked to race. It was a helpful visual for the teachers to understand this connection, and how culture of segregation discourse and whiteness as property could lead to divestment.

After using the concept of redlining to introduce the concepts of racial spaces analysis, I modeled how to analyze school-based examples of racializing space and then had the teachers practice the analysis in small groups. These were real examples from my work with previous schools or from the members of the equity team (though sometimes I condensed them to make them manageable for the activity). I asked the teachers to look at the examples and answer the question, "How is redlining occurring?" Here is one of the examples, about a teacher's response to student behavior.

Charles's Backpack

Charles is an African American kindergartner with special needs who is struggling a bit to get on grade level. One afternoon, he starts yelling at his classmate Ethan, a quiet white boy who is doing very well in the class. The teacher asks Charles to stop yelling, but Charles is clearly upset and won't stop. The teacher again clearly and sternly asks him to stop, but he won't and is now yelling in front of the teacher. Charles is complaining that Ethan put his backpack in the garbage. Even though Ethan has done it before, none of the other students or teachers saw him do it this time, so he isn't reprimanded. Charles huffs and puffs and, though not yelling, keeps mumbling and complaining. Since he won't stop, the teacher reprimands Charles, writes him a referral, and sends him to the office.

Together, the teachers and I used this example to make connections between whiteness and freedom within classroom space. We discussed how Ethan had the right to use and enjoy the privilege of his whiteness. It was known that he had taken Charles's backpack in the past, but his whiteness allowed him to get away with breaking the rules of the classroom space. Alternatively, we discussed how Charles was denied the right to express his frustration—a frustration the faculty at the meeting believed was legitimate—because his manner of expression did not fit with classroom norms. Astutely, some of the teachers even pointed out that Charles's manner of resistance might be coming from ongoing experiences of racism and lack of freedom and voice within school space. One teacher commented, "He has a right to be mad, doesn't he?" Another explained, "I'd be upset, too." In talking through this example, the teachers were able to resist interpreting Charles from a culture-of-segregation perspective. Rather than labeling Charles's behavior as inappropriate, the frame of redlining helped them to contextualize his reaction. They explained that Charles had been redlined and how this could even have affected his ability to get on grade level. For example, one teacher said, "If he's going through this every day, of course he's not doing well in class!" After discussing this example, we had the teachers work in groups—with an equity team member guiding the conversation—to conduct the same analysis on other behavior-related examples. This gave the teachers the chance to practice the analysis and the team members a chance to practice leading these conversations.

In another session with the entire faculty, we moved to analyzing access to curriculum. As with the behavior examples, we examined one together, and then the teachers analyzed additional examples in smaller groups. Here is one of the curriculum examples:

Looking at the Data[3]

A group of fifth-grade teachers at City Elementary are talking about the racial makeup of their math groups. They are discussing the fact that Students of Color are primarily in lower-level groups. The teachers are

Sonya, African American, interventions specialist

Marvin, African American, fifth-grade teacher

Jake, white, fifth-grade teacher

Sonya: How are the groups made up? People are supposed to look at the data but then make decisions to move kids down, and they are usually Kids of Color. They say that they can't do the work even though they tested at that level.

Marvin: And they use "equity" to say they are making the right decision. They say that the kid needs extra language support, so they should be in a group that gives them that support—which are the lower-level groups—versus what the data tell us he can do.

Sonya: And I have seen students in the wrong group. They come to my group to focus on a specific skill, but they can already do it, and I know they have been put in the wrong group.

Marvin: Sometimes the argument has been that certain students can't be together, so one student is moved down.

Jake: We're pigeonholing kids. Sometimes white kids don't do well, and then they still get things. We had a group given this test and the test was blamed when they did poorly on it and we had to retest them. [Jake is discussing when a group of white students scored lower on the test they used to form the groups. The teachers thought it was odd the white students scored so low, so they retested them to see if they would do better the second time around.]

The teachers at City were able to identify culture of segregation and whiteness as property in this example. The City teachers identified how Students of Color were being denied the right of access to higher-level curriculum, even when those students earned scores high enough to give them that right. The faculty at City could see how the argument to move students into lower-level groups was based on culture-of-segregation arguments about Students of Color. They discussed how those students, even when they performed according the norms of whiteness, did not have the right to use and enjoy the privileges of that whiteness. City's teachers also recognized how the white students did have the right to use and enjoy greater access to curriculum because of their white status. The faculty concluded that the teachers in the example were redlining the Students of Color, thus divesting more valuable educational resources from them.

In following sessions, we moved to the teachers analyzing their own experiences. The faculty shared examples of specific instances where they believed racial inequity was occurring. In groups, they examined how redlining might be involved in those instances. The equity team members were the facilitators of the discussions, helping the teachers use racial spaces analysis to reframe their stories. After those group discussions, the entire faculty and I met together to share their stories, answer questions, and talk through the difficult areas of analysis.

Capacity Built? Successes and Limitations

After each training session, the equity team and I reconvened to share insights and discuss any difficulties they had in performing the coach's role. According to the team, a couple of positive results came out of the faculty trainings. One benefit was that it helped the faculty examine their complicity in white supremacy. Some teachers were actually able to point out how they themselves had redlined their Students of Color. For example, in one session, a kindergarten teacher, Kenya, told the story of her work with a young African American boy who had arrived late in the year. She explained that while much of the class could read basic texts and could write words and even some short phrases, the boy only had a basic ability to read letters. Kenya explained how she had, therefore, been limiting him to letter study practice. Talking with her grade-level team, however, helped her realize that restricting him from higher-level curriculum was actually limiting his chance to be successful. So, she started to give him word study and sentence structure practice.

He started to see the point of what he was doing after that. He really began to improve quickly, within just a few weeks.

Kenya's discussion with her PLC helped her to understand how her decision to limit her student's access to higher-level curriculum was linked, in part, to race.

Before that, I was redlining him. . . . I saw a poor, Black boy without much language.

In other words, she used culture-of-segregation logic to restrict his right to use and enjoy higher-level curriculum. An African American teacher herself, she was making a judgment about the boy's academic ability based on his race and where he was from. Kenya's story was not an epiphany only for herself. Sharing her story with the faculty was also an epiphany for some of the other teachers, who started to see their own complicity in redlining.

For instance, the Spanish teacher, Maya, shared a similar self-analysis. She talked about the resistance she got from many of her African American students to practicing Spanish or seeing it as important. The faculty conversations on redlining helped Maya look back at her view of her students.

I have a lot of white students who also don't want to speak in Spanish or do the work, but I don't think about that. The white students are just quiet and sit and don't do any work, but the Black students. . . . It's not loud or anything, but they complain to me.

I asked Maya to retell the story in terms of redlining, and with the help of a colleague, she was able to analyze herself in terms of whiteness as property. She described how she was giving the white students the right to enjoy the privilege of not being seen as resistant and denying that right to her Black students. Maya explained that this could hurt their academic success.

I need to be more careful in the future. I don't think the Black students are doing worse in my class now, but if I reprimand them more, it could hurt them.

An analysis centered on redlining helped both Kenya and Maya frame their complicity in, and subsequent challenge to, letting whiteness dominate their practices. Their original practices—restricting access to curriculum for low-level students and reprimanding more vocally resistant students—were not unusual practices in the school. They were part of the hidden curriculum of whiteness that governed the school's practices. By performing critical analyses of these practices for their colleagues to witness, Kenya and Maya were showing the pedagogical potential of the concept of redlining in countering white dominance.

Another benefit of the equity training was that it helped the school overcome some of the resistance to openly examining whiteness. As explained earlier, the school had already done professional development on white privilege, but it had not given teachers a clear understanding of how they were actively perpetuating privilege in their day-to-day practice. After a few of the faculty sessions, one of the team members, Donna, commented, "Now there is much less resistance to talking about whiteness." She explained that the school now had a language that made it easier to discuss with their colleagues. Talking about whiteness is not, by itself, enough to combat its role in regulating school space. However, dialogue that specifically seeks to overcome resistance to discussing embedded racism can be a useful step in fostering *critical race praxis* (Alemán & Alemán, 2010), which Yamamoto (1997) defines as a "reflective action: infusing antiracism practice with aspects of critical inquiry" (p. 874). The faculty equity trainings helped us begin the work of building the capacity for sustained critical inquiry into whiteness. They gave the equity team a chance to practice using redlining and racial spaces language with their colleagues and to develop their skills as equity leaders and coaches.

Some of the equity team members were even attempting to use the analysis to challenge school decisions that reified white dominance. For instance, the math specialist, Elaine, talked about her attempts to use it when meeting with the professional learning communities. She shared an example of one PLC deciding to separate all the students (across classes) into ability groups for math, which would have resulted in a low group of primarily Students of Color. Rigid ability grouping was still standard practice in many of the classrooms, and the PLC argued that it was a much easier way to group the students. Elaine explained to them, however, how those groups would result in redlining Students of Color. She said, "I just reminded them of the equity trainings, and they said, 'Oh yeah.'" She was then able to get the PLC to reconsider the practice and help them sort their students into more racially and academically heterogeneous groups.

Despite these early successes, much more work is needed to build the capacity to sustain critical race praxis at City. After all, there was still resistance to challenging whiteness. The more explicit forms of that resistance were most often expressed openly to the white team members (usually but not exclusively by other white teachers). Several team members also reported continuing to see Students of Color being reprimanded more harshly than white students, and school data indicated no reduction in the disproportionate number of office referrals for African American students since the beginning of the project. There was a long way to go to make the analysis a more integral part of the school culture. The team had a goal to analyze whiteness as a part of every major educational decision. They wanted to see a critical analysis of whiteness used in all official meetings (e.g., the PLC data meetings, where the teachers discussed the academic achievement of all students across the grade level), but several team members reported that the analysis was not being used in many of the school meetings. The faculty seemed to be able to engage in the analysis in the equity training sessions—where it did not actually have to be implemented—but then would not take it up in their day-to-day practice. Some of the team members tried to engage in the analysis in their own PLC meetings, but they would often be the lone voice in a group, making it difficult to achieve the desired effect. Also, while some team members tried to take on the coaching role and use racial spaces analysis to actively challenge whiteness, several other members mentioned that they did not yet feel prepared to do so. Reflection had not yet turned to schoolwide praxis.

"What Kind of Space Do We Want?": Implications for Praxis

As I continue to work with City, I need to investigate why some teachers and some of the PLCs took up the analysis and others did not. On the positive side, this study has reinforced the idea that racial spaces analysis and the concept of redlining can help teachers develop the racial literacy necessary to engage in critical race praxis. At least some of the teachers have been able to engage in this praxis beyond the project itself. This fits with the cariño-based approach I have been trying to pursue. "This kind of research also aims to leave behind research tools that can be used and reused to continually improve the conditions most in need of attention" (Duncan-Andrade, 2007, p. 617).

Redlining has been a useful organizing concept with which to communicate the research tools of racial spaces analysis. To build on our early successes, the equity team and I need to examine how we can foster even greater capacity for praxis. One thing that might be helpful is examining why some teachers were able to move past only psychological interpretations of racism. Guinier (2004) explains that a psychological view sees racism as irrational, as a person having a "psychological mal-adjustment" (p. 100) that can be cured. However, Guinier (2004) also explains that racism "has not functioned simply through evil or irrational prejudice; it has been an artifact of geographic, political, and economic interests" (p. 98). In other words, racism is also structural. Focusing only on the psychological leads people to ignore racism's structural roots (Guinier, 2004; Leonardo, 2004). In order to develop racial literacy more broadly across the faculty, the team and I need to look at why some of the teachers were able to move beyond psychological explanations and toward the structural understandings necessary for racial literacy. Furthermore, we also need to investigate why some teachers were able to move from understanding to practice. After all, in addition to reflection, critical race praxis requires actual "antisubordination practice" (Yamamoto, 1997, p. 829). Knowing what helped people make that move could give us some direction in guiding the rest of the faculty. That is not to say that I think we will ever get the entire faculty to engage in critical race praxis. Because of the town and district where City is located, it will most likely always be what Urrieta (2009) calls a *whitestream* school, one that is guided by the logic of white supremacy. Within that context, however, some teachers and administrators are already willing to engage in open challenges to whiteness. Therefore, to live up to the ideals of cariño-based research more fully, I need to investigate in more depth what has made them able to conduct praxis in a racial space, so that I can continue to support their efforts and perhaps even use their insights to bring more teachers on board.

Another area for further inquiry is how this project has, so far, mainly focused on the distribution of educational resources. The more equitable distribution of resources is certainly one of the goals of critical race research in education (Lynn & Parker, 2006). Increased access to resources can be beneficial for Students of Color, who will be judged on their ability to perform well on the standard curriculum and who may need the codes of the "culture of power" (Delpit, 1995) to be able to navigate racialized space. However, there are limitations to this focus as well. Soja (2010) explains, "Distributive justice is . . . focused almost solely on outcomes and not on the structure that produces those outcomes" (p. 78). In the context of schools as racial spaces, limiting the focus to distribution does not address how the resources being accessed (e.g., curriculum) are part of the structure of whiteness. Because whiteness is "nothing but oppressive" (Roediger, 1994, p. 13), this prevents the possibility for true equity for Students of Color. Distributive justice might help Students of Color navigate the hidden curriculum of whiteness, but it does not help change how that curriculum is written. Soja (2010) argues that fuller equity comes from what he calls *spatial justice*, which involves having control over how space is organized and governed. As the team and I go forward in our work, we will need to look at how we can create school space where the hidden curriculum of whiteness does not have the same control. We will continue to work on building racial literacy and the structures necessary to embed critical analyses of white supremacy in all the school's decisions. However, by themselves these efforts may not help us answer a question I asked early in our work together: "What kind of space do we want City to be?"

A potential answer to that question might be found in the concept of *community cultural wealth*, which honors the "aspirational, navigational, social, linguistic, familial and resistant capital" of students and their communities (Yosso, 2005, p. 69). Earlier, I mentioned the school's attempt to honor this wealth in a schoolwide project. While a valuable assignment, it currently only serves as an add-on to the school's standard curriculum. To reform the school into a more equitable space, the team and I could help the school utilize the students' cultural wealth in a more encompassing way. In doing so, we might help City "revolutionize the curriculum" (Berry & Stovall, 2013, p. 596) and destabilize the hold of the hidden curriculum of whiteness. To revolutionize the curriculum, Berry and Stovall (2013) argue,

> Educators must be willing to centralize race (with other subordinating factors) in meaningful reflection prior to, in the midst of, and after engaging in work meant to enhance and/or increase the educational/curricular expanse of the student. (p. 598)

Racial spaces analysis and the concept of redlining have been useful in centralizing race at City. These tools have the potential to help school leaders, researchers, and reformers work with schools like City to resist deficit perspectives, center the community cultural wealth of their Students of Color, and therefore increase educational and curricular expanses of their students, particularly when they are used in a cariño-based approach.

Notes

1. It is important to note that both methodologies are evolving. CRSA may indeed apply tools in addition to GIS, and racial spaces analysis may extend its focus beyond teachers.

2. Helen is referring to the seminal essay by Peggy McIntosh (1992), who provides an extensive list of privileges she has as a white woman.

3. This story is condensed from a previous study I conducted, and the fuller data and analysis appears in another publication (Blaisdell, 2016a).

References

Alemán, E. J., & Alemán, S. M. (2010). "Do Latin@ interests always have to 'converge' with white interests?": (Re)claiming racial realism and interest-convergence in critical race theory praxis. *Race, Ethnicity and Education, 13*(1), 1–21.

Annamma, S. A. (2015). Whiteness as property: Innocence and ability in teacher education. *Urban Review, 47*, 293–316.

Ansley, F. L. (1997). White supremacy (and what we should do about it). In R. Delgado & J. Stefancic (Eds.), *Critical white studies: Looking behind the mirror* (pp. 592–595). Philadelphia, PA: Temple University Press.

Berry, T. R., & Stovall, D. O. (2013). Trayvon Martin and the curriculum of tragedy: Critical race lessons for education. *Race, Ethnicity and Education, 16*(4), 587–602.

Blaisdell, B. (2016a). Exorcising the racism phantasm: Racial realism in educational research. *The Urban Review, 48*(2), 285–310.

Blaisdell, B. (2016b). Schools as racial spaces: Understanding and resisting structural racism. *International Journal of Qualitative Studies in Education, 29*(2), 248–272.

Calmore, J. O. (1995). Racialized space and the culture of segregation: "Hewing a stone of hope from a mountain of despair." *University of Pennsylvania Law Review, 143*, 1233–1273.

Chang, R. S., & Smith, C. E. (2008). A tribute to professor John O. Calmore: John Calmore's America. *North Carolina Law Review, 86*, 739–767.

Delpit, L. D. (1995). *Other people's children: Cultural conflict in the classroom.* New York, NY: New Press.

Denzin, N. K. (2001). *Interpretive interactionism.* Newbury Park, CA: Sage.

Dividing Durham (n.d.). *Main Street, Carolina.* Carolina Digital Library and Archives. Retrieved from http://mainstreet.lib.unc.edu/projects/hayti_durham/index.php/map

Duncan-Andrade, J. (2006). Utilizing cariño in the development of research methodologies. In J. Kincheloe, P. Anderson, K. Rose, D. Griffith, & K. Hayes (Eds.), *Urban education: An encyclopedia.* Westport, CT: Greenwood Publishing.

Duncan-Andrade, J. (2007). Gangstas, wankstas, and ridas: Defining, developing, and supporting effective teachers in urban schools. *International Journal of Qualitative Studies in Education, 20*(6), 617–638.

Guinier, L. (2004). From racial liberalism to racial literacy: *Brown v. Board of Education* and the interest-divergence dilemma. *Journal of American History, 91*(1), 92–118.

Harris, C. I. (1993). Whiteness as property. *Harvard Law Review, 106*(8), 1709–1791.

Hillier, A. E. (2003). Redlining and the Home Owners' Loan Corporation. *Journal of Urban History, 29*, 394–420.

King, J. E. (1991). Dysconscious racism: Ideology, identity, and the miseducation of teachers. *Journal of Negro Education, 60*(2), 133–146.

Ladson-Billings, G., & Tate, W. F. (1995). Toward a critical race theory of education. *Teachers College Record, 97*(1), 47–68.

Leonardo, Z. (2004). The color of supremacy: Beyond the discourse of "white privilege." *Educational Philosophy and Theory, 36*(2), 137–152.

Lynn, M., & Parker, L. (2006). Critical race studies in education: Examining a decade of research on U.S. schools. *Urban Review, 38*, 257–290.

Madison, D. S. (2005). *Critical ethnography: Method, ethics, and performance.* Thousand Oaks, CA: Sage.

Mandell, B. (2008). Racial reification and global warming: A truly inconvenient truth. *Third World Law Journal, 28*, 289–343.

McIntosh, P. (1992). White privilege and male privilege: A personal account of coming to see correspondences through work in women's studies. In M. Andersen & P. H. Collins (Eds.), *Race, class, and gender: An anthology* (pp. 76–87). Belmont, CA: Wadsworth Publishing.

Mills, C. W. (1997). *The racial contract.* Ithaca, NY: Cornell University Press.

Omi, M., & Winant, H. (1994). *Racial formation in the United States: From the 1960s to the 1990s.* New York, NY: Routledge.

Pacheco, D., & Vélez, V. (2009). Maps, map-making, and critical pedagogy: Exploring GIS and maps as a teaching tool for social change. *Seattle University Law Review, 8*(1), 273–302.

Pérez Huber, L. (2008). Building critical race methodologies in educational research: A research note on critical race testimonio. *Florida International University Law Review, 4*, 159–174.

Roediger, D. (1994). *Toward the abolition of whiteness.* London, UK: Verso.

Soja, E. W. (2010). *Seeking spatial justice.* Minneapolis, MN: University of Minnesota Press.

Urrieta, L. (2009). *Working from within: Chicana and Chicano activist educators in whitestream schools.* Tucson, AZ: University of Arizona Press.

Yamamoto, E. K. (1997). Critical race praxis: Race theory and political lawyering practice in post–civil rights America. *Michigan Law Review, 95*(4), 821–900.

Yosso, T. J. (2005). Whose culture has capital? A critical race theory discussion of community cultural wealth. *Race, Ethnicity and Education, 8*(1), 69–91.

8

EXPLORING EDUCATIONAL OPPORTUNITY WITH GEOSPATIAL PATTERNS IN HIGH SCHOOL ALGEBRA 1 AND ADVANCED MATHEMATICS COURSES

Mark C. Hogrebe and William F. Tate IV

Using a geospatial perspective to inform educational and community issues has been advocated as a powerful tool for increasing civic understanding and engagement (Hogrebe, 2012; Hogrebe & Tate, 2012a; Tate, 2008a; Tate & Hogrebe, 2011). Hogrebe and Tate (2012a) used the term "*visual political literacy project* to describe a research approach that builds on the psychological and political potential of geospatial methodology as applied to problem spaces in education, health, and human development" (p. 68). From this perspective, exploring educational opportunity and access can be seen as a visual political literacy project. Educational opportunity is an issue that demands awareness, understanding, and engagement of the citizens and leaders in each local community across a region or state. The visualization of educational opportunity and access with geospatial methods can act as a catalyst for bringing about this awareness and engagement.

The study of educational opportunity is particularly suited for the application of spatial methodologies because opportunity occurs in specific locations and places. Exploring educational opportunity in geographic space allows associations to be discovered between particular contexts and the variables that define them. By visualizing educational opportunity on a map in the context where it occurs, patterns with other variables emerge. A number of authors (Dreier, Mollenkopf, & Swanstrom, 2014; Gordon, 2008; Sampson, 2012) have demonstrated that *place matters* in determining social and economic opportunity. These authors have discussed how local policies and ordinances shape neighborhood contexts, which in turn play a critical role in economic and racial segregation and disparity.

A geographic lens frames educational opportunity within neighborhoods, communities, and regions and leads to better understanding of variable relationships and processes. Soja (2010) argued for this *critical spatial perspective* in which social, historical, and economic factors interact within their geographic context. These variable relationships cannot be understood in absence of the space where they occur. It is thus likely that relationships between educational opportunity and other variables differ depending upon the specific local context. Each local context can be a unique combination of demographic, cultural, political, financial, physical, and education-related variables. This uniqueness in local contexts usually moderates or influences relationships between educational opportunity and other variables across geographic space.

In keeping with the theme of using spatial methods to understand educational opportunity as a matter of equity, in this chapter I examine the extent to which districts across Missouri offer access to advanced coursework in mathematics at the high school level. Algebra 1 is viewed as a baseline for college preparatory mathematics at the high school level. School districts must offer mathematics courses beyond Algebra 1 to complete the college preparatory portfolio in this area. This study seeks to determine by using spatial methodologies how equitable the opportunity is to enroll in advanced mathematics courses in districts across the state. Since the local contexts of districts vary, it is essential to understand if advanced mathematics course enrollment is related to key demographic and district variables. Geospatial analysis and geographic information systems (GIS) software is used to see how variable relationships differ as a function of local context. To ensure that all students have an equal opportunity to participate in advanced mathematics courses, we need to discover which local contexts provide limited access to advanced math courses and what some of their distinguishing characteristics are.

Background for Examining Opportunity and Access in Advanced Mathematics Courses

The growth and prosperity that science, technology, engineering, and mathematics (STEM) industries generate for countries and the global economy are without question in today's world (Carnevale, Smith, & Melton, 2011). In addition to the STEM disciplines, even traditional industries like construction, manufacturing, distribution, financial services, and health/medicine are dependent upon a human resource pipeline that provides a continuous supply of technically competent workers. Employees of today must know more than basic mathematics. For example, they need the quantitative skills that enable them to read, understand, and interpret numerical output from medical devices and equipment monitors. In many jobs, workers have to operate and troubleshoot equipment based on numerical process controls. Whether in business, finance, manufacturing, construction, medical, or service and repair industries, employees are likely to use sophisticated software, read and write computer code, and interpret statistical output. Thus, in order to participate in the prospering commercial sectors, students must have knowledge and skills in STEM disciplines.

The foundation for STEM disciplines is built in grades K–12, with an essential common element being mathematical thinking. If the factors and context necessary for the development of mathematical skills and competencies are limited or absent in the school setting, then educational inequity begins to emerge in the early grades (Tate, 2005, 1995).

What are some of the factors that contribute to the emergence of population trends for underperformance by nondominant racial/ethnic groups and/or lower socioeconomic classes on standardized measures of math achievement and other indicators of mathematical proficiency? One answer to this question is that the development of educational inequity among various student groups arises out of differences in opportunities to learn (OTL). Obstacles at school and at home can create limited OTL, resulting in a reduced exposure to critical learning activities.

OTL as an essential educational variable has a long history (Carroll, 1989). In a 25-year reflection on his model of school learning, Carroll (1989) reinforced the importance of *OTL*, which he defined simply as the amount of time allowed for learning. Tate (2005) developed an approach for how mathematics instructional programs should be designed to increase OTL. He adapted the Stevens and Grymes (1993) framework for OTL to use in evaluations of the learning opportunities afforded traditionally underserved students, with a focus on (a) content exposure and coverage, (b) content emphasis, and (c) quality of instructional delivery. He further described how the design of an effective mathematics program requires an innovative portfolio of strategies that allocates appropriate time and implements quality instruction to maximize OTL for students (e.g., Tate & Rousseau, 2007).

Potential obstacles to OTL in the school setting are many. The most obvious one is lack of appropriate curriculum and coursework for students to enroll in at the school (Hudson & O'Rear, 2014; Klopfenstein, 2004; Tate, 2008b; Tate et al., 2012; Wai et al., 2010; Wang, 2013). For example, if advanced mathematics courses are not offered at the high school, then the OTL mathematics necessary for college STEM disciplines are absent. This schoolwide obstacle ensures that students at these schools will not have the necessary time on task in higher-level mathematics and science courses nor the number of these courses essential for adequate preparation (Tate et al., 2012).

In a report on successful K–12 STEM education by the National Research Council (2011), key elements identified for helping students progress in STEM disciplines were coherent standards and curriculum. In each of the STEM subjects, but especially in mathematics and the sciences, advanced courses must be offered throughout the high school curriculum if students are to progress. An extensive review on high school course-taking (Long, Conger, & Iatarola, 2012) cites numerous studies that suggest that taking more advanced credits in high school increases performance on high-stakes exams, the likelihood of high school graduation, and entry to and better performance in college. The results of their own research strongly suggest that taking advanced courses substantially increases the chances of students performing better in high school and beyond. These results were consistent for race, poverty level, gender, and academic ability.

Another school OTL obstacle exists when advanced coursework is offered at the school, but certain groups of students are excluded from these courses because of inappropriate placement decisions or tracking (Faulkner et al., 2014; Museus et al., 2011; Tate, 2008b; Tate et al., 2012). Excluding capable students from access to upper-level courses as a result of placement decisions influenced by something other than academics contributes to educational inequity.

A less apparent school obstacle is placing students in upper-level courses that have sophisticated titles and descriptions but do not teach content at an appropriate cognitive demand level (Tate, 2008b; Tate et al., 2012). More specifically, some schools offer multiple sections of the same course and purposefully offer the courses at different levels of cognitive demand. Some students experience a rigorous college prep treatment of the course, and others a remedial version. Taking courses that are advanced in name only sets students up for failure once they enter college and increases the educational inequity problem.

Other school OTL obstacles include using teachers not qualified to teach in the content area, low teacher expectations, stereotype threat, and an oppositional culture (Tate, 2008b; Tate & Hogrebe, 2011; Tate et al., 2012; Museus et al., 2011). In addition, higher discipline, suspension, and expulsion rates for certain student groups, along with higher dropout rates decreases the OTL when students are absent from the classroom (Museus et al., 2011; Tate, 2008b; Tate & Hogrebe, 2011; Tate et al., 2012). Not being in class reduces time on task and contributes to educational inequity.

Unequal school district funding can be another obstacle that limits OTL. Districts that spend less per student are likely to have larger class sizes and fewer resources to maintain current curriculum materials, laboratories, and technology (Museus et al., 2011; Tate, 2005). A lack of adequate funding can limit the ability to provide the necessary elements for quality teaching, instruction, and building the resources required to create positive OTL.

Finally, disparities in educational equity related to enrollment in advanced high school courses may be associated with socioeconomic status (SES; Hudson & O'Rear, 2014; Klopfenstein, 2004; Tate & Hogrebe, 2011). In their National Center for Education Statistics (NCES) report, Hudson and O'Rear (2014) found that a larger percentage of ninth graders from higher-SES backgrounds planned to take at least four years of high school mathematics. In addition, higher-SES students were socialized to take more mathematics courses in high school because of college expectations, parental encouragement, and personal interest. Higher-SES students experience a form of sponsored mobility that supports their access to more advanced high school courses. Socialization is an important part of the opportunity processes influencing access to higher levels of school mathematics (Smith, 1996). Lower-SES students and other traditionally underserved demographic groups may not actively seek advanced mathematics coursework because of a cumulative effect over their educational history created by obstacles such as lack of access to high-quality teachers and curriculum, inappropriate placement and low expectations, and inadequately resourced schools (Ladson-Billings, 2006; Stiff, Johnson, & Akos, 2011).

Although there are a number of factors that determine whether students enroll in advanced courses as described previously, the prerequisite factor is that these advanced courses must be available for students to enroll in at their high school. Using geospatial methods, the present study examines whether Missouri high school students in different locations across the state have an equal opportunity to enroll in advanced mathematics courses (AdvMathCrs). Subsequent questions seek to determine the spatial distribution of other key district factors that are associated with students' opportunity to participate in advanced mathematics and to understand which local contexts limit access to these courses.

Research Questions

The local contexts in which school districts operate differ in many ways, such as enrollment size, student body demographic composition, teacher workforce experience and competency, and financial resources, to name but a few. Districts also vary on curriculum and instruction issues, including the courses offered. Some districts offer more STEM-related courses such as advanced mathematics, in which case there would be more of an opportunity for students to enroll in these courses. The curriculum in some districts may have few advanced courses, which limits enrollment opportunities for students in these districts and thus increases the potential for educational inequity. Our first research question examines this issue by asking, "To what extent does the offering of AdvMathCrs vary across Missouri districts?"

The number of students enrolled in high schools may relate to AdvMathCrs. Districts with larger enrollments tend to have more resources and options due to economies of scale. With more resources, larger districts should offer more AdvMathCrs than smaller districts. However, this scenario may not always be the case. Some large urban districts may be inadequately funded, while some smaller, well-resourced districts may offer a number of AdvMathCrs. Thus, our second research question asks, "Are the number of AdvMathCrs a function of district enrollment with more courses available in larger districts?"

A district performance measure that may relate to the number of AdvMathCrs offered is the average end-of-course Algebra 1 score that is part of the Missouri Assessment Program by the Missouri Department of Elementary and Secondary Education (DESE; 2014). Variability of Algebra 1 scores is studied with spatial statistics to determine if there is geographic clustering of districts with high and low Algebra 1 scores. It is hypothesized that districts with higher average Algebra 1 scores may have a stronger mathematics program in the lower grades and, therefore, are more likely to offer subsequent higher-level math courses in high school. To confirm or reject this hypothesis we ask our third research question, "Do districts with higher average Algebra 1 scores offer a greater number of AdvMathCrs?"

Another district metric that may relate to the number of AdvMathCrs offered is the amount of annual spending per student. The greater annual district spending per student, the more resources that should be available to provide a sequence of Adv-MathCrs in high school. This assumes that adequate resources are being allocated to the curriculum and instructors. Thus, in our fourth research question we ask, "Do districts that spend more per student provide the resources to offer a greater number of AdvMathCrs?"

District-level student demographics potentially related to the number of Adv-MathCrs offered are the percentage of Students in Poverty and Students of Color historically underserved in STEM subjects. A greater percentage of students with these demographics could indicate a district located in a community with fewer financial resources available to support coursework beyond the essential core curriculum. Missouri provides varied local contexts from large urban and suburban centers to rural areas with varying degrees of low-income and racially diverse students. This variation has the potential to be associated with the number of AdvMathCrs offered across districts. To confirm or refute such relationships, we ask our fifth and final research question, "Are districts that have greater percentages of Students in Poverty or Students of Color historically underserved in STEM subjects able to offer an adequate number of AdvMathCrs?"

Methods

To examine variability of the number of AdvMathCrs with other district factors across Missouri, spatial perspective is used to visualize relationships in geographic space with ArcMap 10.1 (ESRI, 2012). ArcMap is GIS software that integrates spatial and nonspatial data to produce maps. Several spatial techniques described in this section were used to address the research questions and demonstrate how mapping and visualization of variables make relationships more transparent when anchored to the geography in which they occur. In some cases, mapping simple descriptive statistics provides a great deal of understanding. For other questions, spatial statistics are more appropriate for gaining insight and can be mapped to show how relationships vary across locations.

In order to demonstrate the variation in some of the variables, standard deviation units were mapped as categories. Local Moran's I (Mitchell, 2005) was used to examine statistically significant clustering of variables across the state. A significant z score for a local Moran's I indicated that the district is surrounded by other districts with similar values that are not due to chance. When these z scores were mapped, districts with similar values were shown in the same color or pattern to designate a cluster. The cluster may comprise districts with low, medium, or high values.

Geographically weighted regression (GWR; Fotheringham, Brunsdon, & Charlton, 2002) was used to determine significant relationships between the number of AdvMathCrs and Algebra 1 scores, cost per student, and percentage of free or reduced-price lunch students (FRL). GWR is designed to account for spatial dependence in clustered data and whether variable relationships differ by location. Variation in relationships by location is referred to as *spatial heterogeneity*, and GWR incorporates these local spatial relationships in the analysis (for full explanation of GWR see Fotheringham, 2009; Fotheringham et al., 2002). For the present study, the number of AdvMathCrs was a dependent variable for a GWR analysis, and the software program GWR4 (Nakaya, 2014) was used to account for the Poisson distribution of this positively skewed count variable.

An application study of this technique by Hogrebe and Tate (2012b) compared GWR and ordinary least squares in examining the relationships between Algebra 1 scores and various district, student, teacher, and financial variables. The study used GWR and found that variable relationships depended on local context and were not the same across all regions of the state. The models generated by GWR provided a much better fit to the data than the ordinary least squares models.

Data Sources

The data were collected from 493 districts with high schools in Missouri (2011–2012). All variables were aggregated to the district level, which is assumed to approximate a homogeneous local context[1] (Jacob, Goddard, & Kim, 2013). District data were from the following sources: (a) the Missouri Department of Elementary and Secondary Education (DESE; 2014) and (b) the U.S. Department of Education (2014) Office of Civil Rights Data Collection (CRDC) for 2011 to 2012. Variables used in analysis included the following:

- *Algebra I MAP score.* Missouri end-of-course scaled score (DESE).
- *AdvMathCrs.* Number of AdvMathCrs offered, such as trigonometry, analytic geometry, statistics, precalculus, and calculus (CRDC).
- *Annual district spending per student.* District expenditures divided by average daily attendance (DESE).
- *FRL percentage.* Percentage of students that received free or reduced-price lunches (DESE). Our assumption here is that FRL is an indicator of the socioeconomic status of students.[2]
- *Percentage of Students of Color.* Percentage of district enrollment of African American, Hispanic, white, Native American, and Asian students (DESE).
- *District enrollment, grades 7–12* (DESE).

Findings

This section presents the data and analyses that address the research questions, using spatial methods that integrate geographic context with academic and social variables. The results show the impact that location had on the relationship between AdvMathCrs and the other variables. The findings demonstrate the unmistakable role that place had in determining the opportunity to enroll in these courses. Table

8.1 reports variable means and standard deviations that show the average values and variances across all districts in the state. For example, the average number of Adv-MathCrs for all districts was 5.75, with a rather large standard deviation of 12.3. The average percentage of Students in Poverty was almost 55%, with a standard deviation of 15.1. Figure 8.1 is a map of Missouri districts that shows the major metropolitan areas across the state. These metro areas were used as reference points for the larger urban areas that contrast with districts located in mostly rural areas. The St. Louis and Kansas City metro areas on either side of the state comprise a cluster of districts, while a single district encompassing a city represents the other metro areas.

TABLE 8.1
Variable Means and Standard Deviations for All Districts in Missouri

Predictor Variable	Mean	SD	n
Number of AdvMathCrs	57.75	12.32	490
Algebra 1 Scores	202.60	8.56	493
Cost Per Student ($)	9,031.00	1,956.00	493
Students in Poverty (%)	54.77	15.12	493
Students of Color (%)	10.47	16.29	493
Enrollment 9–12	562.00	1,038.00	493

Figure 8.1. Major and mid-size metropolitan areas located in highlighted Missouri districts.

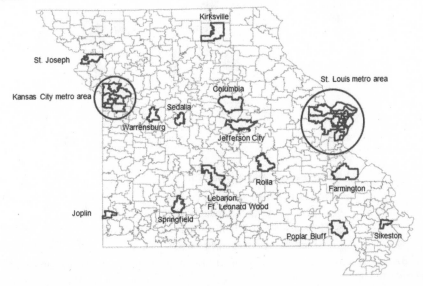

District Variation in Number of AdvMathCrs

Our first research question asked, "To what extent does the offering of AdvMathCrs vary across Missouri districts?" A basic answer to this question was that in order for students to enroll in AdvMathCrs, the courses had to be offered in the district. To answer this question more fully using a geospatial lens, Figure 8.2 shows three categories of district AdvMathCrs offerings based on the mean and standard deviation of offerings in the state: up to the state mean of 5 advanced courses, 6 to 12, and greater than 12 AdvMathCrs. It is interesting to note that almost all of the metro-area districts offered more than five AdvMathCrs. A few districts in the St. Louis metro area and the smaller Sikeston district near the Missouri boot heel region did not offer more than five AdvMathCrs (see Figure 8.3, districts portrayed with no fill). So, for the majority of students living in metro-area districts, there was an opportunity to enroll in at least six or more AdvMathCrs. This finding aligns with the intuitive notion that districts near larger cities had the capacity to offer more AdvMathCrs. However, Figure 8.2 also shows that students in many districts had limited opportunities to take AdvMathCrs. Figure 8.3 demonstrates that even within the large St. Louis metro area, inequity existed among districts in the number of AdvMathCrs offered, leaving many students with limited or no opportunity to advance in higher-level math courses.

Figure 8.2. Distribution of AdvMathCrs.

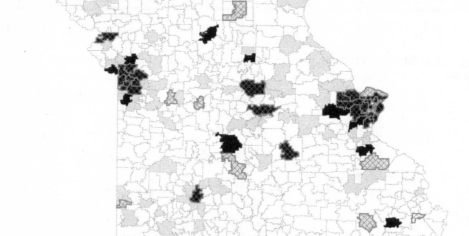

Metro Districts and AdvMathCrs

- ☐ 0 to mean of 5 advanced courses
- ▨ 5.1 to 12 advanced courses +1SD
- ■ Greater than +1SD 12 advanced courses
- ▨ Districts near major metro areas

Note. Darker districts represent a greater number of AdvMathCrs offerings. The cross-hatched areas are districts located near urban areas.

Figure 8.3. Distribution of AdvMathCrs in the St. Louis, Missouri, metro area.

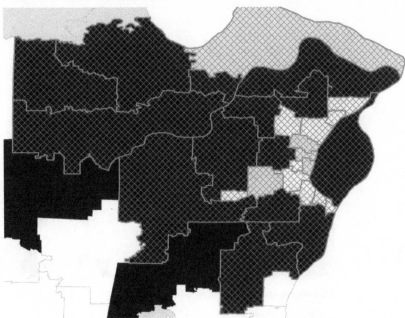

St. Louis Metro Districts and AdvMathCrs

Number of AdvMathCrs

0 to mean of 5 advanced courses

5.1 to 12 advanced courses +1SD

Greater than +1SD 12 advanced courses

Districts near major metro areas

Note. Darker districts represent a greater number of AdvMathCrs offerings. This region includes a range of districts with up to 5 AdvMathCrs and those with greater than 12. The cross-hatched areas are districts located near urban areas.

District Enrollment and AdvMathCrs

Our second research question asked whether the number of AdvMathCrs is a function of district enrollment with more courses available in larger districts. Figure 8.4 maps enrollment in districts by three levels: below 200 students, 200 to 500 students, and more than 500 students. The cross-hatched districts were those that offered more than 12 AdvMathCrs. This overlay clearly shows that almost all districts that offered 12 or more AdvMathCrs had more than 500 students. However, there were still many districts with enrollment greater than 500 students that did not offer at least 12 AdvMathCrs. Only one district with enrollment less than 500 offered 12 AdvMath-Crs. It is quite apparent that students in districts with enrollment under 500 have limited opportunity to take AdvMathCrs.

Figure 8.4. Distribution of districts with the number of AdvMathCrs greater than 12 by enrollment.

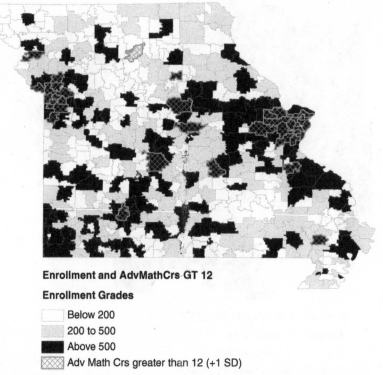

Enrollment and AdvMathCrs GT 12

Enrollment Grades

☐	Below 200
▨	200 to 500
■	Above 500
▦	Adv Math Crs greater than 12 (+1 SD)

Note. Darker shaded districts represent greater student enrollment. The cross-hatched areas are districts that offer more than 12 AdvMathCrs, with most located near urban areas.

Algebra 1 Scores and AdvMathCrs

We then analyzed the relationship between district Algebra 1 scores and the number of AdvMathCrs and hypothesized that districts with higher Algebra 1 scores would have offered more AdvMathCrs. Although Moran's global index (Mitchell, 2005) found significant district clustering of Algebra 1 scores (Moran's $I = .136$, $p < .001$), Figure 8.5 shows that, when mapped, there was not a striking pattern of clustering. District clusters of Algebra 1 scores below the mean, above the mean, and one standard deviation above the mean are dispersed fairly evenly across the state. Higher Algebra 1 scores were not solely clustered in districts from larger metro areas. Rural areas also had districts with higher Algebra 1 scores.

In order to see if there was a significant relationship between districts with higher Algebra 1 scores and AdvMathCrs, a geographically weighted regression program, GWR4 (Nakaya, 2014), was used to determine whether variable relationships differed by location and to account for spatial dependence in the clustered geographic data. AdvMathCrs was a count-dependent variable with a Poisson distribution that

Figure 8.5. Distribution of district Algebra 1 scores.

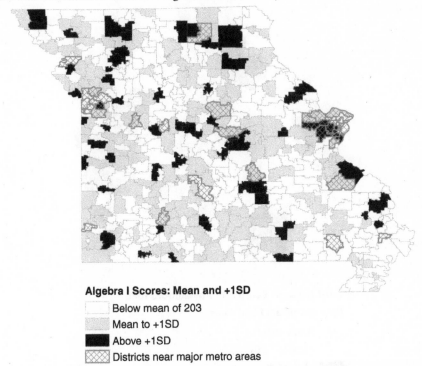

Algebra I Scores: Mean and +1SD

- ☐ Below mean of 203
- ▨ Mean to +1SD
- ■ Above +1SD
- ▨ Districts near major metro areas

Note. Darker districts represent higher scores, while no-fill districts have Algebra 1 scores below the mean. The cross-hatched areas are districts located near urban areas.

was regressed on Algebra 1 scores. Based on model deviance statistics, the GWR4 program produced an approximate R^2 for the overall model of 0.52, which was substantially greater than the ordinary least squares (OLS) R^2 of 0.03. Allowing the Algebra 1 and AdvMathCrs relationship to vary across districts demonstrated that it was dependent on local context. One global OLS model could not adequately describe the variation in the relationship.

Figure 8.6 maps the Algebra 1 score beta coefficient t-test values for each district's local regression. A conservative critical value of 3.08 ($p < 0.001$ in each tail) was used to control familywise Type I errors for multiple statistical tests. The dark areas on the map show the regions where there was a significant positive relationship between Algebra 1 scores and AdvMathCrs. In these areas, higher Algebra 1 scores tended to be associated with more AdvMathCrs, while lower scores point to fewer courses. The areas where this relationship was significant were in and around the St. Louis metro and Springfield areas, to the east of the Kansas City area, and in a cluster of primarily rural districts in the north central region of the state. However, in the other regions, higher Algebra 1 scores at the district level were not consistently associated with more AdvMathCrs offerings.

Figure 8.6. Relationship between Algebra 1 scores and AdvMathCrs using geographically weighted regression.

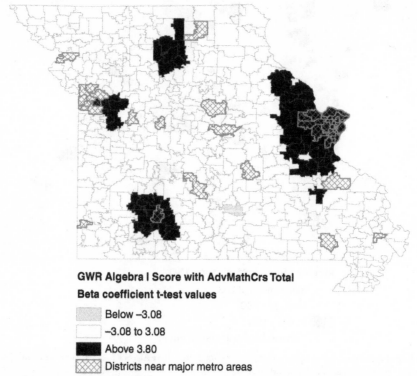

GWR Algebra I Score with AdvMathCrs Total

Beta coefficient t-test values

	Below –3.08
	–3.08 to 3.08
	Above 3.80
	Districts near major metro areas

Note. Dark areas show districts where Algebra 1 scores and number of AdvMathCrs are related positively. The cross-hatched areas are districts located near urban areas.

District Spending per Student and AdvMathCrs

We then wondered whether districts with greater average spending per student offer more AdvMathCrs. The GWR4 R^2 of 0.53 showed a moderately strong relationship between district spending per student and AdvMathCrs. Figure 8.7 maps the t-test values for beta coefficients of spending per student in predicting AdvMathCrs, with significant values being greater than 3.08 or less than –3.08. The lighter shade of gray on Figure 8.7 indicates a negative relationship in some rural district clusters that have higher spending per student without offering many AdvMathCrs. This same pattern was manifested in the St. Louis metro area. For many districts there was no significant relationship between spending per student and more AdvMathCrs. There was one cluster of districts outside of the St. Louis metro area and one around Columbia where a significant positive relationship between spending and AdvMathCrs existed. Thus, only for these two regions was our hypothesis supported that higher district spending leads to more AdvMathCrs. For some other regions, the relationship was negative, while in the remaining regions a significant relationship was not present. Evidently, for most regions in the state, higher spending per student did not lead to

Figure 8.7. Relationship between district cost per student and AdvMathCrs using geographically weighted regression.

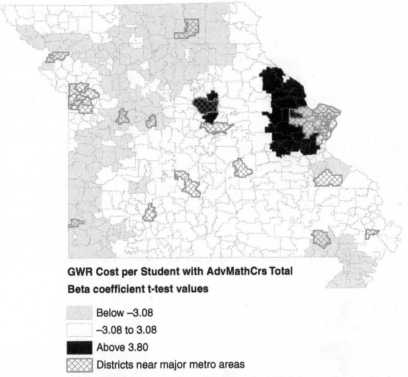

GWR Cost per Student with AdvMathCrs Total

Beta coefficient t-test values

Below −3.08
−3.08 to 3.08
Above 3.80
Districts near major metro areas

Note. Dark areas show districts where cost per student and number of AdvMathCrs are related positively—that is, higher cost is associated with more AdvMathCrs. Lighter shaded districts reveal areas where higher costs do not indicate a greater number of AdvMathCrs. The cross-hatched areas are districts located near urban areas.

more AdvMathCrs being offered, indicating that higher spending does not necessarily translate into more opportunity to enroll in AdvMathCrs.

Student Demographics and Advanced Math Courses

Having so far gained some insight into the limitations of students' OTL in regard to AdvMathCrs, we examine the relationships between student demographics and the availability of AdvMathCrs. Our fifth and final research question asked whether districts with greater percentages of Students in Poverty or higher levels of Students of Color (or both) tended to offer fewer AdvMathCrs. This question suggests that districts with high percentages of Students in Poverty or Students of Color have fewer resources available to support additional coursework beyond the essential core curriculum. The GWR4 R^2 for FRL percentage and AdvMathCrs was 0.59, which indicates a strong relationship. In order to interpret this relationship, Figure 8.8 maps t-test values for the beta coefficients of FRL percentage predicting AdvMathCrs, which describe the direction of the relationship. The lighter shade on Figure 8.8 indicates a negative relationship for many district clusters. A negative relationship means that districts with a higher percentage of FRL students tended to offer fewer AdvMathCrs. In the St. Louis metro area, two scenarios contributed to the negative relationship. First, students in some districts with a higher percentage of FRL students had fewer AdvMathCrs in which to enroll. Conversely, there were also districts in the area that had a lower FRL percentage while offering more AdvMathCrs.

By allowing the relationship of FRL percentage and AdvMathCrs to vary across space, GWR4 also identified a region to the north of the Kansas City metro area where FRL percentage was positively related to AdvMathCrs. In this cluster of districts where the FRL percentage was relatively low, the number of AdvMathCrs tended to be low. This cluster suggests that, in some areas, a lower percentage of FRL students did not guarantee more AdvMathCrs offerings.

The answers to equity questions do not always have to be addressed by inferential methods. The visual power of data displayed spatially can clearly show patterns and regions of inequity. In examining the opportunity for Students in Poverty

Figure 8.8. Relationship between percentage of FRL students and AdvMathCrs using geographically weighted regression.

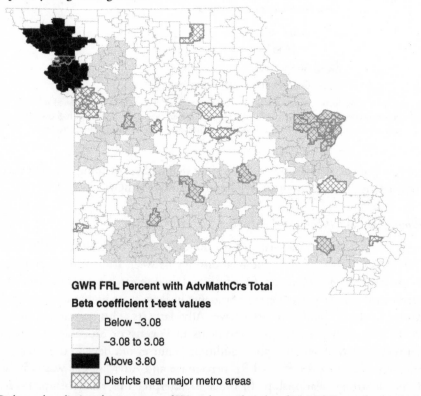

GWR FRL Percent with AdvMathCrs Total

Beta coefficient t-test values

Below −3.08

−3.08 to 3.08

Above 3.80

Districts near major metro areas

Note. Dark areas show districts where percentage of FRL students and number of AdvMathCrs are related positively—that is, a greater percentage of FRL students is associated with more AdvMathCrs. Lighter shaded districts reveal a negative relationship for regions where a higher percentage of FRL students indicate fewer AdvMathCrs. The cross-hatched areas are districts located near urban areas.

and Students of Color to enroll in AdvMathCrs, Figure 8.9 designates districts with greater than 10% Students of Color by cross-hatch, which overlays AdvMathCrs. The resulting pattern reveals that districts with high percentages of Students of Color located near the larger metro areas were likely to offer more AdvMathCrs. For students in these districts, the potential existed for enrolling in AdvMathCrs. However, as the earlier discussion indicated, the opportunity to enroll in AdvMathCrs may not be the same for Students of Color, who face additional barriers even when the courses are available. This particular spatial analysis did not examine the question of internal school dynamics of racial tracking. Still, out of the 124 districts with greater than 10% Students of Color, 61 districts (49%) did not offer more than 5 AdvMathCrs. For almost half of the districts with higher enrollment of traditionally underserved Students of Color, there was limited opportunity for enrollment in AdvMathCrs. The pattern of Students of Color being underserved has been historically documented and continues in our context with relation to OTL mathematics at an advanced level.

Figure 8.9. Distribution of AdvMathCrs in the St. Louis, Missouri metro area.

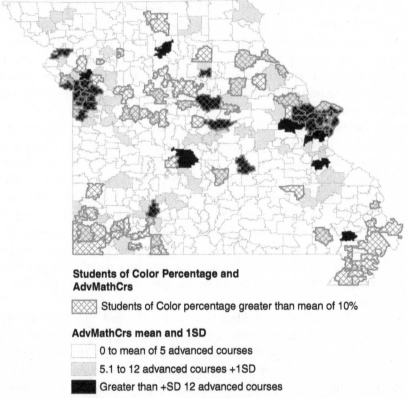

Students of Color Percentage and AdvMathCrs

▨ Students of Color percentage greater than mean of 10%

AdvMathCrs mean and 1SD

☐ 0 to mean of 5 advanced courses

▨ 5.1 to 12 advanced courses +1SD

■ Greater than +SD 12 advanced courses

Note. Darker districts represent a greater number of AdvMathCrs offerings. This region includes districts with up to 5 AdvMathCrs and those with greater than 12. The crosshatched areas are districts where the percentage of Students of Color is greater than the mean percentage of 10 for Students of Color. In 49% of these districts with Students of Color greater than 10%, there were 5 or fewer AdvMathCrs offerings.

Discussion

As presented at the beginning of this chapter, visualization of educational opportunity and access with geospatial methods can be a catalyst for bringing about awareness of inequities and supporting policy formation. Since educational opportunity occurs in specific contexts and places, spatial associations between variables and their location can greatly assist the discovery and clarification of relationships and processes that lead to potential inequities. Specifically for this study, the purpose was to determine the spatial distribution of opportunity to participate in AdvMathCrs in Missouri and to understand which local contexts have relatively limited access.

The spatial analyses showed that the opportunity for students to enroll in AdvMathCrs across Missouri districts was not evenly distributed and appeared to have significant relationships to several key variables. The majority of students living in metro-area districts had the opportunity to enroll in six or more Adv-MathCrs; however, there were exceptions. For example, within the large St. Louis metro area, some districts offered fewer than six AdvMathCrs. One limitation of aggregating to the district level was that there were a few very large districts with more than one high school, and each of these did not necessarily offer the same number of AdvMathCrs. Resources may not have been equally distributed across schools, leaving some schools with more AdvMathCrs than others. However, this was speculative and requires additional spatial analysis of schools within the district. The major takeaway is that opportunity to learn more cognitively demanding mathematics varied across the state. This raises an equity concern for those students attending school districts that failed to offer a full range of college preparatory mathematics.

It was clear from mapping enrollment with AdvMathCrs that all districts (except for one) offering more than 12 AdvMathCrs enrolled greater than 500 students. However, there were many districts with enrollment of 500 students that offered fewer than 12 AdvMathCrs, thus limiting the opportunity for students to take these courses. Equally visible on the map were the districts with enrollment under 500 and that offered few AdvMathCrs. While it may be intuitive that attending schools with smaller enrollment limits course offerings, it was particularly confirming to see the spatial extent of the disparity. Across much of the state, students attending school in smaller enrollment districts had fewer opportunities to take the AdvMathCrs necessary for the development of higher mathematics skills needed in STEM college majors and careers.

The spatial distribution of Algebra 1 scores revealed that high scores were present both in larger metro areas and rural areas. A geographically weighted regression analysis found that there was a significant positive relationship between Algebra 1 scores and AdvMathCrs in four regions but not in others. This positive association was limited to specific regions and depended on the local contexts of districts within the area. So for districts across much of the state, students with higher Algebra 1 scores would not necessarily be able to enroll in subsequent AdvMathCrs. Even though their higher Algebra 1 scores indicated potential for advanced mathematics, they were unlikely to get the opportunity to enroll in AdvMathCrs.

Mapping the GWR results of cost per student demonstrated that, for most districts, higher spending per student was not associated with more AdvMathCrs. In contrast, there were some fairly large regions of rural districts where a negative relationship indicated that higher cost per student did not translate into more AdvMathCrs. Interestingly, there were two regions where a positive relationship suggested that greater cost per student was associated with more AdvMathCrs. It appears that the variation in this relationship across districts exemplified the importance of local context in geographic space and the necessity of accounting for it.

The relationship between the percentage of Students in Poverty in a district and AdvMathCrs was fairly strong and varied across regions. There were several large regions where the relationship was negative, suggesting that higher percentages of Students in Poverty were associated with fewer AdvMathCrs. In one region, the relationship was positive, and in other large regions the relationship was not significant. The variation in the relationship between the percentage of Students in Poverty and AdvMathCrs demonstrated that students in some poorer regions had less opportunity to enroll in AdvMathCrs, but there were other areas where this was not the case. The percentage of Students in Poverty was not consistently associated with the number of AdvMathCrs across all regions.

While historically underserved Students of Color faced many potential barriers to enrolling in AdvMathCrs, it appeared that those attending schools in larger metro areas may have had access to more AdvMathCrs. Attending these metro districts did not ensure that Students of Color could enroll in AdvMathCrs at their particular school, but the likelihood was greater as the courses were offered. The geospatial analysis also revealed that 49% of the districts with at least 10% Students of Color did not offer more than five AdvMathCrs. Many of these districts were located in rural areas of the state.

Implications

Our findings demonstrate the need for using a critical spatial perspective (Soja, 2010) in studying the opportunity to enroll in AdvMathCrs across Missouri districts and regions. The OTL advanced mathematics needed for STEM careers was operationalized by the opportunity to enroll in AdvMathCrs. In districts where few AdvMathCrs were available, the OTL was less likely to support STEM careers for students indigenous to the region. The results of our spatial analyses dramatically show the inequity of AdvMathCrs offerings. Students from districts with smaller enrollment, located in rural regions, and with high percentages of Students in Poverty and Students of Color are much less likely to have access to AdvMathCrs. Students from these local contexts experience the consequences of educational inequity manifested in the lack of opportunities to learn advanced mathematical skills necessary for further STEM education and future careers.

Moses and Cobb (2001) argued that a high-quality mathematics education is required for true economic access and full citizenship. They equated the absence of OTL mathematics in urban and rural communities to the lack of registered African American voters in Mississippi during the early 1960s. Our study suggests this remains a problem in the state of Missouri. The findings show that spatial justice in terms of an equal opportunity to participate in advanced mathematics courses is not distributed equitably across the state. The opportunity to take advanced mathematics courses is a form of spatial justice, and this justice varies by location.

Notes

1. Although there is usually some local context variability within districts, the focus of this study was on the district as the areal unit. Analysis of within-district variability is a legitimate topic for further study.

2. Our assumption is that FRL is an indicator of student socioeconomic status and referred to in the text as *Students in Poverty.*

References

Carnevale, A. P., Smith, N., & Melton, M. (2011). *STEM: Science, technology, engineering, and mathematics.* Washington, DC: Georgetown University Center on Education and the Workforce. Retrieved from http://cew.georgetown.edu/STEM

Carroll, J. B. (1989). The Carroll model: A 25-year retrospective and prospective view. *Educational Researcher, 18*(1), 26–31.

Dreier, P., Mollenkopf, J. H., & Swanstrom, T. (2014). *Place matters: Metropolitics for the twenty-first century* (3d ed.). Lawrence, KS: University Press of Kansas.

ESRI (Environmental Systems Research Institute). (2012). *ArcMap 10.1.* Redlands, CA: ESRI Press.

Faulkner, V. N., Stiff, L. V., Marshall, P. L., Nietfeld, J., & Crossland, C. L. (2014). Race and teacher evaluations as predictors of algebra placement. *Journal of Research in Mathematics Education, 45*(3), 288–311.

Fotheringham, A. S. (2009). Geographically weighted regression. In A. S. Fotheringham & P. A. Rogerson (Eds.), *The Sage handbook of spatial analysis.* Los Angeles, CA: Sage.

Fotheringham, A. S., Brunsdon, C., & Charlton, M. (2002). *Geographically weighted regression: The analysis of spatially varying relationships.* West Sussex, UK: John Wiley & Sons, Ltd.

Gordon, C. (2008). *Mapping decline: St. Louis and the fate of the American city.* Philadelphia, PA: University of Pennsylvania Press.

Hogrebe, M. C. (2012). Adding geospatial perspective to research on schools, communities, and neighborhoods. In W. F. Tate (Ed.), *Research on schools, neighborhoods, and communities: Toward civic responsibility* (pp.). Lanham, MD: Rowman & Littlefield.

Hogrebe, M. C., & Tate, W. F. (2012a). Geospatial perspective: Toward a visual political literacy project in education, health, and human services. *Review of Research in Education, 36*(1), 67–94.

Hogrebe, M. C., & Tate, W. F. (2012b). Place, poverty, and algebra: A statewide comparative spatial analysis of variable relationships. *Journal of Mathematics Education at Teachers College, 3*, 12–24.

Hudson, L., & O'Rear, I. (2014). *Ninth-graders' mathematics coursetaking, motivations, and educational plans.* National Center for Education Statistics (NCES 2015-990). Retrieved from http://nces.ed.gov/pubsearch/pubsinfo.asp?pubid=2015990

Jacob, R. T., Goddard, R. D., & Kim, E. S. (2013). Assessing the use of aggregate data in evaluation of school-based interventions: Implications for evaluation of research and state policy regarding public-use data. *Educational Evaluation and Policy Analysis, 36*(1), 44–66.

Klopfenstein, K. (2004). Advanced placement: Do minorities have equal opportunity? *Economics of Education Review, 23*, 115–131.

Ladson-Billings, G. (2006). From the achievement gap to the education debt: Understanding achievement in U.S. schools. *Educational Researcher, 35*(7), 3–12.

Long, M. C., Conger, D., & Iatarola, P. (2012). Effects of high school course-taking on secondary and postsecondary success. *American Educational Research Journal, 49*(2), 285–322.

Missouri Department of Elementary and Secondary Education (DESE). (2014). *Missouri comprehensive data system, district and school information [state of Missouri education website].* Retrieved from http://mcds.dese.mo.gov/quickfacts/Pages/District-and-School-Information.aspx

Mitchell, A. (2005). *The ESRI guide to GIS analysis: Vol. 2. Spatial measurements and statistics.* Redlands, CA: ESRI Press.

Moses, R. P., & Cobb, C. E. (2001). *Radical equations: Math literacy and civil rights.* Boston, MA: Beacon.

Museus, S. D., Palmer, R. T., Davis, R. J., Maramba, D. C., Ward, K., & Wolf-Wendel, L. (2011). *Racial and ethnic minority students' success in STEM education.* San Francisco, CA, and Hoboken, NJ: Jossey-Bass and Wiley Periodicals.

Nakaya, T. (2014). *GWR4 user manual: Windows application for geographically weighted regression modelling.* Department of Geography, Ritsumeikan University. Retrieved from https://raw.githubusercontent.com/gwrtools/gwr4/master/GWR4manual_409.pdf

National Research Council. (2011). *Successful K–12 STEM education: Identifying effective approaches in science, technology, engineering, and mathematics.* Committee on Highly Successful Science Programs for K–12 Science Education. Board on Science Education and Board on Testing and Assessment, Division of Behavioral and Social Sciences and Education. Washington, DC: National Academies Press.

Sampson, R. J. (2012). *Great American city: Chicago and the enduring neighborhood effect.* Chicago, IL: University of Chicago Press.

Smith, J. B. (1996). Does an extra year make any difference? The impact of early access to algebra on long-term gains in mathematics attainment. *Educational Evaluation and Policy Analysis, 18*(2), 141–153.

Soja, E. W. (2010). *Seeking spatial justice.* Minneapolis, MN: University of Minnesota Press.

Stevens, F. I., & Grymes, J. (1993). *Opportunity to learn: Issues of equity for poor and minority students.* Washington, DC: National Center for Educational Statistics.

Stiff, L. V., Johnson, J. J., & Akos, P. (2011). Examining what we know for sure: Tracking in middle grades mathematics. In W. F. Tate, K. D. King, & C. R. Anderson (Eds.), *Research and practice pathways in mathematics education* (pp. 63–76). Reston, VA: National Council of Teachers of Mathematics.

Tate, W. F. (1995). School mathematics and African American students: Thinking seriously about opportunity-to-learn standards. *Educational Administration Quarterly, 31*, 424–448.

Tate, W. F. (2005). Access and opportunities to learn are not accidents: Engineering mathematical progress in your school. Greensboro, NC: SERVE. Retrieved from www.serve.org/FileLibraryDetails.aspx?id=81

Tate, W. F. (2008a). "Geography of opportunity": Poverty, place, and educational outcomes. *Educational Researcher, 37*(7), 397–411.

Tate, W. F. (2008b). The political economy of teacher quality in school mathematics: African American males, opportunity structures, politics, and method. *American Behavioral Scientist, 51*(7), 953–971.

Tate, W. F., & Hogrebe, M. (2011). From visuals to vision: Using GIS to inform civic dialogue about African American males. *Race, Ethnicity, and Education, 14*(1), 51–71.

Tate, W. F., Jones, B. D., Thorne-Wallington, E., & Hogrebe, M. C. (2012). Science and the city: Thinking geospatially about opportunity to learn. *Urban Education, 47*(2), 399–433.

Tate, W. F., & Rousseau, C. (2007). Engineering change in mathematics education: Research, policy, and practice. In F. Lester (Ed.), *Second handbook of research on mathematics teaching and learning* (pp. 1209–1246). Charlotte, NC: Information Age.

U.S. Department of Education. (2014). *Office of Civil Rights data collection* [Database flat file for 2011–2012]. Available from www2.ed.gov/about/offices/list/ocr/data.html

Wai, J., Lubinski, D., Benbow, C. P., & Steiger, J. H. (2010). Accomplishment in science, technology, engineering, and mathematics (STEM) and its relation to STEM educational dose: A 25-year longitudinal study. *Journal of Educational Psychology, 102*(4), 860–871.

Wang, X. (2013). Why students choose STEM majors: Motivation, high school learning, and postsecondary context of support. *American Educational Research Journal, 50*(5), 1081–1121.

9

GEOSPATIAL PERSPECTIVES ON NEOLIBERAL EDUCATION REFORM

Examining Intersections of Ability, Race, and Social Class

Federico R. Waitoller and Joshua Radinsky

One of the most significant policy issues in recent years has been the deployment of reform strategies to restructure urban public school districts. Increasingly, urban districts are operating under market models of education that include multiple school types, such as charter, contract, magnet, and selective-enrollment schools, in addition to the traditional attendance-area model (Saltman, 2014). Among the populations most vulnerable to changes in public school policies are students who receive special education services, especially those students who experience multiplied effects of structural disadvantages at the intersection of race, ability, and economic means. Exclusion for these students is exacerbated by the interactions of multiple factors, including but not limited to the lack of funding and human resources of urban schools, the mismatch between their cultural repertoires and the cultural repertoires needed to succeed in school, and the lack of opportunities for their families to meaningfully represent themselves in key decisions affecting the education of their children (Waitoller & Artiles, 2013).

In this chapter we examine the possibilities and challenges of using geospatial and temporal analysis to examine inequities at the intersections of ability, race, and social class in neoliberal urban education reform. Our goal is to examine how properties of spatial data representations can mediate the construction of different narratives about Black and Latino students receiving special education services. Policy narratives, and the evidence they employ, can illuminate or obscure the complex forms of exclusion experienced by these students. Thus, it is essential to understand the ways evidence is employed in debates and discussions of these critical issues, and the ways complex interactions are made salient and comprehensible—or, conversely, are ignored or misunderstood.

In the following sections, we discuss neoliberalism in education and its relation-ship to the reconstruction of the urban educational space. Then we discuss the spatial characteristics of special education services and how they are impacted by neoliberal education policy. After discussing our theoretical framework to understand the con-struction of policy narratives, we present examples of data representations from the massive school closings that occurred in Chicago Public Schools (CPS) in 2013 to illustrate how these representations can mediate the construction of policy narratives.

Neoliberalism in Education and the Restructuring of the Urban Space

Beginning in the 1980s, neoliberalism has shaped education policy and practice (Apple, 2001). Neoliberalism is an ideology for capital expansion based on deregula-tion, privatization, and competition, which has transformed the organizing principles of social provisions across the public sector in most Western and developing societies (Ball, 1997). Under neoliberal regimes, the public sector is portrayed as a failing sys-tem that prevents the effective development of markets, which thus needs to be subject to privatization and deregulation. In the neoliberal discourse, the market is depicted as being spontaneous and neutral. Thus, inequities can be resolved through the appli-cation of market forces (Apple, 2001). The government is not absent in this type of control; rather, it exercises supervision at a safe distance (Fischman, Ball, & Gvirtz, 2003). Olssen (1996) wrote, "Neoliberalism has come to present a positive conception of the state's role in creating the appropriate market by providing the conditions, laws and institutions necessary for its operation" and in seeking "to create an individual who is [an] enterprising and competitive entrepreneur" (p. 340). Thus, the role of the state is to ensure that a market regime is applied and follow by its entire constituency.

Neoliberal policies and practices have a profound impact in the production of space, locally and globally. The impact that these policies and practices have in urban cities is of particular interest in this chapter. Neoliberalism aims to resolve social conundrums (e.g., unemployment and educational inequities) through a *spatial fix*, reconstructing the urban space for capital accumulation (Harvey, 2009). As Soja (1989) noted,

> We are now faced with a situation in which industrialization and economic growth, the foundations of capitalist accumulation, are shaped primarily by and through the social production of urbanized space, planned and orchestrated with increas-ing power by the state and expanding to encompass more and more of the world's population resources. (p. 96)

Yet the production of space is uneven, as capital investment is disparately distributed in the urban space, creating centers and peripheries (Brenner & Theodore, 2002). Take, for instance, the efforts of urban centers like Chicago to become global cit-ies (Sassen, 2005). Global cities function as command centers of global financial markets, coordination, and decision-making; they are hubs for the concentration of transnational financial companies and corporate interests (Sassen, 2005). These cities disproportionally concentrate both middle- and upper-class professionals and low-paid workers, embodying the juxtapositions of wealth and poverty inscribed in the segregated geographies of their urban landscapes. Accumulation of capital and power in the hands of a few is achieved by dispossession of public land and wealth (Harvey, 2005). Through gentrification processes, white and also African American and Latino middle-class professionals claim and occupy certain urban spaces in which poor and working-class racial minorities live. Yet, while some low-income communities experience rapid change and displacement due to gentrification, others show the opposite: multigenerational poverty and a lack of economic development over many decades. In both cases, the neoliberal restructuring of the urban space results in the uneven distribution of resources and opportunities for well-being. Because the vast majority of affected populations are low-income African American and Latino communities, neoliberal restructuring acts as a structural manifestation of whiteness and the historical oppression of People of Color (Stovall, 2013). This restructuring has implications for, and is intimately connected to, urban education policy.

Urban Education Policy and Neoliberalism

As Lipman (2011) noted, urban education policy is tightly intertwined with the making of the global city, and therefore with the restructuring of urban space. Indeed, education is one of the public sectors profoundly impacted by neoliberalism. Through the deployment of accountability, testing, and school choice regimes, neoliberal education policies restructure the media through which public education is provided. As Apple (2007) wrote, "The movement toward marketization and choice requires the production of standardized data based on standardized processes and products so that comparisons can be made and so that consumers have relevant information to make choices" (p. 111). The assumption is that, using data from standardized assessments, demographics, and other quantitative measures (e.g., dropout rates, graduation rates), families and students choose from a portfolio of schools that include but are not limited to charter schools, magnet schools, selective-enrollment schools, military schools, gifted centers, and traditional neighborhood schools with attendance boundaries (Saltman, 2014). Schools whose students cannot reach established achievement targets, or those that lose student enrollment, are "turned around," restructured, or closed.

Over time, the closing of "poorly performing" or low-enrollment schools and the opening of new charter, selective-enrollment, and turnaround schools restructures the urban educational space, producing geographies of uneven educational opportunities. Following neoliberal patterns of uneven urban restructuring discussed previously, these school actions tend to affect areas of the city in which working-class and poor racial minorities live. The restructuring of educational opportunities exemplifies Bell's (1980) interest in convergence, as it is argued that "reforming schools" is beneficial for marginalized communities but also attracts middle-income and affluent families. As Stovall (2013) explains,

It is in the best interests of white policy makers to shift the curricular focus of schools in ways that make them attractive to traditionally marginalized communities, while at the same time rendering them less accessible to the least desired segments of the population by way of academic admissions requirements, lottery systems (to regulate the number of "undesirables"), and inaccessible housing. (p. 39)

While children from affluent families access the best school options through selective enrollment requirements, marginalized communities' guaranteed access to schools is diminished. Thus, some families adopt what Stovall (2013) calls the *politics of desperation*, defined as "the complex assemblage of thoughts and actions that guide educational decisions in periods of housing and schooling uncertainty, especially when available choices have not been defined by affected communities" (p. 40).

An extensive critique of neoliberalism in education is beyond the scope of this chapter, and a plethora of these critiques are published elsewhere (e.g., Apple, 2001; Ball, 2006; Lipman, 2011). For the purpose of this paper, we turn to an area that has had little attention: how the neoliberal restructuring of urban education shapes the spatial dimensions of special education services.

The Spatial Dimensions of Special Education Services

While spatial perspectives can illuminate many aspects of urban educational practice, particular elements of special education services have uniquely spatial characteristics. The centrality of space cuts through the history of special education (Danforth, Taff, & Ferguson, 2006). Access to certain spaces, and placement into spaces deemed therapeutic, has always been debated as a matter of individual rights, "a careful arrangement of a specialized environment, a curative geography" (Danforth et al., 2006, p. 2). For instance, a key provision of the Education for All Handicapped Act of 1975 (PL 94-142) is the Zero Reject provision, which ensures that all children with disabilities have access to a free appropriate and public education (FAPE), guaranteeing access to a space: the school.

Within the school, another key provision in PL 94-142 that takes on spatial dimensions is that of access to the least restrictive environment (LRE). The LRE provision requires schools to provide a continuum of alternative placements, offering a range of spaces in which the student can receive services, including a separate facility, a separate classroom that serves only students with disabilities, and the general education classroom. Services provided in such spaces are operationalized in schools based on spatiotemporal calculations. That is, each student's individual education plan (IEP) indicates the percentage of minutes of the school day the student spends in general education spaces or in separate settings. Further, these services are referred to in explicitly spatial terms, such as *pull-out*, *push-in*, and *self-contained classroom* models of instruction. In determining this calculation of minutes, different social spaces are produced within the school as sites within which access (to peers, curricula, or both) is more or less restricted. For instance, the gymnasium, playground, lunchroom, library, and art classroom might be identified as spaces in which particular students will interact with peers who do not share their disability label, affording certain social interactions to students. It is not surprising, thus, that debates about inclusion of students with special needs in the general education classroom have been essentially a debate about space and its inherent qualities (Dorn, Fuchs, & Fuchs, 1996).

In addition, schools provide individuals with important spatial properties of specialized technologies and services. Elevators enable wheelchair access to spaces that staircases deny, and technologies (such as audio players) installed in one region of a classroom provide access to texts for learners whose vision is impaired. Specialized technologies may be available within a school building or might need to be accessed from a central district location. Further, some professionals are located within a school building (e.g., special education teacher, case manager, speech pathologist), while others may share their time among multiple schools (e.g., speech therapist, occupational therapist, psychologist). To those located within the school building, spaces are assigned according to their expertise (e.g., the speech pathologist classroom, the social worker office, and the nurse room).

In addition to these spatial characteristics of special education service within schools, distinct spaces are sometimes produced for students receiving special education services in the transit to and from school. Some students are bused to a school farther from their home than a neighborhood school in order to receive the services they need. Distinct spaces are produced in the traversal of these bus routes, the social and physical space of the bus itself, and the temporal and spatial arrangement of pickup and drop-off locations and times. For some students, sensory or mobility differences (e.g., a student using a wheelchair) produce spaces in the walk to school that have different properties than those experienced by their peers. For example, street crossings may require more time or effort to traverse, producing spaces of differential risk and anxiety.

All of these spatial properties of special education services exist within the context of urban communities, and thus intersect with spatialities of race and class. Public schools in urban areas are hypersegregated by race, mapping to and often exceeding the hypersegregation of residential communities (Orfield, Kuscera, & Siegel-Hawley, 2012). Thus, examining the impact of neoliberal policies in the spatial dimension of special education services provides a window into the relationships among race, ability differences, and spatial restructuring.

Impact of Neoliberal Restructuring of Urban Space on Special Education Services

The neoliberal restructuring of the urban space through education policies affects special education services, perpetuating old and creating new racial disparities within the special education system. Take, for instance, the case of CPS. Since the early 2000s, CPS has served as a means to restructure the urban space (Lipman, 2011). Through the deployment of neoliberal policies discussed previously, CPS in recent years has opened more than 130 charter school campuses while "turning around" over 30 and closing more than 100 schools. Both school actions tend to disproportionly impact the south and southwest areas of the city, where low-income and working-class Black and Latino students live and attend schools. Due to this uneven spatial restructuring of educational opportunities, Black and Latino students receiving special education services are more vulnerable to neoliberal education policies than their white peers receiving the same services. In this section, we examine examples of this differential impact of neoliberal policies.

The massive closing of schools that occurred in CPS in 2013 disproportionly affected Black students receiving special education services. Of the total students impacted by the 50 school closings that occurred in 2013–2014, 80% were African American, representing over one quarter of all African American children living in Chicago between the ages of 5 and 14 (Radinsky & Waitoller, 2013). Further, while the average proportion of students with IEPs in a given school in CPS is 13%, the average proportion of students with IEPs in the closed schools was 17% (de la Torre et al., 2015). Indeed one third of the closed schools had special education programs serving Black students with extensive support needs (i.e., autism, intellectual disabilities, multiple disabilities, sensory impairments). These programs have specialized personnel and resources and lower teacher-student ratios to better serve these students.

In part, special education programs were impacted by the school closings due to a utilization formula that was not sensitive to special education classrooms with low student-teacher ratios. The 2013 closings were explained as a response to underenrollment in neighborhood schools, and the utilization formula was employed to provide evidence of underenrollment by dividing total enrollment by the number of functional classrooms. The use of averages and standardized formulas to justify neoliberal policy decisions is a current reiteration of historical efforts to normalize students (Dudley-Marling & Gurn, 2010). In neoliberal education policy, deep structural and historical injustices are mathematized (Artiles, 2011), benefitting those students that compose the norm for comparison (i.e., white, middle-class, nondisabled students) and further marginalizing those who do not conform to such a norm. For instance, many Black and Latino parents of students receiving special education whose schools were closed found that their new school did not have adequate services to meet their children's needs and had to look for another school in the middle of the school year (de la Torre et al., 2015).

Beyond this marginalization from such normalizing discourse, school closings have direct impacts on special education spaces and students receiving these services. The opening of charter schools and closing of neighborhood schools can result in fewer school options for them to be included in schools with their general education peers. While neighborhood schools provide guaranteed access to a school near students' homes, charter schools work on a lottery system, which does not guarantee services near students' residences. Furthermore, this lottery system is sometimes trumped by a *steering-away mechanism*—strategies that schools employ to implicitly suggest that parents move their children to other schools (Welner & Howe, 2005). Steering-away mechanisms can include but are not limited to charter schools communicating to parents that the school does not have the services the child requires, applying repetitive disciplinary measures to the student (e.g., suspension), or not providing services required in the student's IEP (Welner & Howe, 2005). These mechanisms can force parents to move their children to another school where they may receive better services.

Further, charter schools in Chicago tend to enroll a selective profile of students receiving special education services (Waitoller, Maggin, & Trzaska, in press). Charter schools enroll disproportionately lower rates of students receiving special education, who required more extensive educational supports, and significantly higher proportions of students with learning disabilities (LD), who tend to require less intense supports (Waitoller et al., in press). Thus, closing neighborhood schools and opening charter schools directly decreases school options for Black and Latino students who require more extensive supports.

In addition, the opening of charter schools and closing of neighborhood schools has implications for the types of services offered for students receiving special education. Students receiving special education services in charter schools tend to spend a larger portion of the school day in the general education classroom than their peers in neighborhood schools. This is the case even for students with extensive support needs. For instance, in 2011–2012, 59% of students with autism attending charter schools spent more than 80% of their school day in the general education classroom, while the same rate for their peers attending neighborhood schools was only 25% (Waitoller, Maggin, & Radinsky, 2015). Interestingly, charter school administrators continue to reveal their struggles understanding the Individuals with Disabilities Education Act (IDEA), providing services to students with special education needs, obtaining adequate special education funding from their home state or district, and hiring certified special education teachers (U.S Government Accountability Office, 2012). Thus, charter schools' higher rates of inclusion in nonspecialized classrooms raises equity concerns about whether charter schools are providing the required learning supports for students with extensive support needs. In other words, are they being placed in the general education setting due to a commitment to inclusive education, or due to the lack of individualized and specialized services available in charter schools?

Persistent racial disparities exist in Chicago charter schools in regard to the inclusion in general education classrooms of students receiving special education services (Waitoller et al., 2015). When compared to their peers in other racial groups receiving special education services, African American students in charter schools are less likely to be placed in the general education classroom for more than 80% of the school day and more likely to spend less than 40% of their time in a general education setting (Waitoller et al., 2015). These data, mirroring disparities in other schools, suggest that the expansion of charter schools has had little impact in addressing the racial disparities historically evidenced in special education.

The equity issues discussed in this section underscore the significance of analyzing and debating the implications of neoliberal education policies with clear consideration for intersections of race, disability, and spatial restructuring. Black and Latino students receiving special education, over time (as these policies advance), may be less likely to attend school close to home, more likely to experience longer commutes, and more likely to change schools in search of the services they require. Inherently, policy narratives rely on representations of places, people, and practices. These narratives can either illustrate or ignore these intersecting impacts, including their spatial dimensions. Thus, we turn now to discuss the role of data representations in mediating the construction of these policy narratives.

Data Representations as Mediational Artifacts for Constructing Policy Narratives

Narratives play a crucial role in the ways in which educational policies recruit proponents and gain legitimacy. They are built from structural components that bring coherence across a text or an argument (Hill, 2005): they tell about the social actors involved, the roles that they perform, the places they inhabit, and their problems and solutions. Policy narratives often employ data representations (e.g., tables, graphs, maps) to contest or support arguments about people, places, policies, and outcomes. A key assumption of our approach is that such data representations are not just "innocent bystanders" in these discursive contexts: they are authored texts, infused with a host of assumptions and perspectives (Lynch, 1990). The design of data representations is a nuanced and creative practice, in which particular concepts, relationships, actors, and places can be foregrounded or backgrounded, highlighted or obscured (Lemke, 2000; Tufte & Weise Moeller, 1997). Thus, data representations can have a great deal of agency in the ways they mediate discourse and the construction of policy narratives. Meanings are not straightforward and implicit in the data themselves; rather, they are "emplotted" (Wertsch, 1998) in the discourse of planning meetings and public debates. Rather than simply ask whether stakeholders understand the facts represented by data, we need to examine the ways data are infused with meanings, translated, and employed in policy narratives across contexts.

Making sense of the spatial aspects of special education services, urban communities, and neoliberal policies—in order to engage in meaningful debates of these policies—requires representations of data with which to emplot these layered spatial relationships. Proportional relationships, such as the relative percentages of students with IEPs in charter and neighborhood schools, can be visualized with proportional column graphs or pie charts. Temporal change, such as decreasing enrollments in schools, can be shown with time-series graphs, "small multiples" (Tufte, 1990), or tables of numbers. Spatial relationships such as relative locations of schools, lengths of commutes, or layouts of rooms within school buildings can be made visible using maps. Each of these types of representations makes some relationships visible while obscuring others (Lynch, 1990).

The mobilization of these narratives and their data representations occurs within political discourses of race, power, and privilege in urban contexts. That is, the institutional and structural factors that contribute to the spatial construction of race (and the racialization of space) are challenged, legitimated, or normalized in these narratives (Mitchell, 2000). Ideologies such as whiteness and ableism contribute to this construction by informing the design and interpretation of data representations, which can be employed to build "common sense" by universalizing particular facts and marginalizing others (Fairclough, 2003). For instance, on the one hand, data representations that do not account for race can be used to justify technocratic solutions that ignore the legacies of historical disinvestment in spaces where Black and Latino youth attend schools (Ladson-Billings, 2006). In addition, they can obscure the racial dimension of accumulation by disposition processes (Harvey, 2005). On the other hand, data representations that do not account for students' (dis)ability *and* race can be used to evade the discussion of the detrimental effects of school actions (e.g., closing schools) on Black and Latino students receiving special education. Thus, studying and deconstructing the design and interpretation of data representations and the narratives they support contribute to build counternarratives that challenge racial privilege. It contributes to unraveling how racism and ableism and their ties to legal, political, and economic power operate in sync to create unjust geographies. From this theoretical stand, we turn now to examine a set of representations about special education services in CPS amid the closing of neighborhood schools.

Spatial Data Representations as Mediators of Policy Narratives

The examples that follow belong to an emerging study that examines the construction of narratives about special education services and neoliberal policies through the collaborative design of data representations with stakeholders. They are part of an initial phase prior to beginning the collaborative design work. The purpose of this analysis is to examine properties of data representations that support different narrative elements and that mediate the description of some of the intersecting spatialities of special education policy and neoliberal urban schooling policies. These representational practices are particularly central to addressing the complex forms of inequities experienced by students living at the intersections of race and special education identification in urban contexts where neoliberal policies dominate.

In the first part of this section we present two data representations that are embedded in two different published reports as examples. The first example is a page from a data briefing in the form of a PDF made public by CPS in March 2013, to explain the district's decision to close 54 neighborhood elementary schools (later reduced to 50). The second example is an interactive web page from a site called SchoolCuts.org, which was created the same year by a group of stakeholders engaged in the public debate about school closings. As such, these two texts are in dialogue with each other. Both of these examples embed a map that includes the school and accompanying text that adds more information. We select here a page from each of these sources that focuses on a school on Chicago's far South Side, Owens Elementary, which was closed as part of the district's mass school closings in 2013. In the second part of this section, we examine these cases and offer alternative representations as an example of ways that policy concerns about the provision of special education services could be made more visible in such reports.

Example 1: CPS Briefing Page

The CPS briefing page (see Figure 9.1) belongs to a 66-page document from CPS in which one page was dedicated to each of the actions involving a closing school and one or more "receiving" schools. This representation offers several elements with which to construct the setting of a policy narrative. The area visible in the map suggests a spatial setting for the narrative: about a square mile surrounding both schools, showing nearby streets (five of which are labeled) and two parks (unlabeled). Spatially, the map affords characterizing the proximity of the two schools to each other with reference to streets, but no other spatial relationships are available (e.g., location in the city, identifying markers of the surrounding neighborhood, or a scale legend).

Temporally, the text suggests a 10-year process of declining enrollment at Owens (the closing school), and various "recent" and "new" upgrades at Gompers (the receiving school), as temporal backdrops to the proposed actions.

There are three characters in this policy narrative. First, though the two schools can be seen as settings, they also can be constructed as characters: entities who take actions (e.g., "Gompers will offer. . . .") or are subjected to the actions of others ("requires $8.8 million to maintain" and "received $5.6 million"). Owens (the closing school) is constructed as problematic (e.g., "enrollment has declined" and "requires $8.8 million"), and Gompers, as "higher performing," "upgraded," and having "new" features, is construed as comparatively better. Second, students are indirectly implied as characters, mentioned in their proportional representation of meeting or exceeding standards, and as the potential recipients of "a smooth and safe transition." Third, CPS is constructed as the primary active character (e.g., "recommends to close this

Figure 9.1. Representations of the closing school (Owens), the welcoming school (Gompers), and the neighborhood in which they are located.

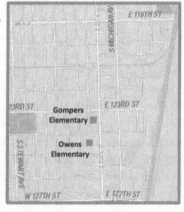

Owens Elementry
Why CPS recommends to close this school:

- Enrollment has declined by 31% over the last 10 years (474 to 328)
- Building is 68% utilized
- Building requires $8.8 million to maintain and update
- Future school will offer a full K–8 grade continuum with cohesive vision and curriculum

Gompers Elementry
As a welcoming school, Gompers will offer:

- A higher performing school with 68% of students meeting or exceeding ISAT standards (versus 57% at Owens)
- A new STEM program
- Upgraded science and computer labs
- New engineering and media labs
- A PreK program
- Air conditioning in every classroom
- A building that has received $5.6 million in recent facility investment
- A school safety plan to provide a smooth and safe transition for all students

school"), though the text does not explicitly position CPS as the one that would actually close the school. CPS, as the author of the policy narrative, thus constructs its own character as a relatively passive "recommender" of actions and observer of processes beyond its control, but obscures its implicit role as the responsible agent overseeing all of these processes, and now planning to close a school. This obscuring of the agency of CPS in enacting these policies belies the active role the district has played in broader city efforts to make Chicago a "global city," which have included dismantling public housing and disinvesting in working-class and poor neighborhoods (Lipman, 2011).

The narrative's plot presents problems and solutions. The text constructs particular problems at Owens requiring resolution: a 31% decline in enrollment over 10 years, a space that is 68% utilized, and $8.8 million that would be required to "maintain and update." Solutions to these problems (and, implicitly, to others not mentioned) are suggested in the characteristics of Gompers: the Owens students would move to a "higher performing" school, one with "a new STEM program" and new or upgraded science, computer, engineering, and media labs. The text offers a narrative about a "smooth and safe" move of students from Owens to Gompers, though the visual representation does not present any information about what makes those school routes safe or unsafe. The relative safety or danger of different routes, and the declining enrollments of schools in African American communities, are implicitly constructed as preexisting problems to be solved by CPS, rather than as problems resulting from policy decisions such as opening charter schools, closing neighborhood schools, and other neoliberal policies that contribute to pushing Black and Latino working-class families from the city (Lipman, 2011).

Example 2: SchoolCuts.org Web Page

Each page on SchoolCuts.org integrates multiple data sources to enable users to look up a range of information about each of 133 schools that would be impacted by proposed CPS actions: either closing or receiving schools. The site is clearly organized to be used in crafting responses to the arguments put forward by CPS for closing schools. This is evident in phrases found in each page such as, "CPS believes," "According to CPS," "CPS will consider only," and "To learn more about how CPS utilization calculations may not be accurate, see . . ." (see SchoolCuts.org). While in Figure 9.1 the reasons for closing schools are represented as undeniable facts, Figure 9.2 makes clear that these reasons come from the CPS perspective and therefore are contestable. Thus, Figure 9.2 unravels CPS's attempt to exercise power by universalizing their reasons for closing schools.

Figure 9.2 shows a section of the page containing information about Owens Elementary (the closing school). The page offers several resources for constructing a spatial and temporal setting for a policy narrative. Like the CPS page, it depicts the school and its closest neighbor school, Gompers, and identifies them as "closing" and "receiving" schools, respectively. At a further zoom distance, the map offers two spatial references: inner and outer circles defining one-mile and one-and-a-half-mile distances from the school, and circles representing all other schools in the roughly six

Figure 9.2. The map and demographics section of the SchoolCuts.org page for Owens.

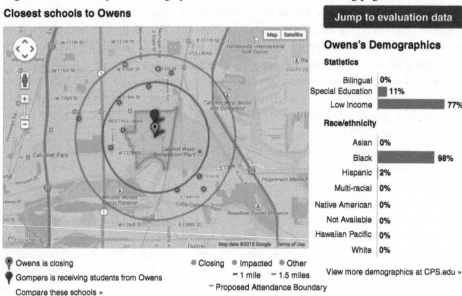

square miles of the map. This affords constructing a narrative set in a neighborhood with multiple schools, where the distances among the schools are a relevant aspect of the setting. In addition, the map includes the proposed attendance boundary of the receiving school after the proposed closing is completed. Together with the inner and outer radii of different distances, these elements afford constructing the distances students will walk to school as a meaningful aspect of the policy. This portion of the web page offers little in the way of temporal setting for a narrative, but the other sections (not shown here) provide different annual data going back between 2 and 12 years.

Like the CPS page in Figure 9.2, schools can be constructed as characters in policy narratives with this page. The focal schools are subjects of active sentences under the map ("Owens is closing," "Gompers is receiving students from Owens"), and the other schools on the map are color-coded as "impacted" or "other" (color codes not reproduced in grayscale figure, see online figures at SchoolCuts.org). Using the other sections of the page, CPS again can be constructed as a character, in that it is given agency in phrases such as "CPS believes" and "by CPS calculations." Students can be constructed as characters less directly, using the "Owens's Demographics" graphs that depict the student body as proportions of students that are bilingual (0%), special education (11%), or low income (77%), and that fall into eight "race/ethnicity" categories (98% Black, 2% Hispanic).

While there is no text like the bullet-point lists on the CPS page, a plot is clearly communicated: "Owens is closing," "Gompers is receiving students from Owens," and other schools in the area are either impacted or not (as coded by color on the website) by the larger process of "school cuts." Unlike the CPS page, no causes or predicted effects of these actions are explicitly provided. (Other elements on the larger page offer implicit counterpoints to some of the claimed causes and effects named on the CPS page, but these are not examined here.) However, the distance-circles, attendance-boundary shape, and additional schools on the map afford constructing distances as relevant potential problems or solutions.

Discussion of the Examples and Alternative Representations

Policy narratives employing these texts might construct the closing of Owens as a problem or a solution—for either school, and/or for people living in the mapped community served by the schools. Spatially, what problems and solutions, for what actors and places, can be narrated with these data? How are intersections of race, class, and special education made visible or invisible?

The SchoolCuts.org page shows that 11% of Owens's students are labeled as "special education," and an informed reader might see this percentage as slightly below the CPS average. However, a map like Figure 9.3, which shows the proportions of students with IEPs in each of eight categories, reveals that roughly half of Owens's students with IEPs are in categories of autism (black) or developmental delay (dark gray). This suggests different representations of characters and plot elements in a policy narrative, and additional considerations of spatial dimensions: lower

Figure 9.3. CPS students with IEPs by school, 2012–2013 (percentages of all IEPs in each category).

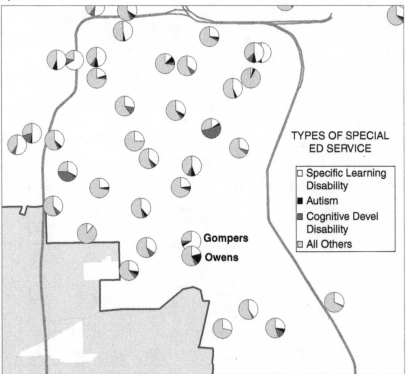

student-teacher ratios, and relatively more classroom space, are often required to meet the needs of students in these two categories. This suggests that the calculation of utilization rates and "empty seats" ought to be reconsidered, shifting the terms of the "problem" to be constructed in the CPS briefing's narrative.

At the neighborhood level, Figure 9.3 reveals that the proportion of students with autism at Owens is greater than that of any nearby school, and much greater than that of Gompers, the receiving school. What will happen when this larger population of students with autism moves from one school to another? How will efforts to include students with autism in the general education classroom in Owens be disrupted by closing it and transferring students?

Similarly, a racial-proportions data map of public schools in the Chicago area (Figure 9.4) might support different narratives than the school-level demographics available in the SchoolCuts.org page. The latter shows that 98% of Owens's students are labeled African American, which might support a policy narrative about the school being segregated. Figure 9.4 supports a narrative of hypersegregation not just of Owens, but of public schools for several miles around. This in turn might suggest a different set of plot elements about closing and receiving schools than those outlined in the CPS briefing: students are moving from one segregated school to another, and hypersegregation is not one of the problems being addressed.

Figure 9.4. Cook County public schools: Student population by race categories.

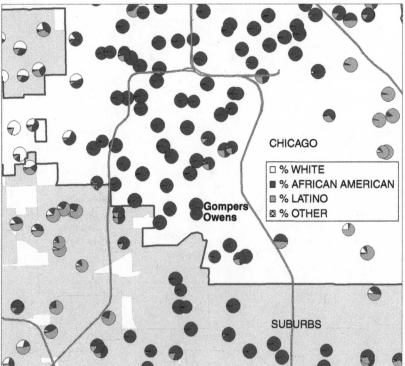

Demographic and political dynamics affecting segregated African American communities might have more to do with the proposed actions (and their causes and consequences) than the plot points suggested in the CPS and SchoolCuts pages. Further, this broader racial perspective begs the question of how the school closings may exacerbate the long-standing racial disparities evidenced in special education services. These inequities include the overrepresentation of African American students in special education categories, their disproportional placement in more restrictive settings (e.g., self-contained special education classrooms) and the disproportional amount and severity of discipline measures experienced by these students (Losen & Orfield, 2002).

Conclusion

In this chapter, we examined the use of data representations to construct narratives about Black and Latino students receiving special education. We contextualized our analysis within the neoliberal restructuring of urban education and its implications for inequities at the intersections of ability, race, and class and for the spatial dimensions of special education services. Too many policy debates render these spatialized concerns invisible. It is not enough to call for the inclusion of special education data in policy debates. Rather it is essential to attend to the kinds of narratives these data enable stakeholders to construct. This attention requires empirical research to better understand the ways narratives are constructed and spatialized and the ways these processes interact with specific concerns for students in urban schools receiving special education services.

We provided examples of data representations only to illustrate the ways data artifacts mediate policy narratives. These examples highlight the importance of attending to the narrative affordances of data representations as they impact policy deliberations about special education. However, there are many narrative elements that remain invisible in these representations. Importantly, none of them offers any direct representation of the intersections of race, class, and special education, which requires more detailed combinations of multiple sets of data. These kinds of representations may be essential for confronting and counteracting the erasure of African American and Latino students with disabilities from policy narratives and deliberations. Combining proportional representations by both race and disability categories is complex for mapped data; such cross-tabulations are usually presented in numerical tables, but such representations do not afford the kinds of community-level perspectives that maps afford. The collaborative design project mentioned previously will explore ways of designing and narrating such representations of intersectionality, to discover how layered impacts of race, class, and disability may be constructed across representations, or made more directly visible through map design.

Furthermore, there are other perspectives that are lacking in each of these representations. For example, while these maps offer alternative spatial perspectives on schools, neighborhoods, and the larger urban area, neither offers spatial perspectives of the school building or grounds, which are an important context of the decisions about school closings and receiving schools. Particular programs, room and building configurations, and equipment can construct radically different spaces for students receiving specialized services, as we discussed earlier. In addition, the examples do not offer representations of class or privilege, displacement or disinvestment, or accumulation by dispossession (Harvey, 2005), which are highly relevant contexts of these policies that are also missing in the narratives.

We argue that the construction of data representations is an important strand of critical analysis that should be undertaken in close coordination with exploring the construction of narratives about race, disability, and urban space. This chapter contributes to a growing body of literature on critical race spatial analysis (e.g., Pacheco & Vélez, 2009; Vélez, Solórzano, & Pacheco, 2007), offering collaborative data design as a valuable context for examining the construction of space, within the contested arena of public education policy deliberations. Further, our chapter encourages special education researchers, critical race scholars, and political economy scholars to examine how spatial representations can obscure, neglect, or elucidate complex forms of inequities at the intersections of race and ability and their relationship with the production of the urban space.

References

Apple, M. W. (2001). *Educating the "right" way: Markets, standards, God, and inequality.* New York, NY: RoutledgeFalmer.

Apple, M. W. (2007). Ideological success, educational failure? On the politics of No Child Left Behind. *Journal of Teacher Education, 58*(2), 108–116.

Artiles, A. J. (2011). Toward an interdisciplinary understanding of educational inequity and difference: The case of the racialization of ability. *Educational Researcher, 41*(9), 431–445.

Ball, S. J. (1997). Policy sociology and critical social research: A personal review of recent education policy and policy research. *British Educational Research Journal, 23*(3), 257–274. doi: 10.2307/1502044

Ball, S. J. (2006). *Education policy and social class: The selected works of Stephen J. Ball.* London, UK: Routledge.

Bell, D. (1980). *Brown v. Board of Education* and the interest convergence dilemma. *Harvard Law Review, 93*, 517–533.

Brenner, N., & Theodore, N. (2002). Cities and the geographies of "actually existing neoliberalism." *Antipode, 34*(3), 349–379. doi: 10.1111/1467-8330.00246

Danforth, S., Taff, S., & Ferguson, P. M. (2006). Place, profession, and program in the history of special education curriculum. In E. Brantlinger (Ed.), *Who benefits from special education: Remediating (fixing) other people's children* (pp. 1–25). Mahwah, NJ: Lawrence Erlbaum Associates.

de la Torre, M., Gordon, M. F., Moore, P., & Cowhy, J. (2015). *School closings in Chicago: Understanding families' choices and constraints for new school enrollment.* Chicago, IL: University of Chicago, Consortium on School Research. Retrieved from https://ccsr .uchicago.edu/publications/school-closings-chicago-understanding-families-choices-and-constraints-new-school

Dorn, S., Fuchs, D., & Fuchs, L. S. (1996). A historical perspective on special education reform. *Theory Into Practice, 35*(1), 12–19.

Dudley-Marling, C., & Gurn, A. (Eds.). (2010). *The myth of the normal curve.* New York, NY: Peter Lang.

Fairclough, N. (2003). *Analysing discourse: Textual analysis for social research.* London: Routledge.

Fischman, G., Ball, S. J., & Gvirtz, S. (2003). *Education, crisis and hope: Tension and change in Latin America.* New York, NY: RoutledgeFalmer.

Harvey, D. (2005). *A brief history of neoliberalism.* Oxford, UK: Oxford University Press.

Harvey, D. (2009). *Social justice and the city* (2d ed.). Athens, GA: University of Georgia Press.

Hill, J. H. (2005). Finding culture in narrative. In N. Quinn (Ed.), *Finding culture in talk: A collection of methods* (pp. 157–202). New York, NY: Palgrave McMillan.

Ladson-Billings, G. (2006). From the achievement gap to the education debt: Understanding achievement in U.S. schools. *Educational Researcher 35*(7), 3–12.

Lemke, J. L. (2000). Mathematics in the middle: Measure, picture, gesture, sign, and word. In M. Anderson, V. Cifarelli, A. Saenz-Ludlow, & A. Vile (Eds.), *Semiotic perspectives on mathematics education.* Mahwah, NJ: Lawrence Erlbaum Associates.

Lipman, P. (2011). *The new political economy of urban education: Neoliberalism, race, and the righ to the city.* New York, NY: Routledge.

Losen, D. J., & Orfield, G. (2002). *Racial inequities in special education.* Cambridge, MA: Harvard Education Press.

Lynch, M. (1990). The externalized retina: Selection and mathematization in the visual documentation of objects in the life sciences. In M. Lynch & S. Woolgar (Eds.), *Representation in scientific practice* (pp. 19–68). Cambridge, MA: MIT Press.

Mitchell, D. (2000). *Cultural geography.* Oxford, UK: Blackwell.

Olssen, M. (1996). In defense of the welfare state and publicly provided education: A new Zealand perspective. *Journal of Educational Policy, 11*(3), 337–362.

Orfield, G., Kucsera, J., & Siegel-Hawley, G. (2012). *E pluribus . . . separation: Deepening double segregation for more students.* Los Angeles, CA: Civil Rights Project.

Pacheco, D., & Vélez, V. N. (2009). Maps, mapmaking, and critical pedagogy: Exploring GIS as a teaching tool for social change. *Seattle Journal for Social Justice, 8*(1), 273–302.

Radinsky, J., & Waitoller, F. R. (2013). *Chicago Public Schools actions: Impact on students.* Retrieved from www.createchicago.org/

Saltman, K. J. (2014). Neoliberalism and corporate school reform: "Failure" and "creative destruction." *Review of Education, Pedagogy, and Cultural Studies, 36*(4), 249–259. doi: 10.1080/10714413.2014.938564

Sassen, S. (2005). The global city: Introducing a concept. *Brown Journal of World Affairs, 11*(2), 27–43.

Soja, E. W. (1989). *Postmodern geographies: The reassertion of space in critical social theory.* New York, NY: Verso.

Stovall, D. (2013). Against the politics of desperation: Educational justice, critical race theory, and Chicago school reform. *Critical Studies in Education, (54)*1, 33–43.

Tufte, E. R. (1990). *Envisioning information.* Cheshire, CT: Graphic Press.

Tufte, E. R., & Weise Moeller, E. (1997). *Visual explanations.* Vol. 36. *Images and quantities, evidence and narrative.* Cheshire, CT: Graphics Press.

U. S Government Accountability Office. (2012). *Charter schools: Additional federal attention needed to help protect access for students with disabilities.* (GAO-12-543). Washington D.C. Retrieved from www.gao.gov/products/GAO-12-543

Vélez, V., Solórzano, D., & Pacheco, D. (2007). *A critical race spatial analysis along the Alameda Corridor in Los Angeles.* Paper presented at the American Education Research Association Annual Conference, April 9–13, Denver, CO.

Waitoller, F. R., & Artiles, A. J. (2013). A decade of professional development research in inclusive education: A critical review and notes for a research program. *Review of Educational Research, 83*(3), 319–356. doi: 0034654313483905

Waitoller, F. R., Maggin, D. M., & Radinsky, J. (2015). *A longitudinal comparison of students receiving special education in urban neighborhood and charter schools.* Presented at the annual meeting of the American Educational Research Association, Chicago, IL.

Waitoller, F. R., Maggin, D. M., & Trzaska, A. (in press). A longitudinal comparison of enrollment patterns of students receiving special education in urban neighborhood and charter schools. *Journal of Disability Policy Studies.*

Welner, K., & Howe, K. (2005). Steering toward separation: The policy and legal implications of "counseling" special education students away from choice schools. In J. Scott (Ed.), *School choice and student diversity: What the evidence says* (pp. 93–111). New York, NY: Teachers College Press.

Wertsch, J. V. (1998). *Mind as action.* New York, NY: Oxford University Press.

10

CONCLUSION

Critical Spatial Analysis in Education: Today and Tomorrow

Deb Morrison, Subini Ancy Annamma, and Darrell D. Jackson

The authors in this book have been working in the area of critical spatial analysis for varied amounts of time; some are pioneers of this work in education while others are relative newcomers. The broad call for papers that framed this book allowed authors to explore new dimensions of entrenched and systemic racial inequities in educational settings and to search for solutions. Authors were asked to address the broad research question, "How does space impact educational inequity?" In addition, authors were asked to consider such subquestions as

- How does spatial analysis improve understanding of how social inequities (at a variety of scales, including institutional and structural) are distributed and can be disrupted?
- Where and how are people using spatial analysis to disrupt educational inequity?
- What types of spatial analysis tools are in use or could be used for spatial analysis of educational equity?

Authors took this guidance and within their various research contexts across the United States engaged with a variety of partners to provide the extensions of theory and methodology and examples of the application of critical spatial analysis of racial injustices found in this collection.

Several key features that unite the research in this collection are the concern about the entrenched inequities in education and how spatial analysis has been brought to bear on these injustices to illuminate heretofore new perspectives on old problems. The varied theoretical and methodological approaches utilized in these examples of critical spatial analysis widen the utility of these chapters for critical scholars. Here authors steeped themselves in social, cultural, and historical perspectives on educational inequities, enriching existing research in their respective areas by also integrating a spatial lens to their work at various scales of space and time.

Several themes emerge from the collective work of the contributors to this book. First, addressing the question, "What does it mean to be critical?," authors approached different educational research contexts using a wide variety of theoretical grounding from a rich scholarly history of critical research. While many of the authors used Soja's critical spatial analysis as a jumping-off point, or framed their work in Vélez and Solórzano's critical race spatial analysis (CRSA), either explicitly or implicitly, they mostly rooted themselves in critical race theory (CRT) with references to tenets such as whiteness as property. All authors accounted for race within their research, though some explicitly called out white supremacy and differentiated this from white privilege. Finally, many of the authors engaged in intersectional work, centering race but also addressing poverty, dis/ability, or other dimensions of oppression. The attention to issues of oppression and power given by the authors in this book provides multiple perspectives on what it means to engage in critical scholarship, and more specifically, critical spatial scholarship.

Second, authors also reconceptualized mapping and space within educational research, broadening it from simply exploring external spaces to considering internal geographies, as well as recognizing the critical potential of maps to address racialized inequities. In particular, many of the authors investigated the ideas of internal space versus external space. Annamma, Hidalgo, Blaisdell, and Waitoller and Radinsky all examined, either explicitly or implicitly, the internal spaces, which were coconstructed by external interactions with geography. Several authors examined the idea of unjust geographies and discussed how sociospatial thinking was more likely to be developed within such spaces. This is in contrast to Blaisdell's work, where privileged teachers were encouraged to examine white supremacy, as these teachers' own construction of sociospatial practices may maintain or disrupt such unjust geographies. Such work, juxtaposed together, highlights how the privileged may differ in sociospatial thinking from oppressed communities and how we may learn from both perspectives. However, to truly learn from the varied perspectives, we must engage in critical methods for collecting and analyzing data.

Third, we come to the theme of innovative critical methods. All of the authors weave narratives of countercartographies, which were theoretically grounded in critical theory. The authors using qualitative methodologies unearthed geographies of hope (e.g., Hidalgo) or resistance (e.g., Annamma). To do this, most authors situated historically oppressed participants as "knowledge generators." Blaisdell situated his teachers, who were privileged and needed work in deconstructing white supremacy, as both learners and knowledge generators. Such reframing of evidence collection recentered power with research participants instead of making such work the sole ownership of researchers.

Similar to the innovative critical qualitative methods, many authors reimagined the use of traditional quantitative methods from critical perspectives. Morrison and Garlick examined the use of data categorization, statistical representations, and spatial tools in general, highlighting key areas of attention in use with respect to power and the reproduction of the status quo. Waitoller and Radinsky examined data representations and how varied narratives can be constructed on the same data, given differences in positionality and historicity of perspectives. Hogrebe and Tate used geographic information systems (GIS) to address a research question centered on systemic issues of racism by examining the opportunities for historically marginalized students to participate in STEM subjects based on the math course availability across a state. Each of these authors took existing tools and used them to speak to larger communities of scholars—to speak the language of power—about ways we should rethink issues of justice in education and how we go about investigating them. This work represents the paradox of how we communicate with those in power while maintaining our own ethics and moral guidelines of acting to ensure justice in our research efforts.

A fourth, and final, theme arising from the collective work of authors in this book is an examination of mapping means. The spatial display and analysis of data allows us to communicate what we see as educational injustice with each other and with participants in our studies. The (co)construction of maps or spatial products given as examples in this book is a type of evidence generation and often also a type of data analysis that is not portrayed only in words or images but also can be spread across a landscape and sometimes across time so that it can be juxtaposed with other information for a deeper understanding of connections in the lived experiences of People of Color in situations of educational inequity. Thus maps have provided our authors both with analytic and communicative paths that were not available to them prior to engaging in critical spatial analysis work. For example, redlining, a practice illuminated in CRT research, was illustrated for both the material ways this spatial practice segregated Communities of Color (Solórzano & Vélez) but also allowed for a metaphorical understanding of ways teachers segregate within racially diverse classrooms through acts of discourse (Blaisdell).

Looking Forward

We imagine a number of ways that the work presented here may contribute to future work in critical spatial analysis of racial injustice in education. We want to challenge all scholars to work toward dismantling inequities from a deep, explicit critical framing. We all need to constantly interrogate our own biases in theory and methods if we are all to continue to work toward liberation of marginalized students in education. As such, we collectively have found it important to root our work in critical analyses of race, given the centrality of racism in reproducing inequity in educational opportunities and outcomes.

We hope that this work inspires scholars to apply a spatial lens to issues of racial injustices in education within their own research contexts. The authors included here were excited to engage with each other in multiple contexts during the creation of this book in order to share ideas on what we were all doing in our own locales. By sharing our efforts, we hope to mentor others into our community of critical race spatial researchers both in an effort to broaden the application of such work and to deepen the methodological possibilities and rigor within the field.

Ultimately our goal is that such research efforts will lead to action—engaging communities as partners in analyzing problems of concern to them and implementing solutions for change. Through such collaborations, our goal is not only to call out injustices we see across the landscapes of America but also to reclaim these spaces, both external and internal, so that People of Color can truly share in the opportunities that our nation can offer.

Subini Ancy Annamma, PhD, is an assistant professor in the Department of Special Education at the University of Kansas. Her research and pedagogy focus on increasing access to equitable education for historically marginalized students and communities. Specifically, she examines the social construction of race and ability, how the two are interdependent, how they intersect with other identity markers, and how their mutually constitutive nature impacts education experiences. She centers this research in urban education and juvenile incarceration settings and focuses on how student voice can identify exemplary educational practices.

Benjamin Blaisdell, PhD, is a teaching associate professor in the Department of Special Education, Foundations, and Research at East Carolina University. Blaisdell's scholarship employs critical race theory as means of examining and challenging white supremacy in public schools. He draws on critical and performance ethnography to highlight the interplay between structural issues and teacher practices. His goals are to promote teacher agency and highlight the efforts of racially literate teachers and administrators. Blaisdell earned his PhD from the University of North Carolina at Chapel Hill. Currently he teaches undergraduate- and graduate-level courses on diversity and social foundations of education and works as a racial equity coach for schools in North Carolina.

Graham S. Garlick, MS, is a geographic information systems (GIS) consultant with TREE Educational Services. He earned his master's degree in geography at the University of Victoria, specializing in analytical land evaluation methods, and has worked in the field of GIS for over 15 years. Garlick has collaborated with Deb Morrison on educational research work for several years, contributing his skills around spatial analysis and mapmaking to various projects. He is deeply interested in exploring the spatial dimensions of educational (in)justice.

Leigh Anna Hidalgo, MA, is a PhD candidate in the University of California, Los Angeles's Cesar E. Chavez Department of Chicana/o Studies. Her research focuses on labor, self-employment, and activism among historically marginalized communities. Specifically, she examines the contradictory ways that race, racism, and nativism intersect to hypercriminalize and surveil informal workers at the same moment where geopolitical forces have displaced a growing number of laborers out of formal work and onto street corners. Her theoretical framework draws on four disciplines—urban planning, geography, ethnic studies, and anthropology—and primarily utilizes critical race theory. She centers this research on cocreating augmented fotonovelas as visual counterstories that highlight informal workers' voices as they struggle to obtain legitimization of their businesses and organize to collectively pursue democratic futures.

Mark C. Hogrebe, PhD, is an educational researcher in the Department of Education at Washington University in St. Louis, Missouri. His interests include research and evaluation methodologies in applied settings, education in the STEM fields, and using geographic information systems (GIS) to give geospatial perspective to education data. His research projects integrate data from different sources into GIS technologies that help researchers understand and communicate complex spatial relationships. He received his PhD in educational psychology from the University of Georgia and has taught courses in applied statistics, research design, and GIS methodologies.

Darrell D. Jackson, JD, PhD, is an associate professor at the University of Wyoming College of Law. Immediately prior, he was a scholar-in-residence and fellow at the University of Colorado Law School. He earned his PhD in educational foundations, policy, and practice from the University of Colorado (Boulder) School of Education. He received his JD from George Mason University School of Law, where he was editor-in-chief and cofounder of the *George Mason University Civil Rights Law Journal*. Jackson's research surrounds supporting historically marginalized communities (HMCs) as they struggle to obtain an equitable share of power within truly democratic societies. His theoretical framework is formed at the intersections of three primary disciplines—law; education; and race, cultural, or ethnic studies—and primarily utilizes critical race theory. Using counternarratives from HMCs and legal analysis that suggests protecting those whose interests are often overlooked, he critically analyzes institutional status quo.

Deb Morrison, PhD, is a research associate at the University of Washington. She earned her doctoral degree in science education, curriculum, and instruction from the University of Colorado (Boulder) School of Education. She also has a master of science in environmental and plant science from the University of Western Ontario. Morrison's research interests lie at the crossroads of justice, environmental literacy, and teacher education. She is particularly passionate about environmental justice challenges intersecting issues of race, culture, and climate science. In her positionality as a white science teacher, teacher educator, and researcher, Morrison believes that praxis is a personal responsibility and seeks to engage in ethical research and its translation into practice.

Joshua Radinsky, PhD, is associate professor of the learning sciences and curriculum studies at the University of Illinois at Chicago. His research applies sociocultural theory and design-based research methods to the study of teaching, learning, and argumentation with data visualizations. His work is centered in Chicago Public Schools (CPS), in middle school and high school social studies classrooms, in professional development with CPS teachers and postsecondary instructors, and in collaborative advocacy with community stakeholders. Curriculum design focuses on using census data and geographic information systems data maps to study African American and Latino migrations.

Daniel G. Solórzano, PhD, is professor of social science and comparative education, Graduate School of Education and Information Studies, University of California, Los Angeles and is the director of the Center for Critical Race Studies. His teaching and research interests include critical race theory in education, racial microaggressions, critical race pedagogy, and critical race spatial analysis. He has authored over 100 research articles and book chapters on issues related to educational access and equity for underrepresented student populations in the United States.

William F. Tate IV, PhD, is the Edward Mallinckrodt Distinguished University Professor in Arts and Sciences, dean of the Graduate School of Arts and Sciences, and vice provost for graduate education at Washington University in St. Louis. He is an urbanist and social scientist interested in the application of epidemiological and geospatial models to explain the social determinants of science, technology, engineering, and mathematics attainment and related developmental outcomes. He is a past president and fellow of the American Educational Research Association. He served as an editor of the association's *American Educational Research Journal.*

Verónica N. Vélez, PhD, is an assistant professor at Woodring College of Education and Fairhaven College of Interdisciplinary Studies, Western Washington University (WWU). Before joining WWU, Vélez worked as a postdoctoral research fellow and the Director of Public Programming at the Center for Latino Policy Research at the University of California Berkeley. Her research interests include critical race theory and Latina/o critical theory in education, the politics of parent engagement in educational reform, particularly for Latina/o (im)migrant families, participatory action and community-based models of research, and the use of GIS technologies to further a critical race research agenda on the study of space and educational (in)opportunity.

Federico R. Waitoller, PhD, is an assistant professor of special education at the University of Illinois at Chicago. His research agenda focuses on urban inclusive education. His work examines (a) how the production of the urban space affects the educational experiences of Students of Color with disabilities and (b) the role of teacher learning and school/university partnerships in developing capacity for inclusive urban education.